GREAT IDEAS IN THE LAW

Justice: Due Process of Law

Isidore Starr

Photo and Cartoon Credits. Page numbers in bold precede related credit lines.
ii-iii William Lizdas. **x** H. Armstrong Roberts. **xiv** H. Armstrong Roberts.
2 William Lizdas. **4** FUNKY WINKERBEAN by Tom Batiuk © Field Enterprises,
Inc., 1974. Courtesy of Field Newspaper Syndicate. **8** Yoichi R. Okamoto/
Photo Researchers. **15** Flip Schulke, Black Star. **28** Wayne Miller, Magnum.
37 Wide World Photos. **43** Reproduced by permission of the Arizona *Republic*.
51 The New York Times. **53** Wide World Photos. **58** © Washington Star
Syndicate, Inc., Permission granted by King Features Syndicate, Inc. **62** Robert
A. Isaacs/Photo Researchers. **69** Reproduced from the Collections of the
Library of Congress. **74** © 1973 Jules Feiffer. **76** Yoichi R. Okamoto/Photo
Researchers. **78** United Press International Photo. **82** Drawing by Ross; ©
1970. The New Yorker Magazine, Inc. **86** Reproduced from the Collections
of the Library of Congress. **90** (top and bottom) Culver Pictures, Inc. **91** Culver
Pictures, Inc. **97** Yoichi R. Okamoto/Photo Researchers. **99** The New York
Times. **106** The New York Times. **116** Reproduced from the Collections of
the Library of Congress. **130** William Lizdas. **134** William Lizdas. **135** Wide
World Photos. **139** Wide World Photos. **148** Yoichi R. Okamoto/Photo Researchers. **174** William Lizdas. **177** United Press International Photo. **182**
Reproduced from the Collections of the Library of Congress. **186** Reproduced
from the Collections of the Library of Congress. **196** Wide World Photos. **199**
Culver Pictures, Inc. **214** Wide World Photos.

COPYRIGHT © 1981 By WEST PUBLISHING CO.
50 West Kellogg Boulevard
P.O. Box 3526
St. Paul, Minnesota 55165

Printed in the United States of America

Library of Congress Cataloging in Publication Data

Starr, Isidore.
  Justice, due process of law.

  (Great ideas in the law)
  Bibliography: p.
  Includes index.
  SUMMARY: Examines the rights considered essential by the Supreme Court for the
accused to be assured due process of law in criminal and delinquency proceedings and in
school and administrative hearings.
    1. Due process of law—United States. 2.   Justice—
United States. 3.   Juvenile courts—United States. 4.   School discipline—United States.
[1. Due process of law. 2. Justice, Administration of. 3. Juvenile courts. 4. School
discipline] I. Title. II. Series.

K F4765.Z9S7   347.73   81-1968
ISBN 0–8299–1020–4   347.307   AACR2

To Kay

On Our Fortieth Anniversary
Who suffered many an injustice
So that justice could triumph

ACKNOWLEDGMENTS

An author may write a book, but it requires the talents of many people to give it life. I wish to express my appreciation to the editorial and production departments of West Publishing Company for their distinctive contributions to the publication of this volume.

Members of the editorial department read the manuscript with care and their suggestions improved the clarity and accuracy of the ideas. Their legal training was especially helpful in pinpointing refinements in the reasoning of the courts.

Several members of the textbook production group assisted in the designing of the "windows," as well as in the placement of the cartoons and pictures. Their ideas contributed to the attractiveness of the format of the book and to the planning of all those important details which move the manuscript from edited copy to bound volume.

A NOTE TO THE READER

The material in this book deals with those due process of law issues in the criminal courts, the juvenile courts, and the schools which have reached the United States Supreme Court. As is to be expected in controversies involving interpretation of important constitutional issues, the nine justices tend to differ in their views. Such decisions by a divided Court often evoke critical reactions by the public and the media.

Each of us has the constitutional right to disagree with the rulings of the Court. *At the same time, however, each of us has the responsibility to try to understand what the Court has actually said and why the justices have said it.* Then, and only then, does criticism become worthy of consideration.

To assist the reader in understanding the rulings of our highest court, I have tried to present as fairly as possible, space permitting, the range of judicial opinions—majority, dissenting, and concurring. Since judicial opinions are not written for the general public, they are not easy reading. But the effort expended in reading these cases is worthwhile because it improves our understanding of the law of the land; it exposes us to the reasoning skills of sophisticated jurists; and it shows the judicial process at work in resolving value conflicts in our society.

ISIDORE STARR

CONTENTS

Introduction   xi

SECTION I **THE COURTROOM AS THEATER: THE CURTAIN RISES   1**

Introduction   2

1 The Set: The Courtroom   7

2 The Leading Players: Judge, Prosecutor, Defendant, Defense Attorney   11

3 The Supporting Players: Witnesses, Victim, Court Reporter, Bailiff, and Clerk   23

4 The Audience: The Public and the Press   31

5 Drama in the Courtroom: The Play Begins, The Plot Unfolds   39

6 Disorder in the Courtroom: Disrupting the Play   47

7 The Jury Hands Down a Verdict   55

8 Behind the Scenes: Plea Bargaining   73

SECTION II **THE COURTROOM AS THEATER: THE CURTAIN FALLS   79**

Introduction   80

9 Sentencing and Punishment   81

10 Capital Punishment: Cruel and Unusual?   **89**

11 Due Process Guidelines for Imposing the Death Penalty   **105**

12 Concluding Thoughts on Capital Punishment   **123**

13 The Critics Review the Play   **127**

SECTION III JUSTICE IN THE JUVENILE COURTS   131

Introduction   **132**

14 Due Process Rights of a Juvenile   **137**

15 The Nature of Proof in a Delinquency Proceeding   **147**

16 Jury Trials in Juvenile Proceedings   **153**

17 Transfer of Juvenile Cases to Criminal Courts   **161**

18 Compensating the Victim   **167**

19 Concluding Thoughts on Juvenile Justice   **169**

SECTION IV JUSTICE IN THE SCHOOLS   175

Introduction   **176**

20 Suspensions and Expulsions   **179**

21 Corporal Punishment   **195**

22 Questions Answered and Questions Raised   **207**

Concluding Thoughts   209

Appendixes

A. The Anatomy of a Criminal Case:
The Record of *Mapp* v. *Ohio*   **213**
B. Constitutional Amendments Cited in
the Text   **258**
C. Glossary   **260**
D. Bibliography   **265**
E. Table of Cases Cited in the Text   **269**

Index   **271**

INTRODUCTION

We, the people of the United States, in order to form a more perfect Union, establish justice . . .

Preamble to the Constitution of the United States

I pledge allegiance to the flag of the United States of America and to the Republic for which it stands, one Nation under God, indivisible, with liberty and justice for all.

Pledge of Allegiance

You will find justice represented as a woman in famous paintings and in sculpture. You will find her sitting in front of courthouses or government buildings. In one hand, she holds scales and, in the other, a sword or book. The scales represent the weighing of right and wrong or the evidence presented by the opposing sides. The sword is used to enforce the law and to punish the lawbreaker. The book may be either the Bible or the Law.

Who is she? She is Themis, Greek Goddess of Justice, who used to sit at the side of Zeus on Mount Olympus to make sure that Justice prevailed.

Why is it that there are times when Justice wears a blindfold and times when the blindfold is gone? Interpretations differ. According to one account, Justice originally did not wear a blindfold so that she could see what was going on around her. By observing the human drama, she could ferret out the guilty and protect the innocent. In the Middle Ages, widespread corruption led some of the jesters to place a blindfold over her eyes to indicate that the Goddess was blind to the injustices going on around her. In Raphael's famous Renaissance painting in the Vatican, we see Justice peering out from under her blindfold.

With the passage of time, the blindfold was interpreted to mean that Justice was impartial because the Goddess was not supposed to be interested in the color, religion, or wealth of the parties before her. Justice was her only concern. With the civil rights revolution of recent times, the blindfold at times has been dropped to indicate that the poor and the disadvantaged in our society can stand before the Goddess and demand intervention through the balancing of the scales.*

*This account of Justice is based on Andrew Simmonds, "The Blindfold of Justice," American Bar Association Journal, vol. 63 (September 1977), p. 1164 and "Blindfolded Justice" in The Docket Sheet of the Supreme Court of the United States, vol. 15 (April-May 1978), p. 5.

The main steps leading to the United States Supreme Court Building in Washington, D.C. are flanked by two figures: a figure of a woman symbolizing the authority of the law and a figure of a man representing contemplation of justice. Together, the message these figures convey is that justice and authority complement each other.

Justice is referred to in both the Pledge of Allegiance and the Preamble to the Constitution; the former pledges "justice for all," and the latter states that one purpose of the Constitution is to "establish justice."

What does justice mean? To some, justice is fairness; to others, it is equality. Still others associate justice with the equal distribution of the wealth of society. A poor person thus may refer to his or her condition as unjust when comparing that condition to another person's wealth. A losing team may claim "foul" or "unfair" because of a call made by the referee or umpire in a game. A young person growing up in a neighborhood or school district without the cultural, recreational, or educational advantages that other districts have may claim that he or she is unjustly denied equal opportunity.

Americans assume that their founding fathers were concerned with justice. This book will explore the concept of justice as put forth by the founding fathers and interpreted by the United States Supreme Court. The book will focus on the specific concept of justice as it applies in the courtroom and in the school, a concept known as due process of law. The Supreme Court has ruled over the years that due process of law includes certain rights which are stated in the Fourth, Fifth, Sixth, and Eighth Amendments to the United States Constitution. The rights enumerated in these amendments were originally thought applicable in federal criminal proceedings only; the Supreme Court has ruled, however, that certain of these rights are applicable (that is, the right must be protected) in the state courtroom proceedings by virtue of the Fourteenth Amendment due process clause. You will note that the amendments (see Appendix B, pp. 258–259) list numerous rights.

Are all of these rights essential for justice to be done? Or are only certain of these rights essential for fairness and due process of law?

This book examines the rights that the Supreme Court considers essential in order for an accused in a criminal proceeding, a juvenile in a delinquency proceeding, and a student in a school or administrative hearing to be assured due process of law.

As you read the discussion of cases and the excerpts from the opinions in the cases, ask yourself the following questions: do you agree or disagree with the concept of due process of law that the Justices of the Supreme Court have shaped? Has the Supreme Court balanced the rights of the accused and the rights and needs of the community to ensure justice? Do you think that the results in the cases discussed were "just" for all parties to the proceedings?

The Courtroom as Theater:

The Curtain Rises

All the world's a stage
And all the men and women merely players.

Shakespeare, As You Like It.

There is no doubt that very generally throughout the country, for several generations, trials at law satisfied the natural human craving for melodrama. At least jury trials did. . . . In the jury trial, everything was brought down to the intelligence level of . . . the spectator. It was good drama for it was realistic. The actors were no mere marionettes. They exulted when they won verdicts and they suffered genuinely when they lost. . . . A gratification of the instinct for drama and entertainment is a part of every complete social environment. . . . Seen as a form of drama, one comes to understand better the nice balancing of procedural rights which were worked out, the rules tending to make it an all-star cast, the alternation of the forces of good and evil, and the exquisite prolongation of suspense.

Anonymous, Journal of the American Judicare Society, *February, 1940, quoted in Marcus Gleisser,* Juries and Justice. South Brunswick and New York: A. S. Barnes and Company, 1968.

INTRODUCTION

The courtroom is, in a sense, a theater in which a play is performed. On the stage appear the actors: judge, jury, prosecutors, defendant, defense counsel, court reporter, bailiff, clerk, and witnesses. A railing separates the actors from the audience or public. The scene appears something like the one in the accompanying illustration, although the arrangements may differ.

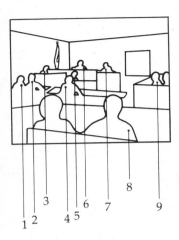

1 Defendant
2 Defense attorney
3 Clerk of the court
4 Prosecutor
5 Court reporter
6 Judge
7 Witness
8 Spectator
9 Jury

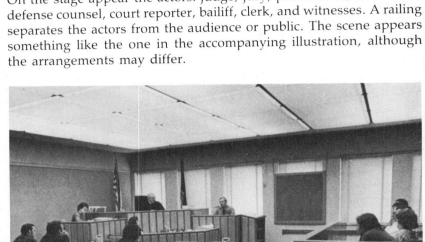

As in all theaters, the courtroom has props, costumes, and sets. Can you think of any?

The courtroom set consists of the witness stand, jury box, railing, tables for the lawyers, and the judge's bench. The Bible, law books, judge's gavel, court stenographer's machine for recording the proceedings, and evidence such as knives, guns, counterfeit money, and fingerprints all serve as props. The costumes include the judge's robe and the clothes worn by the other actors in the courtroom drama.

The play that unfolds in this theater may be a tragedy or a comedy. More often than not, it is a tragedy in which the life or liberty of the accused is at stake. There are times, however, when the defendant decides to make a mockery of the proceedings. When this happens, there may be moments of comedy which, in most cases, do not help the defendant but disrupt the presentation of the play.

Can you suggest a title for the play unfolding in the courtroom?

People who have been asked this question sometimes respond with such titles as

"Let's Make a Deal,"
"Truth or Consequences," or
"This is Your Life."

The following titles, however, are probably more descriptive of what actually takes place:

"The Trial,"
"Criminal Justice,"
"Due Process of Law."

The drama that takes place in the courtroom deals with the subject of justice and injustice. When the play proceeds according to the cues and directions established by the law, *due process of law* has taken place.

Throughout history, various methods of trying a person were developed to probe the issue of guilt. Ancient societies and primitive people, as well as those of medieval Europe, used trial by ordeal to decide the guilt or innocence of an accused. The ordeal was an appeal to the judgment of God to assist the authorities by pointing the finger at the guilty and protecting the innocent.

Members of the nobility or people of high rank who were accused of a crime underwent ordeal by fire. They had to walk barefoot over red-hot irons, carry a red-hot iron over a certain distance, or plunge their hands into boiling water. If the wounds healed within a prescribed period of time—usually three days—it was regarded as an act of divine intervention and the accused was declared innocent. If the wounds did not heal, the accused was considered guilty.

Common people who were accused of a crime underwent ordeal by water, which usually consisted of being thrown into deep water. According to some accounts, if the accused people floated, they were guilty because the water had rejected them. If the accused sank, they were innocent because the water had received them. (The ordeal of plunging an accused's hand into boiling water, referred to variously as ordeal by fire and ordeal by water, was also used to determine the guilt or innocence of common people.)

As you read these descriptions of ordeals, how do you feel? Why? Are there societies today that resort to similar ordeals?

Another method used to determine guilt or innocence was compurgation, or "wager of law." The accused or prisoner had to bring a number of neighbors or friends who would swear that the accused was telling the truth. The number of required oath swearers depended on the severity of the crime. In some cases, the number of compurgators was eleven, with the twelfth being the accused. The oath that the compurgators were required to swear called upon God and was considered a very serious matter. If the oath swearers were not convincing, the accused was judged guilty.

In the ordeal by battle, the contestants fought each other on the assumption that the innocent person would be assisted by God and would therefore win. If the contestants were very young or very old, permission was granted to hire a champion to fight in their place. Perhaps this is one explanation of the use of lawyers to champion the cause of their clients who are not skilled in the procedures of the law.

It took a long time for some societies to move away from trial by ordeal to our present system of trial under due process of law. The phrase "due process of law" has an extensive history. On June 15, 1215, English barons forced King John to sign the Great Charter (Magna Carta) limiting his power. Through this important document, the king promised that no one would be prosecuted except "by the lawful judgment of his peers, or by the law of the land." The phrase "the law of the land" has become associated with the phrase "due

FUNKY WINKERBEAN

By Tom Batiuk

process of law," or the process due a person under the law. Just as the Magna Carta declared that justice would not be delayed, denied, or sold to anyone, due process of law means that an accused must be tried according to those processes that have been set up to determine guilt or innocence.

The United States Constitution has incorporated the concept of due process or the law of the land in the Bill of Rights. The Fifth and Fourteenth Amendments explicitly mention due process. The concept of "judgment of his peers" is not mentioned specifically but has been incorporated in the Sixth Amendment requirement of a jury trial. In time, the American court system developed to include a judge, jury, and lawyers to represent each side.

The notion of the precise meaning of due process—i.e., how it is given to an accused and what rights must be protected—is still being developed and changed. In interpreting the first eight amendments of the Bill of Rights, the Supreme Court is constantly defining and refining the rights of the accused.

It must be noted, however, that the personal rights guaranteed by the first eight amendments were originally thought to be protected only from federal action which violated them. A defendant accused of violating a *federal* law and tried in a *federal* court thus was guaranteed a jury trial and the assistance of counsel because of the rights given to citizens under the Fifth and Sixth Amendments. The Fifth Amendment states that no person can be deprived of life, liberty, or property without due process of law; the Sixth Amendment guarantees a jury trial and the right to assistance by counsel.

But what happens if an accused is charged under a *state* law and will be tried in a *state* court? To answer this question, the Justices of the Supreme Court have turned to the meaning of the due process clause of the Fourteenth Amendment.

The Fourteenth Amendment, ratified in 1868, says in part, ". . . nor shall any State deprive any person of life, liberty or property, without due process of law. . . ."

What does this mean in specific rights? Is the accused in a state trial entitled to the same rights as the accused in a federal trial?

As mentioned in the previous paragraphs, the Supreme Court has looked to the provisions of the first eight amendments for guidance on the rights essential for a fair trial, or due process of law, in state and federal courts. Over the years, the Supreme Court has incorporated certain provisions of the first eight amendments into the concept of Fourteenth Amendment due process by holding that the particular right is *fundamental* to due process. It also contends that the accused in a state proceeding must therefore be given this right in order to receive due process under the Fourteenth Amendment.

Later discussions will demonstrate the provisions of the Fourth,

Fifth, Sixth, and Eighth Amendments that have been held necessary for due process and are now applicable in state trials or proceedings through the Fourteenth Amendment due process clause. These amendments set forth those rights essential to the notion of fairness in trying the accused; at the same time, they provide the meaning of due process of law.

1 THE SET: THE COURTROOM

The courtroom set may be a local, state, or federal trial court or a state or federal appellate court (court of appeal). The trial court is the stage upon which the drama is played for the first time. It is in the trial court (referred to as a court of original jurisdiction) that the witnesses, the attorneys, the plaintiff, and the defendant appear to present the evidence. In an appellate court, the case is reviewed, or heard, for the second (or even the third) time. At the appellate level, however, the case is heard through written arguments (briefs) presented by the attorneys, with the defendant not present. An additional difference is the number of judges who listen to a case. As a rule, one judge presides over a trial in the trial court, while several judges hear an appeal.

Each state has a court system, which includes trial courts, known as municipal, district, or superior courts, and appellate courts, which may include intermediate courts of appeal. All states have a supreme court as the highest appellate court in the state.

The federal court system consists of trial courts, known as district courts, and appellate courts, including courts of appeals and the United States Supreme Court, the highest court in the nation. There are also such special courts as the United States Court of Claims and the Tax Court. Although the United States Supreme Court is primarily an appellate court, it has the power of original jurisdiction to act as a trial court in cases in which an ambassador, public minister, or consul is a party or in cases in which one state sues another.

As a rule, an accused who has been found guilty has a number of appeals available. In the federal system, a person found guilty in a United States District Court can first appeal to the United States Court of Appeals and then to the United States Supreme Court. If the trial has taken place in a state court, the case can be appealed to the state court of appeals and eventually to the highest state court. As in the case of Gideon (pp. 14–17), an accused who loses in the highest court of the state can try to persuade the Supreme Court of the United States to hear the appeal. The Supreme Court will do this if the case involves a federal constitutional issue.

Aside from having trial and appellate courts, each state has a juvenile court, a "trial courtroom" in which cases involving juveniles are heard.

Two major types of cases may be heard in the courtroom: civil and criminal. Civil actions—the majority of cases tried in United States courts—may involve negligence, fraud, inheritance rights, bankruptcy, defamation, or breach of contract. Criminal actions may

An informal portrait of the present Supreme Court, *left to right:* John Paul Stevens, Lewis F. Powell, Jr., Harry A. Blackmum, William H. Rehnquist, Thurgood Marshall, William J. Brennan, Jr., Warren E. Burger, Potter Stewart, and Byron R. White.

involve any offense or misconduct which the state legislature has defined by statute as a crime. Crimes range from such violent acts as murder, assault, and rape, to such white-collar crimes as tax fraud, embezzlement, and price fixing.

Civil and criminal cases are distinguished by (1) the parties to the action and (2) the judgment rendered.

PARTIES TO THE ACTION

In civil cases, one private party sues another private party. The case is thus cited (titled) as *Jane Doe* v. *Richard Roe.*

The party suing (Doe) is the plaintiff; the party being sued (Roe) is the defendant. In criminal cases, the state prosecutes a person for having committed an act which the state has defined by statute as a crime. The criminal case is thus cited as, for example, *The People of the State of Arizona* v. *Miranda* or, in shortened form, *Arizona* v. *Miranda.*

JUDGMENT RENDERED

In a civil case, the plaintiff has been injured by the defendant and therefore is seeking some remedy or compensation. The remedy is usually in the form of money for damages. There are other remedies, however, such as the injunction (an order by the court to stop the defendant from doing an act) and the declaratory judgment (an opinion by the court which defines or clarifies the legal rights of the parties). On the other hand, upon a finding of guilty in criminal cases, judgment takes the form of punishment by a fine, imprisonment, or both.

In which court do you think a juvenile proceeding belongs? When a juvenile is charged with committing an offense, is it a criminal or civil case? If a juvenile is truant, neglected, or disobedient, is the action a criminal or civil one?

The juvenile court is not regarded as a criminal court, and a proceeding involving a juvenile is considered an administrative proceeding of a civil nature. A juvenile court proceeding handles acts committed by juveniles which, if committed by adults, would be tried as a criminal case. They also handle status offenses, acts which are offenses because of the age of the person committing the act—for example, truancy and possession of intoxicating beverages. Our system of justice reflects the philosophy that the age of juveniles requires treating them differently than adult criminal defendants.

In recent years, however, the juvenile court proceeding has begun to resemble a criminal trial in a number of ways. The juvenile courts will be examined in Section III because they constitute a special kind of courtroom drama.

2 THE LEADING PLAYERS: JUDGE, PROSECUTOR, DEFENDANT, DEFENSE ATTORNEY

Who is the most important person in the courtroom?

The defendant in a criminal trial whose life or liberty is at stake might say, "I am the most important person because without me there would be no trial." The defendant's lawyer might also claim this role because people often attend a trial to see a famous defense lawyer in action. Or, the prosecutor might claim to be most important because he or she represents the people of the United States or the people of a state in bringing to justice those individuals who are accused of committing a crime.

On further reflection, however, the judge appears to be the most important person in the courtroom by acting as director of proceedings. He or she sustains or overrules motions and objections made by the lawyers; rules on the admissibility of evidence such as photos, tests, and demonstrations; and decides whether a witness can testify. If anyone—lawyer or member of the public—interrupts the proceedings, the judge can hold that person in contempt after appropriate warnings. In jury trials, the judge instructs the jurors on the rules of law that apply to the case, and in a nonjury case the judge determines guilt or innocence. In either a jury or a nonjury trial, the judge determines the sentence (except in some capital punishment cases) when a defendant is found guilty.

What are the qualities of a good judge?

THE JUDGE

Obviously, a good judge should know the law and be fair so that either side has an equal opportunity to present its position. Most judges have spent a number of years as practicing attorneys—in private practice or as government attorneys—before coming to the bench. Judges interpret the law in applying it to the case before them. Ideally, they must be versed in all areas of the law and must have a "seasoned" judgment.

The Code of Judicial Conduct, adopted in most states, provides the following standards (canons) for the conduct of judges in office.

Canon

1. A Judge Should Uphold the Integrity and Independence of the Judiciary.
2. A Judge Should Avoid Impropriety and the Appearance of Impropriety in All His Activities.
3. A Judge Should Perform the Duties of His Office Impartially and Diligently.
4. A Judge May Engage in Activities to Improve the Law, the Legal System, and the Administration of Justice.
5. A Judge Should Regulate His Extra-Judicial Activities to Minimize the Risk of Conflict with His Judicial Duties.
6. A Judge Should Regularly File Reports of Compensation Received for Quasi-Judicial and Extra-Judicial Activities.
7. A Judge Should Refrain from Political Activity Inappropriate to His Judicial Office.

Would you add any standards to this list?

Judges may be biased in different ways. Like all human beings, judges carry their prejudices with them. Some are called hanging judges, because they tend to favor the prosecution. Others are known as bleeding hearts, because they tend to be lenient toward defendants who they feel are victims of society and have never really had a chance to go straight. Some judges may have racial biases, others may have religious prejudices, and still others may have prejudices based on the sex of the individual.

In general, we expect our judges to be honorable men and women who are honest, fair, and impartial and who apply the law equally to all defendants regardless of race, creed, sex, age, economic status, or national origin. How can we choose judges with these qualifications? One way is to elect them in the same way we choose other public officals.

Do the previously listed canons or standards governing judicial conduct discourage elections of judges?

Many states which follow the election method find it satisfactory. However, critics of election of judges point out that it is not dignified for judges to engage in politics and that campaigning for office involves considerable expense and precious time. Critics fear that rather than remaining impartial, judges may reflect the positions of the majority that elected them. These critics favor selection of judges by appointment as it is done in the federal system. Under the federal system the president of the United States appoints judges, and the Senate confirms the choice by a majority vote. In some states, judges are appointed by the governor. Critics argue, however, that judges can be appointed for political reasons and that the best men and women may not be chosen.

To counter this argument, plans have been proposed that the person making an appointment should choose from a list proposed by a committee of the bar association (professional association of attorneys), a committee of prominent citizens, or a combination of the two. Some states have a merit system, which requires appointed judges to run periodically on their record so that voters have the opportunity to either retain them or vote them out of office.

Do you think that judges should be elected or appointed? Why? Can you think of a plan for selecting judges that would guarantee ability and honesty?

THE PROSECUTOR

Prosecutors are powerful figures in the courtroom drama because they decide who will be charged, what crime the defendant will be charged with, and when the criminal proceedings will begin. If the prosecutors believe that an accused is innocent or that the evidence is not sufficient to result in a conviction, they will not prosecute. Prosecutors are not required to get convictions regardless of the guilt or innocence of the accused; rather, as officers of the court, their responsibility is to see that justice is done.

In criminal proceedings, prosecutors represent the people of their states or of the United States. A federal prosecutor is a United States Attorney or an Assistant United States Attorney; a state or local prosecutor is generally an Attorney General, Assistant Attorney General, District Attorney, or County Attorney. Federal prosecutors are appointed; state prosecutors are either appointed or elected.

Most state supreme courts have adopted a code of professional responsibility which establishes standards for the conduct of attorneys. The rule relating to the duty of the public prosecutor's conduct is as follows:

1. A public prosecutor or other government lawyer shall not institute or cause to be instituted criminal charges when he knows or it is obvious that the charges are not supported by probable cause.
2. A public prosecutor or other government lawyer in criminal litigation shall make timely disclosure to counsel for the defendant, or to the defendant if he has no counsel, of the existence of evidence, known to the prosecutor or other

government lawyer, that tends to negate the guilt of the accused, mitigate the degree of the offense, or reduce the punishment.

Do you think it is fair to require a prosecutor to disclose to the accused evidence favorable to his or her defense? If you decided to have a career in law, would you like to become a prosecutor? a judge? a defense attorney?

THE DEFENDANT

Although the defendant believes that he or she is the most important person in the courtroom, the judge has the most influence

---

Is the defendant the most important actor in the courtroom?

---

over the drama in the courtroom. Some defendants have very little impact on the proceedings, even though it is their life and liberty that is at stake. A few defendants nevertheless have had an important influence on the development of our sense of justice and due process procedures. These defendants have managed to affect the role of the defense attorney in the courtroom by challenging the laws governing their own defense.

Since the state is represented by prosecuting attorneys, should the defendant be represented by an attorney as well? A defendant who can afford an attorney will be represented, but what about a defendant who cannot afford one? Can that defendant receive a fair trial?

GIDEON V. WAINWRIGHT
Does an indigent defendant accused of a felony have the right to court-appointed counsel?

Clarence Earl Gideon was poor and had been in trouble with the law for most of his life. In 1961 he was arrested in Florida for breaking and entering a poolroom with intent to commit petty larceny. At his trial he asked the judge to appoint an attorney to represent him, but the judge refused. Under Florida law at that time, an indigent accused of a crime was entitled to the assistance of counsel only if charged with a capital offense—a crime for which the death penalty might be given. Since Gideon had not committed a capital offense, the judge refused his request.

Gideon defended himself to the best of his ability, but the jury found him guilty and he was sentenced to five years in jail. This was not the end of Gideon's case, however. He obtained law books and prepared an appeal to the Florida supreme court. After losing in the state supreme court, he prepared a petition to the United States Supreme Court asking the nine justices to consider his appeal.

"An Ex-Con Overturns the Law"

Michael Durham

He was a small-time crook who had already spent most of his adult life in jail. On August 4, 1961 he stood trial in the circuit court of Bay County, Florida. Before pleading not guilty, he asked Judge Robert L. McCrary Jr. to appoint a lawyer to defend him. The judge denied the request, and Gideon then protested: "The United States Supreme Court says I am entitled to be represented by counsel."

Gideon was wrong. He was not entitled to counsel. The U.S. Supreme Court had said the opposite in 1942 in its decision on *Betts* vs. *Brady*, which stated that no man accused of a felony was automatically entitled to counsel unless he was a victim of "special circumstances."

Gideon was not such a victim. He was mature, sane, literate and, by now, reasonably familiar with courtroom procedure. Nor were the charges complicated. Many states have laws guaranteeing lawyers to defendants, but not Florida.

Gideon was his own lawyer at his trial and lost his case before a six-man jury. He was given the maximum five-year sentence. With so many years of jail behind him he was not unduly distressed by a few more. But he had picked up a crude sense of justice and considerable jailhouse knowledge of the law.

"I knew the Constitution guaranteed me a fair trial," he says, "but I didn't see how a man could get one without a lawyer to defend him." Also, he really felt he was not guilty of the poolroom robbery. He began to work up a burning indignation at what had happened to him. He read

Clarence Earl Gideon in the
Panama City, Florida courthouse.

diligently in the jail library's law books and got the counsel of the other jailhouse lawyers. He, Clarence Earl Gideon, was going to take his case to the U.S. Supreme Court. He couldn't have picked a better time. The Florida supreme court promptly denied Gideon's petition for a writ of habeas corpus, which would free him on the ground that he was illegally imprisoned. But he then sent an appeal to the Supreme Court. Though handwritten and badly spelled, it fell upon fertile soil. Uncomfortable with two decades of *Betts* vs. *Brady*, the Court in its own sophisticated way had been groping toward Clarence Earl Gideon's simple feeling about the importance of a lawyer to a poor man charged with a crime. "Although he did not know it," writes Anthony Lewis in his book, *Gideon's Trumpet*, "Clarence Earl Gideon was calling for one of those great occasions in legal history. He was asking the Supreme Court to change its mind. . . ."

Source: Adapted from Life, *June 12, 1964, pp. 83ff. Life © 1964. Time, Inc. All rights reserved.*

. . . March 18, Justice Hugo L. Black read the decision affirming Gideon's claim that every indigent charged with a crime serious enough to rate a lawyer is entitled to one. When the news came to the state prison at Raiford, fellow prisoners crowded around Gideon offering congratulations and cigarets and thanks. "The majority of the men in there with me," says Gideon, "had been convicted without a lawyer to defend them, and nine out of ten saw a way of getting out if I did." Gideon recalls, somewhat sententiously, that his only thought at the time was: "This decision is the most important thing to happen since the Fourteenth Amendment."

The first impact of *Gideon* vs. *Wainwright* has already affected hundreds of convicts in Florida jails. Anthony Lewis reports that "by Jan. 1, 1964, 976 prisoners had been released outright from Florida penitentiaries, the authorities feeling they could not be successfully retried. Another 500 were back in the courts, and petitions from hundreds more were awaiting consideration." Of course there was always the chance that a retrial could get them a stiffer sentence.

There were a few compensations for his loneliness. *Gideon's Trumpet* is one. When he was given an advance copy of the book he held it in his hands and wept. And when a young man, walking with his wife, stopped to stare at him. "You're Gideon, aren't you?" the young man asked him. "I should thank you. You just got me out of prison."

Gideon's sad face broke into a rare smile. "That made me feel pretty good," he beamed.

Gideon died January 18, 1972.

In the petition, he claimed that he had been denied due process of law because the state of Florida denied him the assistance of counsel. Although the petition was written in pencil without the help of a lawyer, the Court decided to hear Gideon's case. Since only lawyers are present in appellate courts, Gideon could not appear at the Supreme Court. Besides, he was in prison and could not be released to go to Washington. Since Gideon needed a lawyer, the Justices of the Supreme Court engaged Abe Fortas, a prominent Washington, D.C. attorney who later became a Justice on the Supreme Court, to represent Gideon in his appeal.

The issue raised in Gideon's appeal was whether an indigent without assistance of counsel is denied due process. Put another way, the issue was whether an indigent accused of a serious crime had the right to counsel provided at state expense. The question was settled in a unique fashion. The Sixth Amendment provides for the assistance of counsel (an attorney) in criminal prosecutions. The Supreme Court has interpreted the amendment as requiring the government of the United States to furnish counsel in federal criminal prosecutions. Gideon's case started out as a prosecution under state law and therefore did not come under this rule. However, when Gideon appealed to the U.S. Supreme Court, claiming that he had been denied due process of law under the Fourteenth Amendment, his case involved the *federal Constitution* and had to be determined under *federal constitutional law*. Gideon's argument was that the Sixth

Amendment (right of counsel) applies to state action by reason of the Fourteenth Amendment, which says that no state can deprive a person of life or liberty *without due process of law.*

Would the Supreme Court support Gideon's argument? Twenty years earlier, the Supreme Court had ruled that states must furnish lawyers to defendants when there are special circumstances which pose a handicap to the defendant, such as illiteracy, ignorance, or youth, or where public hostility threatens the life of the defendant. But Gideon's statement to the Court failed to mention any such special circumstances.

After hearing the arguments, the Justices unanimously decided that an indigent defendant accused of a serious crime must be afforded the assistance of an attorney. Gideon's personal struggle resulted in a victory for all future indigent defendants accused of serious crimes. Justice Black expressed the reasons for this new principle of law as follows:

"*[R]eason and reflection require us to recognize that in our adversary system of criminal justice, any person haled into court, who is too poor to hire a lawyer, cannot be assured a fair trial unless counsel is provided for him.* This seems to us to be an obvious truth. Governments, both state and federal, quite properly spend vast sums of money to establish machinery to try defendants accused of crime. *Lawyers to prosecute are everywhere deemed essential* to protect the public's interest in an orderly society. Similarly, there are few defendants charged with crime, few indeed, who fail to hire the best lawyers they can get to prepare and present their defenses. That government hires lawyers to prosecute and defendants who have the money hire lawyers to defend are the strongest indications of the widespread belief that *lawyers in criminal courts are necessities, not luxuries. The right of one charged with crime to counsel may not be deemed fundamental and essential to fair trials in some countries, but it is in ours.* From the very beginning, our state and national constitutions and laws have laid great emphasis on procedural and substantive safeguards designed to assure fair trials before impartial tribunals in which every defendant stands equal before the law. *This noble ideal cannot be realized if the poor man charged with crime has to face his accusers without a lawyer to assist him.*

[emphasis added]

Justice Black was noted for his use of eloquent language. Which of his words and phrases appeal to your thoughts and feelings?

The new rule applied to defendants accused of *serious crimes or felonies.* Is an indigent defendant who is accused of a misdemeanor also entitled to the assistance of counsel? Nine years after the Gideon decision, the Court heard *Argersinger* v. *Hamlin.*

ARGERSINGER v. HAMLIN
Is an indigent accused of a misdemeanor entitled to court-appointed counsel?

Jon Richard Argersinger was arrested in Florida and charged with carrying a concealed weapon, a crime punishable by six months in prison and a $1,000 fine. Because Argersinger could not afford an attorney, he was tried without one, found guilty, and sentenced to ninety days in jail. Like Gideon, he appealed his case to the Florida courts and, finally, to the Supreme Court of the United States. He used the same argument—that he had been denied due process. The issue now before the justices was: Should every indigent defendant accused of a crime be assigned counsel?

If you were a Supreme Court Justice, interested in balancing the scales of justice, how would you handle this tough issue? Is it practical to offer every accused who cannot afford a lawyer the assistance of court-appointed counsel? Are there enough attorneys to go around?

The Supreme Court ruled unanimously that an indigent defendant could not be "imprisoned for any offense whether classified as petty, misdemeanor, or felony, unless he was represented by counsel at his trial." Justice Douglas spoke for the Court, but several of the Justices wrote concurring opinions.

Gideon v. *Wainwright* and *Argersinger* v. *Hamlin* clearly show that the Supreme Court regards the right to counsel as "fundamental and essential to a fair trial." The *Gideon* case held that the Sixth and Fourteenth Amendments extend the right to counsel to all indigents tried for serious crimes in state courts. The *Argersinger* case extended this right to any state proceeding in which a convicted defendant is imprisoned. The Justices concluded that when an indigent accused is confronted by the government's prosecutorial "machinery," the defendant must have "the guiding hand of counsel" to balance the scales of the adversary system.

One would think that the *Gideon* and *Argersinger* cases had settled once and for all the issue of an indigent's right to counsel in state courts. This was not so. In the law, decisions in one or two important cases may answer specific questions, but, at the same time, the Court's opinions may raise additional problems which may or may not have been foreseen at the time. One such issue relating to the right to counsel emerged in a recent case and the Court had to rethink its position.

Is an indigent accused entitled to counsel when tried under a penal law *authorizing* imprisonment, a fine, or both?

SCOTT v. ILLINOIS
Must an indigent be represented by court-appointed counsel if the sentence may be a fine instead of prison?

Aubrey Scott, an indigent, was convicted of shoplifting merchandise valued at less than $150 and was tried and convicted under an Illinois law which provided for a fine of up to $500 or one year in jail, or both. Scott received a bench trial and was fined $50. He argued that his conviction was unconstitutional because he had not been represented by counsel.

Now we have an entirely different issue. Scott was not given a prison term but had been fined for his offense. However, the statute under which he had been tried did *authorize* a prison term. Did this uncertainty about the nature of the penalty fall within the *Argersinger* rule? How can one determine the penalty before the case is heard? It is possible, of course, under the *Argersinger* rule, for a judge to decide in advance that the accused will not be given a prison term and counsel therefore need not be provided. But does this situation not create great uncertainty in the law? And is a fine not a penalty that could be so severe as to impoverish a defendant or be beyond his or her reach of payment?

Five Justices, with Justice Rehnquist delivering the opinion of the Court, refused to extend the *Argersinger* rule to cover the issue raised in the *Scott* case. Actual imprisonment, not fines or mere threats of imprisonment, is the factor which determines the constitutional right to appointment of counsel. A fine, declared the Court, is different in kind from actual imprisonment and does not warrant representation by counsel.

Although the opinions of the Justices in the *Argersinger* case had upheld the right to counsel despite the social cost and lack of available lawyers to accommodate defendants, Justice Rehnquist concluded that "any extension [of *Argersinger*] would create confusion and impose unpredictable, but necessarily substantial, costs on fifty quite diverse States."

Four Justices dissented from this ruling and reasoning. Speaking for himself and Justices Marshall and Stevens, Justice Brennan attacked the expense argument as follows:

This Court's role in enforcing constitutional guarantees for criminal defendants cannot be made dependent on the budgetary decisions of state governments. . . . In any event, the extent of the alleged burden on the States is, as the Court admits, . . . speculative.

Perhaps the strongest refutation of . . . alarmist prophecies that an authorized imprisonment standard would wreak havoc on the States is that the standard has not produced that result in the substantial number of States that already provide counsel in all cases where imprisonment is authorized. . . . In fact, Scott would be entitled to appointed counsel under the current laws of 33 states.

Justice Brennan went on to say that many crimes, such as the one with which Scott was charged, carry "the moral stigma associated with common-law crimes traditionally recognized as indicative of moral depravity." Conviction of such crimes, whether accompanied by fine or imprisonment, disqualifies a person from licenses or occupations requiring "good moral character." Therefore, the right to counsel "perhaps the most fundamental Sixth Amendment right," must be extended rather than restricted, as the majority have done in this decision.

Justice Blackmun's dissent recommended that an indigent defendant in a state criminal case be represented by counsel whenever the charge is one punishable by more than six months imprisonment or where the defendant is actually subjected to a prison term.

FULLER v. OREGON
Should an indigent be required to repay the state for a court-appointed lawyer?

In Oregon, a man named Prince Eric Fuller was charged with committing a serious crime. Fuller informed the judge that he could not afford an attorney and was provided with the assistance of a court-appointed lawyer. Fuller's lawyer hired an investigator to assist him in the case.

At the conclusion of the court proceedings, Fuller was found guilty. As part of his sentence, Fuller was required to reimburse the court for the fees and expenses of the court-appointed attorney and the investigator.

Under Oregon law, the court was required to ensure that the convicted person pay these costs and that the payment did not impose "manifest hardship on the defendant or his family." The law applied only to those poor persons who were convicted and not to those found not guilty. Fuller appealed his case, claiming that the Oregon law violated the equal protection clause of the Fourteenth Amendment since it treated persons who were found guilty and those not guilty differently.

The U.S. Supreme Court upheld the provisions of the Oregon law. Although two justices dissented (Marshall and Brennan), the majority saw no problem in differentiation. In addition, the majority of the Supreme Court saw no merit in Fuller's argument that such laws might discourage indigent defendants from asking for the assistance of court-appointed attorneys.

FARETTA v. CALIFORNIA
Does the defendant have a right to defend himself?

Anthony Pasquall Faretta was charged with grand theft. Although the judge appointed a public defender at the arraignment to represent Faretta, the defendant subsequently asked the judge for permission to defend himself. Faretta told the judge that he had a high school education and that he felt public defenders had such heavy case loads that they could not devote adequate time to his case. The judge tried to talk him out of this request but agreed to consider it when Faretta persisted. Later the judge asked Faretta whether he had done any research, and Faretta indicated that he had consulted law books about choosing jurors and rules of evidence. After listening to Faretta for a while, the judge concluded that Faretta had not made "an intelligent and knowing waiver of his right to the assistance of counsel." The judge ruled that Faretta had no constitutional right to conduct his own defense. In November 1974 the case reached the United States Supreme Court.

On June 30, 1975, the Supreme Court ruled that Faretta could defend himself. Three justices disagreed with this ruling. Justice Stewart, writing for the majority, said that the defendant has *an independent constitutional right to represent himself if he intelligently and voluntarily chooses to do so.* He noted that the constitutions of thirty-six states offer the right of self-representation to a defendant and that the federal government should also recognize this right. To force a lawyer upon an unwilling defendant, he stated, "is contrary to his basic right to defend himself if he truly wants to do so." Justice Stewart then went on to say:

It is undeniable that in most criminal prosecutions defendants could better defend with counsel's guidance than by their own unskilled efforts. But where the defendant will not voluntarily accept representation by counsel, the potential advantage of a lawyer's training and experience can be realized, if at all, only imperfectly. To force a lawyer on a defendant can only lead him to believe that the law contrives against him. Moreover, it is not inconceivable that in some rare instances, the defendant might in fact present his case more effectively by conduction of his own defense. Personal liberties are not rooted in the law of averages. The right to defend is personal. The defendant, and not his lawyer or the State, will bear the personal consequences of a conviction. It is the defendant, therefore, who must be personally free to decide whether in his particular case counsel is to his advantage. And although he may conduct his own defense ultimately to his own detriment, his choice must be honored out of "that respect for the individual which is the lifeblood of the law."

Chief Justice Burger and Justices Blackmun and Rehnquist disagreed. The dissenters thought that defendants who undertake their own defense would be put at a disadvantage against a well-trained and well-prepared prosecutor. Since our system is an adversary system, they believe that the opposing sides should be as evenly matched as possible. Chief Justice Burger wanted to leave the determination of whether self-representation might serve the interests of justice to each individual case. In his dissenting opinion, Justice Blackmun said that he found nothing in the Constitution which gives individuals the right to defend themselves whenever they choose. He then concluded that: "If there is any truth to the old proverb that one who is his own lawyer has a fool for a client, the Court by its opinion today now bestows a *constitutional right* on one to make a fool of himself."

THE DEFENSE ATTORNEY

The preceding cases underscore the important role of the defense attorney in the legal process. The cases have established that an indigent defendant accused of a felony or a misdemeanor involving a prison sentence is entitled to the assistance of a court-appointed lawyer. A defendant also has a right to defend himself or herself (the right *not* to have an attorney) under certain circumstances.

Defense attorneys become involved in courtroom proceedings through several different routes. They can be hired directly by the defendant. An accused who can afford it can select and hire an attorney from among the most experienced and successful in the country. An accused with more limited financial means can also contact and engage his or her own lawyer.

An attorney can be appointed by the state to defend an accused person who cannot afford an attorney. In some states—California and Illinois, for example—there are public defenders who are employed by the state to defend an accused, just as the district attorney is employed by the state to prosecute the accused. In other states, legal aid organizations supported by both private and public funds offer assistance to those who cannot afford a lawyer. In addition, there are law firms which engage in what is referred to as *pro bono publico* work, which means work for the good of the public. Such law firms ask some of their members to devote a part of their time to assisting the poor.

Even though court-appointed attorneys are now required in many cases, some defendants argue that legal aid and public defenders are so overburdened with cases that they are unable to fully prepare the kind of defense that is necessary for complex adversary proceedings. This argument could be countered with the statement that prosecuting attorneys are also overworked and are unable to represent the people's case as effectively as possible. Obviously, if the adversary system is to work properly, both sides should have the best available representation in court. If that does not happen, the system has to be improved or changed in the interests of justice.

THE SUPPORTING PLAYERS: WITNESSES, VICTIM, COURT REPORTER, BAILIFF, AND CLERK

3

Rounding out the cast of characters in the courtroom drama are a number of participants who do not have featured roles. Each of these players, however, makes an important contribution to the play, and each player's presence helps to guarantee the right to a fair and public trial. The court reporter, bailiff, and clerk ensure that the courtroom procedures are followed and that the testimony is accurately reported. The witnesses and the victim testify regarding the crime and present the judge or jury with information which will either acquit or convict the defendant.

THE WITNESSES

Witnesses give testimony at the trial. They are sworn in by promising to "tell the truth, the whole truth, and nothing but the truth." In many courts the oath ends with the phrase "so help me God." This oath is relatively old and reflects the religious background of court trials. The phrase "so help me God" is derived from an older oath meaning "so smite me God." In other words, witnesses were expected to tell the truth or face a punishment which supposedly came from Heaven but which was carried out by the ruler. Today, witnesses who lie on the witness stand may be convicted of *perjury*, a crime punishable by fine or imprisonment. Those witnesses who do not believe in God may declare that they affirm that the testimony that they give will be the truth.

Witnesses can testify only about events they saw or heard directly. The *hearsay* rule, which governs what witnesses may testify to, limits testimony to what a witness knows from personal observation. Secondhand, or hearsay, evidence is prohibited, because the only way to verify a hearsay statement is to call as a witness the person who originally made it. In this way, the statement can be acknowledged under oath and the person can be examined and cross-examined. An exception to the hearsay rule can occur, however, when a statement is considered more likely than not to be truthful because of the circumstances under which it was made. A deathbed statement is an example of such a possible exception.

It is customary to call expert witnesses to the stand to give specialized statements about facts or interpretations of facts. For example, ballistics experts testify about guns and bullets, psychiatrists testify as to the mental state of the accused, and physicians testify regarding the medical condition of the defendant or victim.

As a general rule, witnesses in a case do not sit in the courtroom but sit in the witness room, which is removed from the proceedings.

Why would witnesses be separated from the proceedings?

It is important to prevent witnesses from hearing what others say. If witnesses were to hear one another, they might consciously or unconsciously change their testimony to conform to or contradict what they had heard.

THE VICTIM

The victim in a criminal proceeding can play an important role in the trial. This role depends on the facts and circumstances surrounding the commission of the crime. In a homicide case, the victim's body is used as evidence. In cases of arson, rape, mugging, robbery, burglary, larceny, or assault and battery, the victim may be able to offer important testimony for the state. This will depend, of course, on whether the victim is able to remember the incident accurately or actually saw the defendant commit the crime.

When the victim is the state's star witness, the testimony is assumed to be incriminating. In such cases, the defense counsel will use every available strategy during cross-examination to show that the witness is lying, has a defective memory, or is really not sure of what happened. In other words, the defense will try to break down the witness.

Is it fair to try to break down the witness?

Under the adversary system, the defense must try to raise reasonable doubts in the minds of the jurors concerning the guilt of the defendant. The defense lawyer's tactics may cause the victim additional anxiety. But when life or liberty is at stake, the defendant must have the right, within the rules of due process of law, to make a vigorous defense.

Recently there has been increased concern for the welfare of the victim. The argument has been made that we are overly concerned with the due process rights of the defendant and too little concerned with the plight of victims who have suffered physical injury or loss of property.

Do you agree? Why or why not? If you agree, what suggestions do you have for assisting the victims of crime?

We could say, "Let the victims sue their assailants in a civil case for damages." But there are problems with that idea. If the defendant is sent to jail, he or she will probably not be able to pay a judgment, even if the victim wins the civil case. Of course, if the defendant is wealthy, the victim might be able to collect damages. But lawsuits are expensive, and many victims cannot afford an attorney to bring a civil suit for damages.

There has been a growing awareness of the need to develop programs granting public compensation to victims of muggings, stabbings, homicide, and other violent crimes. Two philosophies underlie this movement, according to *The Challenge of Crime in a Free Society: A Report by the President's Commission on Law and Enforcement and Administration of Justice* (p. 41):

The first argues that the government is responsible for preventing crime and therefore should be made responsible for compensating the victims of the crimes it fails to prevent. The second approach, an extension of welfare doctrines, rests on the belief that people in need, especially those in need because they have been victimized by events they could not avoid, are entitled to public aid.

According to this report, the first modern victim-compensation programs were established in 1964 in Great Britain and New Zealand. Two years later, the first U.S. state to follow this lead (California) initiated a program for victims of limited financial means. In 1966, New York State also instituted a victim-compensation program, but only for those who would suffer serious financial hardship as a result of crime. Other states have now adopted various forms of victim-compensation laws.

What do you think about this trend? Does your state have such a program? Are you satisfied with it?

A recent government report shows that by the end of 1976, eighteen states had enacted victim-compensation laws: Alaska, California, Delaware, Hawaii, Illinois, Kentucky, Louisiana, Maryland, Massachusetts, Minnesota, New Jersey, New York, North Dakota, Pennsylvania, Tennessee, Virginia, Washington, and Wisconsin. In general, those who are eligible for compensation under these laws are the actual victim; a third person who pays the victim's medical expenses; and the spouse, children, or parents of a homicide victim. Payments are generally limited to medical expenses, such as doctor bills, hospital, emergency room, and aftercare treatment, which have not been reimbursed in any way. In addition, payments may cover loss of earnings by the victim, loss of support by the victim's dependants, and funeral and burial expenses occurring as a direct result of the crime. Some states provide compensation for psychological and vocational rehabilitation, while a few compensate for "pain and suffering."

The maximum award in most states is $10,000; in Louisiana it is $50,000. To be eligible for these awards, the applicant must have been an innocent victim of a crime and must not be related to the offender. In addition, as a rule, the victim must have sustained a minimum loss (usually $100) in expenses or two weeks' loss of earnings. Table 1 summarizes the victim compensation programs in fifteen states.

THE COURT REPORTER

Table 1

Selected Provisions of
Victim Compensation
Statutes in 15 States, 1976

The court reporter performs a vital role in keeping an accurate *verbatim* (word for word) account of all that takes place in the courtroom. The court reporter's record of the proceedings is official. Any mistake

	ALASKA	CALIFORNIA	DELAWARE	HAWAII	ILLINOIS	KENTUCKY
Is coverage restricted to violent crimes resulting in injury or death?[a]	Yes	Yes	Yes	Yes	Yes	Yes
How soon after the crime must a claim be filed?	2 yrs.	1 yr.	1 yr.	18 months	2 yrs.	90 days
Must the crime be reported to the police?	Yes	Yes	No[b]	Yes	Yes	Yes
Which losses are eligible for reimbursement?						
(a) medical expenses	(a) Yes	(a) Yes	(a) Yes	(a) Yes	(a) Yes	(a) Yes
(b) loss of earnings or support	(b) Yes	(b) Yes	(b) Yes	(b) Yes	(b) Yes	(b) Yes
(c) pain and suffering	(c) No	(c) No	(c) Yes	(c) Yes	(c) No	(c) No
(d) funeral and/or burial expenses	(d) No	(d) Yes	(d) Yes	(d) Yes	(d) Yes	(d) Yes
In death cases, are dependents eligible for award?	Yes	Yes	Yes	Yes	Yes	Yes
Must claimant show financial need?	No	Yes	Yes	No	No	Yes
What is the minimum loss required?	No minimum	Lesser of $100 or 20 percent of victim's net monthly income	$25	No minimum	$200	$100 or two weeks earnings
What is the maximum limit on compensation[d]	$10,000	$10,000	$10,000	$10,000	$10,000	$15,000
Are reimbursements received by the victim through insurance, etc. deducted from the award?	Yes	Yes	Yes	Yes	Yes	Yes
Is victim ineligible if related to the offender?[e]	Yes	NA[f]	NA[f]	Yes	Yes	Yes

Sources: New York Legislative Commission on Expenditure Review (1975) and National District Attorneys Association (1976)

[a]Most States also extend coverage to persons who are injured or killed while trying to prevent a crime or assist a law enforcement officer.
[b]Cooperation with law enforcement authorities is required.
[c]Compensation limits correspond to those in the workman's compensation provisions.

in the record becomes critical, especially if the case is appealed to a higher court. Court reporters are specially trained for their jobs because of the great responsibility involved.

THE BAILIFF OR MARSHAL

The bailiff, or marshal, is an officer of the court assigned to the important job of assisting the judge in maintaining order in the courtroom. In state and local courts, this task is generally performed by the bailiff; in federal courts, it is done by the marshal. The bailiff is in charge of the defendants and of bringing in witnesses at the proper time.

THE CLERK

The court clerk assists the judge in many ways: keeping a record of the docket (the list of cases to be tried), announcing the entrance

LOUISIANA	MARYLAND	MASSACHU- SETTS	MINNESOTA	NEW JERSEY	NEW YORK	NORTH DAKOTA	PENNSYL- VANIA	WASHING- TON
Yes	Yes	Yes	Yes	Yes	Yes	Yes	Yes	Yes
1 yr.	180 days	1 yr.	1 yr.	1 yr.	1 yr.	1 yr.	1 yr.	180 days
Yes	Yes	Yes	Yes	Yes	Yes	Yes	Yes	Yes
(a) Yes	(a) Yes	(a) Yes	(a) Yes	(a) Yes	(a) Yes	(a) Yes	(a) Yes	(a) Yes
(b) Yes	(b) Yes	(b) Yes	(b) Yes	(b) Yes	(b) Yes	(b) Yes	(b) Yes	(b) Yes
(c) Yes	(c) No	(c) No	(c) No	(c) No	(c) No	(c) Yes	(c) No	(c) No
(d) Yes	(d) Yes	(d) No	(d) Yes	(d) No	(d) Yes	(d) Yes	(d) Yes	(d) No
Yes	Yes	Yes	Yes	Yes	Yes	Yes	Yes	Yes
Yes	Yes	No	No	No	Yes	No	No	No
$100 or two weeks earnings	$100 or two weeks earnings	$100 or two weeks earnings	$100	$100 or two weeks earnings	$100 or two weeks earnings	$100	$100 or two weeks earnings	No minimum[c]
							$10,000 for injury	No
$50,000	$45,000	$10,000	$10,000	$10,000	$15,000	$25,000	$15,000 for death	maximum[c]
Yes	Yes	Yes	Yes	Yes	Yes	Yes	Yes	Yes
Yes	Yes	Yes	Yes	Yes	Yes	Yes	Yes	Yes

[d]Maximum compensation limits are often set for particular types of losses (e.g., for burial expenses).
[e]Restrictions are usually extended to prohibit compensation to victims who had been living with or maintaining a sexual relationship with the offender.
[f]Not assertained.

This material was drawn from James Garofald and L. Paul Sutton, Compensating Victims of Violent Crime: Potential Costs and Coverage of a National Program. *Washington, D.C.: U.S. Government Printing Office, 1977.*

The Court Reporter and the Chessman Case

Larry Millett

His name was Ernest Perry and for more than 30 years he labored in obscurity as a court reporter in Los Angeles. But when Perry died in 1948, his work suddenly became the focus of one of the most celebrated legal battles in American history.

In April, 1948 Perry had been assigned as court reporter for the trial of Caryl Chessman. Chessman was the man Los Angeles newspapers had dubbed the "Red Light Bandit" because he was accused of using a flashing red light atop his car to make his victims believe he was a police officer. During a five-day crime spree, Chessman had allegedly accosted several couples parked in secluded areas. The couples were robbed and the women were forced to perform sex acts.

After a three-week trial, Chessman was convicted of 17 felonies, including kidnapping and attempted rape. The judge then sentenced him to death, a punishment provided by California law for conviction of kidnapping.

But just two days before that sentence was handed down, Ernest Perry had dropped dead of a heart attack. Before he died, Perry had managed to transcribe only about a third of his shorthand notes from the trial. That meant someone else would have to be found to transcribe the rest of the notes so that a complete transcript of Chessman's trial would be available for purposes of appeal.

It became apparent that transcribing Perry's notes would not be easy. Perry did not use the stenographic machine that is used by almost all court reporters today. Instead, he took handwritten notes, using an old-style shorthand that was difficult

Caryl Chessman in 1960, shortly before he was executed.

to decipher. Perry also used his own private symbols—a sort of shorthand within a shorthand—that added to the difficulty of reading his notes.

A court reporter named Stanley Fraser, who had known Perry and was familiar with his style, was finally called in to decipher the notes. But the accuracy of Fraser's transcript soon came into question. This touched off a seemingly endless series of appeals as Chessman tried to show that the transcript of his trial contained numerous errors.

Finally, in November, 1957, a special hearing was held to determine once and for all whether the Perry-Fraser transcript was accurate. The hearing lasted 55 days and produced enough testimony to fill 6,000 pages. When it was all over, the judge certified the transcript as accurate.

Once the transcript question was resolved, Chessman's appeal effort lost steam.

On May 2, 1960—after spending a record 12 years on death row—Chessman was executed in the gas chamber at San Quentin Prison.

of the judge, performing duties assigned by the judge, generally seeing that the courtroom is ready for the trial, and announcing the case to be tried. Some of these functions may be performed by the bailiff, depending on local court procedure.

4 THE AUDIENCE: THE PUBLIC AND THE PRESS

The public and the press make up the audience at a trial. A railing separates the audience from the actors or players, and the press generally sits in the same section as the public. At important trials, a section is set aside for the press, since seats are at a premium.

The presence of the press means that information about the crime and the trial is carried to the public, who can make their own judgment about the fairness of the trial. The public, who are allowed into almost every proceeding, can listen to the testimony firsthand and carry their views outside the courtroom if they think that justice has not been done.

Americans take public trials for granted. We assume that all trials should be open to the public so that the citizens and the press can observe what is going on in the courtroom and evaluate whether justice is being done and whether all the players are performing according to the directions prescribed by the law.

A brief look into history discloses that criminal trials have not always been open to the public. In eighteenth-century France the King had the power to issue *lettres de cachet*—documents ordering the arrest and imprisonment without trial of any person whose name appeared on them. The documents could be issued in blank without the name of any person to the police. King Louis XV is reported to have issued more than 150,000 of these arrest warrants.

The Spanish Inquisition of the thirteenth century employed torture and secret proceedings to ferret out heretics, while the Star Chamber in seventeenth century Britain was a power unto itself grilling suspects and witnesses in private. The public trial was used by the Star Chamber only after all the evidence had been obtained by a variety of means.

It is against this background that the common law of England incorporated the "ancient rule that Courts of Justice are public." By the seventeenth century the public trial was generally accepted under the common law, and, after the settlement of the American colonies the principle of open trials was gradually incorporated into some of the state constitutions. Knowledge of past abuses in criminal proceedings led to the formulation of that famous sentence in the Sixth Amendment of the Bill of Rights that "In all criminal prosecutions, the accused shall enjoy the right to a speedy and public trial."

What does this sentence mean? Do press and public have the right to be present at *every* trial? Let us suppose that the defendant does not want the press and public admitted. Should this request be granted?

A recent case confronted these questions and the differing opinions of the Supreme Court Justices testify to the difficulties posed in interpreting general principles.

GANNETT CO. v.
DEPASQUALE
**Can the court
exclude public and
press from pretrial
judicial proceedings?**

On July 16, 1976, Wayne Clapp, who lived in upstate New York, went fishing with two companions and did not return. Three days later the police found Clapp's bullet-ridden boat but failed to find his body or Clapp's companions. Between July 20 and August 6, the two local newspapers, both owned by the Gannett Company, ran stories about the crime in which the following facts and theories were presented to the readers:

1.   There were three suspects: Jones, an adult; and Greathouse and his wife, both juveniles.
2.   Clapp had probably been shot and his body had been dumped overboard.
3.   Greathouse had a criminal record and was on probation in Texas.
4.   The Michigan police apprehended the three suspects at a place where Clapp's truck was parked.
5.   The New York police theorized that Clapp had been shot with his own pistol, robbed, and thrown into the lake.
6.   Greathouse, after his capture, led the Michigan police to the place where he had buried Clapp's revolver.
7.   Ammunition had also been found at the hotel where the Greathouses had been staying.
8.   The suspects were extradited and arraigned in New York.
9.   The Grand Jury indicted both men on three counts: second-degree murder, robbery, and grand larceny. The woman was indicted for grand larceny. The murder charges were based on the theory that the two men had shot Clapp with his own gun and had weighted his body with anchors and tossed it into the lake. They then made off with the gun, truck, and credit card. It was mentioned that Clapp's body had not been recovered.
10. Both men pleaded not guilty, and their attorneys were given ninety days to file pretrial motions.

The attorneys for the defendants filed several pretrial motions. They asked the court to suppress statements made by the defendants to the police because the statements had not been made voluntarily. In addition, they moved to suppress such physical evidence as the gun, because they argued that it was found as the result of an involuntary confession. They also asked Judge DePasquale to exclude the public and the press from the pretrial hearing, because the adverse publicity of the newspaper stories had created an environment which made it difficult for the defendants to have a fair trial. The District Attorney did not oppose this motion, and Ritter, a reporter for the Gannett papers, raised no objection. The motion was granted.

The following day, Ritter wrote the judge, saying that the press has a constitutional right to cover such hearings and requesting that the judge make available the transcript of the hearing. The request was denied. The judge took the position that to open the pretrial hearing to the public and the press would pose a "reasonable probability of prejudice to these defendants." He concluded that the right to a fair trial had priority over freedom of the press and a public trial.

Do you side with the judge or with the newspapers? Why? Which constitutional amendments are involved? Does history help your position? Do you consider the newspaper stories prejudicial to the accused?

The newspapers challenged the judge's ruling under the First, Sixth, and Fourteenth Amendments which guarantee the right to freedom of the press and the public's right to open trials. They lost in New York State's highest court, the Court of Appeals. The next step was an appeal to the United States Supreme Court.

By this time, an interesting development had occurred. While the case was moving its way toward the highest courts, the defendants engaged in a plea-bargaining agreement under which they pleaded guilty to a lesser offense. A transcript of the pretrial hearing was then made available to the newspapers. The defendant in the case, the trial judge, argued that the issue was now *moot* (abstract and hypothetical because it no longer involved a real dispute). Since courts tend to stay out of moot issues because they seem to have been settled before the case is heard, the defendant in this case asked the higher courts to dismiss the case. Both the New York State Court of Appeals and the United States Supreme Court concluded, however, that the constitutional questions raised by the facts were so important that they required an answer.

If you were a member of the Court, how would you pose the issue to be decided? How would you answer the question?

The opinion of the Court as delivered by Justice Stewart stated the issue as follows:

The question presented in this case is whether members of the public have an independent constitutional right to insist upon access to a pretrial judicial proceeding, even though the accused, the prosecutor and the trial judge all have agreed to the closure of that proceeding in order to assure a fair trial.

The four dissenters, however, posed the issue in this way:

. . . whether and to what extent the Constitution prohibits the States from excluding, at the request of a defendant, members of the public from such a (pretrial) hearing.

Can you detect the difference in these two ways of looking at the facts?

Justice Stewart's opinion for the Court concluded that the public does not have an independent constitutional right to attend a pretrial hearing when defendant, judge, and prosecutor decide that exclusion of the public is necessary for a fair trial. The right to an open trial is personal to the accused, he said, and was not intended to be invoked by the public. It is true, of course, that the public has an interest in seeing that all the rights of the Sixth Amendment are respected, but this does not mean that the public has a constitutional right to attend pretrial hearings. At least eight states have adopted a code which provides for closed pretrial hearings when necessary to protect the accused against prejudicial pretrial publicity. Since such hearings seek to screen out illegally seized evidence or coerced confessions before the actual trial, the opinion continued, it could very well be that potential jurors will be exposed to evidence which would be inadmissible at the trial.

As for the argument that the First and Fourteenth Amendments give public and press a constitutional right to attend criminal proceedings, Justice Stewart concluded that it was not necessary in this case to decide that issue. In the first place, neither the spectators nor the public objected to the judge's exclusion order. When the counsel for the newspapers did object, the judge weighed the competing interests of free press and fair trial and decided that considering the facts of the case free press was outweighed by the defendant's right to a fair trial. The order was temporary because, as Justice Stewart pointed out, once the danger of prejudicial publicity was over, the public and press would be given access to the pretrial transcript.

Chief Justice Burger's concurring opinion differentiated between a *trial* and a *pretrial* hearing, stating that the public has no constitutional right to be present at the latter where decisions are made concerning the inclusion and exclusion of evidence at the trial which follows.

Justice Powell's concurring opinion concluded that the trial judge respected the First Amendment right of freedom of the press by holding a hearing on the exclusion order. The counsel for the newspapers was given an opportunity to present his case and, after weighing the facts and arguments, the judge could reasonably conclude that here was a "unique situation" demanding that public and press be excluded from the hearing.

Under our federal system, according to Justice Rehnquist's concurring opinion, lower courts are free to decide for themselves whether to open or close judicial proceedings if the parties agree that it is desirable, and the Supreme Court should stay out of such local issues.

What is of special interest here is that the Court's opinion speaks for only two Justices: Stewart and Stevens. Each of the three concurring opinions accentuates different views of the problem and the solution. This was not the case with the four dissenters. Justice Blackmun, speaking for Justices Brennen, White, and Marshall, found the newspaper stories factual and to the point, with little editorializing. There was little in the record he concluded, to show an "unabated buildup of adverse publicity."

As Justice Blackmun pointed out, the public trial guarantee of the Sixth Amendment serves several important purposes. It guards against the use of courts "as instruments of persecution." By subjecting all participants in a criminal proceeding to public scrutiny, the open trial "serves to guarantee the fairness of trials." It is necessary that the citizenry have access to the judicial process so that it can judge its strengths and weaknesses. It is for this reason, concluded Justice Blackmun, that the right to a public trial is too important to be left to the decision of the defendant. This view is supported both by the history of the common law and by developments in American legal practices.

Justice Blackmun's discussion of the societal values associated with open trials makes several important points:

It is true that the public trial provision serves to protect every accused from the abuses to which secret tribunals would be prone. But the defendant himself may benefit from the partiality of a corrupt, biased, or incompetent judge, "for a secret trial can result in favor to as well as unjust prosecution of a defendant."

Open trials also enable the public to scrutinize the performance of police and prosecutors in the conduct of public judicial business. Trials and particularly suppression hearings typically involve questions concerning the propriety of police and government conduct that took place hidden from the public view. Any interest on the part of the prosecution in hiding police or prosecutorial misconduct or ineptitude may coincide with the defendant's desire to keep the proceedings private, with the result that the public interest is sacrificed from both sides.

Public judicial proceedings have an important educative role as well. The victim of the crime, the family of the victim, others who have suffered similarly, or others accused of like crimes, have an interest in observing the course of a prosecution. Beyond this, however, is the interest of the general public in observing the operation of the criminal justice system. Judges, prosecutors, and police officials often are elected or are subject to some control by elected officials, and a main source of information about how these officials perform is the open trial. And the manner in which criminal justice is administered in this country is in and of itself of interest to all citizens.

The same rule of open trials, declared Justice Blackmun, applies to pretrial hearings for the following reasons:

I, for one, am unwilling to allow trials and suppression hearings to be closed with no way to ensure that the public interest is protected. Unlike the other provisions of the Sixth Amendment, the public trial interest cannot adequately be protected by the prosecutor and judge in conjunction, or connivance, with the defendant. The specter of a trial or suppression hearing where a defendant of the same political party as the prosecutor and the judge—both of whom are elected officials perhaps beholden to the very defendant they are to try— obtains closure of the proceeding without any consideration for the substantial public interest at stake is sufficiently real to cause me to reject the Court's suggestion that the parties be given complete discretion to dispose of the public's interest as they see fit. The decision of the parties to close a proceeding in such a circumstance, followed by suppression of vital evidence or acquittal by the bench, destroys the appearance of justice and undermines confidence in the judicial system in a way no subsequent provision of transcript might remedy. But even when no connivance occurs, prosecutors and judges may have their own reasons for preferring a closed proceeding.

The dissenters conceded that there may be times when a criminal hearing may have to be closed to the public and press. Such a decision must not be made lightly; it must be "narrowly drawn," and the following guidelines, as a minimum should be observed:

1. The accused must show that an open hearing will create "a substantial probability" that there will be irreparable damage to the right to a fair trial.
2. The accused must show "a substantial probability" that there are no realistic alternatives to a closed trial which will protect the right to a fair trial.
3. The accused must show that there is "a substantial probability" that a closed trial or hearing will be effective in protecting against prejudicial developments.

Having based the dissent on the Sixth and Fourteenth Amendments, which, he said, protects access by public and press to a judicial hearing, Justice Blackmun saw no need to discuss the implications of the First Amendment to this case. He pointed out that if any member of the public is excluded from a trial, "the court must provide a reasonable opportunity to that person to state his objection.

His dissent concludes with a summary of the importance of open hearings.

It has been said that publicity "is the soul of justice." J. Bentham, A Treatise on Judicial Evidence 67 (1825). And in many ways it is:

open judicial processes, especially in the criminal field, protect against judicial, prosecutorial, and police abuse; provide a means for citizens to obtain information about the criminal justice system and the performance of public officials; and safeguard the integrity of the courts. Publicity is essential to the preservation of public confidence in the rule of law and in the operation of courts. Only in rare circumstances does this principle clash with the rights of the criminal defendant to a fair trial so as to justify exclusion.

The right to a fair trial is a precious and hard won victory over the capricious and arbitrary methods used in the past. Modern technology, however, has created conditions which seem to impinge on principles which characterize a fair trial. For example, television coverage and newspaper stories relating to criminal conduct can prejudice a community to the point where it becomes impossible to impanel an impartial jury.

Judge Hugh Stuart

This is not mere conjecture; it is a reality. In the case of Sam Sheppard, accused of murdering his wife (*Sheppard* v. *Maxwell*, [1966]), the Supreme Court decided, with one Justice dissenting, that massive pretrial publicity by the newspapers had prejudiced the accused's chances for a fair trial before an impartial jury. On the other hand, ten years later in *Nebraska Press Association* v. *Stuart* (1976), a unanimous Court condemned a judge's gag order prohibiting newspapers from reporting confessions and other facts "strongly implicative" of the accused. The Justices reasoned that a gag order on the press is so extreme a measure that it should be used only after all else has failed, such as continuance of the trial, change of venue, and searching *voir dire* [questioning of jurors by attorneys before the trial to determine whether they have bias or prejudice which would affect the fairness of the trial] of prospective jurors.

Those who concluded that the Supreme Court in the Stuart case preferred freedom of the press over the right to a fair trial were doomed to disappointment when they read the case of *Gannett Co.* v. *DePasquale.* As we have seen, the four dissenters followed in the spirit of the Stuart decision by maintaining that the press cannot be excluded from criminal proceedings except in unusual circumstances. Yet, the majority of five Justices wrote four opinions, and it is difficult to conjecture how far the Justices will go in closing criminal proceedings to public and press and when that might occur.

RICHMOND NEWSPAPERS v. VIRGINIA
Can the court exclude the public and the press from a criminal trial?

In the *Gannett* case, the Court majority concluded that the Sixth Amendment's provision for a public trial did not guarantee the right of the public and the press to attend *pretrial hearings related to the suppression of evidence.* However, in *Richmond Newspapers, Inc.* v. *Virginia*, decided on July 2, 1980, seven of the Justices concluded that the First and Fourteenth Amendments guaranteed *the right of the public and of the press to attend criminal trials*, except where the circumstances make it impossible for defendants to receive a fair trial. Justice Rehnquist dissented, while Justice Powell did not take part.

Why did the Court seem to change its mind? The *Gannett* ruling was attacked both by the press and by commentators as an infringement on the press, as well as a violation of the historic right of the public to see justice in action. In addition, some of the Justices seem to have differed over the nature and scope of the *Gannett* ruling. Thus the decision in *The Richmond Newspapers, Inc.* case appears to have been an effort by the Court to clarify its position on open trials.

5 DRAMA IN THE COURTROOM: THE PLAY BEGINS, THE PLOT UNFOLDS

The players are now ready to perform their roles and the action begins. A court officer (the clerk or the bailiff) starts the criminal proceedings by announcing: "All Rise! Oyez! Oyez! Oyez! [Hear ye! Hear ye! Hear ye!] The Court of (city, county, state) is now open and in session, the Honorable Judge _____ presiding. All persons having business before the court come to order."

Do you know which of the courts in your community try criminal cases?

The title or name of the case is then announced and, in the case of a jury trial, jury selection begins. After the selection and swearing in of the jury (a method which varies according to jurisdiction), the trial is ready to begin.

Do you know how juries are selected in your community?

The judge asks: "Is the state ready? Is the defendant ready?" If both sides answer yes, the prosecutors begin to unfold the plot with their opening statement. The defendant's lawyers follow with their statement. The attorneys for the prosecution and for the defense outline for the judge and jury the main points which each hopes to prove. The emphasis at this stage is on the facts which are to be presented.

The prosecution calls its first witness, who is sworn in (as are all witnesses), and the questioning (referred to as direct examination) begins. After each prosecution witness is questioned, the defendant's attorney has the right to cross-examine the witness. When the prosecution completes its case, the state's attorney declares: "The state rests."

At this point the defendant's attorney may move to have the charges dismissed because the evidence and testimony presented by the prosecution did not sustain the charges against the defendant. If the judge grants this motion, the trial is over. If the motion is denied, the defense presents its case.

The defendant's attorney now calls the witnesses for the defense, and the prosecution has the right to cross-examine each of them. During cross-examination attorneys try to impeach the credibility of witnesses, that is, throw doubt on their believability by showing that they lied or told only part of the story, or that they are confused or have unreliable memories.

Each side then has the opportunity to make a closing statement. As a rule, the defense attorney begins, followed by the prosecutor. Since the state carries the burden of proving that the accused is guilty beyond a reasonable doubt, the prosecutor is allowed to close the arguments before the jury.

The judge instructs the jury on the law relating to the case. The bailiff conducts the jurors to the jury room where they deliberate on the verdict. The foreperson chairs the discussion and, after the jury returns to the courtroom, delivers the verdict to the judge.

Before imposing sentence, the judge usually waits for the pre-sentence report, a document which tells the judge a great deal about

STAGES OF TRIAL

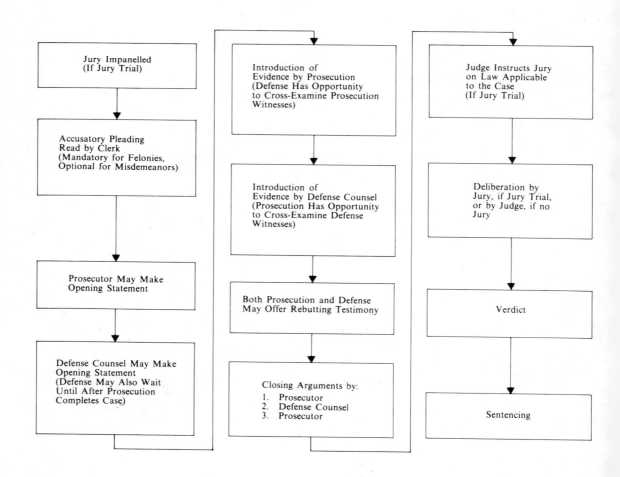

the offender's background, schooling, family, friends, employment, and any past offenses. This is crucial in helping to decide the nature of the sentence and whether the offender will be placed on probation.

If the verdict is guilty, the judge, as a rule, imposes the sentence. (In some states, juries also have the power to impose the sentence in such serious crimes as murder, rape, or robbery.)

LAWYERS' OBJECTIONS

Movie and television courtroom dramas are marked by lawyers objecting and judges either sustaining or overruling the objections. Objections are generally technical matters, but the following examples will illustrate why they are made.

1. As a rule, hearsay evidence is not permitted. Suppose a witness says that he heard John Doe tell Richard Roe that he had a gun. Would you, as a judge, permit this testimony? Or would you insist that John Doe or Richard Roe be brought to the courtroom so that they could be questioned and cross-examined?
2. What is wrong with the question, "Ms. Jones, while walking down the street, you saw John Doe hold up Jane Dow at gun point, did you not?" This can be objected to as a leading question because the answer is being suggested in the form of a question. The witness is being led (or told what to say) by the lawyer. As a rule, such leading questions are not permitted, unless the witness is hostile to the side which is doing the questioning.
3. Lawyers are not permitted to harass witnesses. A lawyer who shouts at a witness, "You are a liar and a thief," will find his opponent objecting to these remarks.

ADMISSIBILITY OF EVIDENCE AND TESTIMONY

Not all evidence or testimony is admitted at a trial. As previously discussed, hearsay testimony and leading questions can be objected to by the attorneys, and the objections may be sustained by the judge. Other important rules for the unfolding of the drama are outlined in the following paragraphs.

THE MIRANDA RULE

Throughout history torture and threats have been used to force confessions, often from the innocent. With this in mind, the founding fathers included in the Bill of Rights the clause in the Fifth Amendment known as the "privilege against self-incrimination," which states: ". . . nor shall be compelled, in any criminal case, to be a witness against himself."

This prohibition is directed against all federal government law-enforcement officials. Under the Fourteenth Amendment's due process of law clause, the same prohibition applies to state and local police officers.

In the now famous case of *Miranda* v. *Arizona* decided in 1966, the U.S. Supreme Court, in a five-to-four ruling, handed down a set of standards relating to admissibility of confessions. These standards were designed to ensure that a confession was made willingly, voluntarily, and knowingly. In order that any statement or confession may be admitted at trial, the police must now inform a person taken into custody of the following rights:

1. You have the right to remain silent.
2. Any statement you make may be used as evidence against you.
3. You have the right to counsel before being questioned.
4. If you cannot afford an attorney, one will be appointed for you before questioning, if you so wish.
5. Do you understand these rights?
6. If you do, are you now willing to talk to us?
7. If you agree to talk, you may stop talking at any time.

An accused can, of course, waive these rights. If he or she does not make a voluntary and knowing waiver, any confession or statements will not be admitted at the trial.

An interesting legal point arises when an accused confesses and then, upon learning of his rights, withdraws the confession. The Supreme Court, in a five-to-four ruling in 1971 (*Harris* v. *New York*) decided that the confession can be introduced to show that the accused is lying, if he takes the stand in his own defense.

A typical Miranda Warning Card carried by law enforcement officers.

MIRANDA WARNING
1. YOU HAVE THE RIGHT TO REMAIN SILENT.
2. IF YOU GIVE UP THE RIGHT TO REMAIN SILENT, ANYTHING YOU SAY CAN AND WILL BE USED AGAINST YOU IN A COURT OF LAW.
3. YOU HAVE THE RIGHT TO SPEAK WITH AN ATTORNEY AND TO HAVE THE ATTORNEY PRESENT DURING QUESTIONING.
4. IF YOU SO DESIRE AND CANNOT AFFORD ONE, AN ATTORNEY WILL BE APPOINTED FOR YOU WITHOUT CHARGE BEFORE QUESTIONING.

WAIVER
1. DO YOU UNDERSTAND EACH OF THESE RIGHTS I HAVE READ TO YOU?
2. HAVING THESE RIGHTS IN MIND, DO YOU WISH TO GIVE UP YOUR RIGHTS AS I HAVE EXPLAINED TO YOU AND TALK TO ME NOW?

Ernesto Miranda is killed; subject of landmark case

Ernesto Miranda, whose rape conviction was overturned by the U.S. Supreme Court in 1966 in a landmark decision, was stabbed to death Saturday night in Phoenix in a fight over a barroom card game.

Miranda, 34, was stabbed in the chest and abdomen, police said.

He was stabbed by one of two men he had beaten in a fistfight minutes earlier in the La Amapola Bar, 231 S. Second St. Patrolman Gordon Costa said.

The killer, believed to be an illegal Mexican immigrant, was being sought in the downtown area.

Minutes after the slaying, police went to the Nogales bar, 21 S. Second St., and arrested a man suspected of handing the knife to the killer.

The man, Fernando Zamora Rodriguez, 23, who was staying at the Hayes Hotel, 335 E. Jefferson, gave police a statement and was booked into Maricopa County jail for investigation of murder, according to Detective Calvin Lash.

Miranda and two men had been drinking and playing cards at the bar when they argued over who owned some change lying on the bar, witnesses told police.

"Ernie beat both of them up, but Fernando slipped the other guy a knife and he stabbed him," said Mary Ann Estrella, 21, barmaid at the La Amapola. "They were playing cards. They tried to get his money.

"Ernie went to the rest room to wash his hands because they were bloody from the fight," she said. "Fernando gave the

Ernesto Miranda

other man a knife and then Fernando's girl friend left with him (Fernando)."

When Miranda returned, Miss Estrella said, "The guy pulled the knife and went after Ernie. Ernie tried to take it away. He stabbed him twice. Ernie just fell down."

Witnesses described the knife as a collapsible weapon with a six-inch, hook blade like those used in cutting linoleum or harvesting lettuce, police said. The knife was not found.

Before being booked, Rodriguez was read — in English and Spanish — a list of his rights from a card carried by all policemen as a result of the 1966 Miranda decision. The card is known as a "Miranda card."

Miranda's conviction for kidnaping and rape was overturned by the Supreme Court on grounds he was not advised of his rights against self incrimination at the time of his arrest and his rights to counsel before questioning.

Source: Arizona Republic, *February 1, 1978, pp. 1, 10. Reprinted with permission of the Arizona* Republic.

He was later retried, convicted and re-sentenced to 20 to 30 years in prison for the crimes, committed in 1963. He also served a concurrent term for an unrelated $8 robbery of a housewife.

Miranda was paroled in 1972. He was arrested in July 1974 on charges of possession of dangerous drugs (three amphetamine pills) and a firearm while on parole. That arrest came after he was stopped for a routine traffice violation. The charges were dropped in October 1974 after a Superior Court judge ruled that the search violated Miranda's rights because police had no reasonable cause to search the car.

Miranda attempted to capitalize on the Supreme Court decision after being released from prison. He sold autographed "Miranda cards" around the Maricopa County Superior Court building.

He originally sold the cards for $1.50, but recently raised the price to $2, one officer said.

When Miranda was arrested in 1963, he was 23 and was working in a produce warehouse.

He had served a year in federal prison for taking a stolen car across state lines.

Miranda was asleep one morning in April 1963 when policemen knocked on the door of his rented house and said they wanted to take him to headquaters.

"I didn't know whether I had a choice . . . " he said in a 1973 interview. "I get in the car and asked them what it was about. They said they couldn't tell me anything. Once we got there they started interrogating me about a kidnap case, telling me that they weren't sure that I had committed the crime or not, but that they had certain information and wanted to get it straightened out.

"This went on for a couple of hours. In the process, I was taken out of one interrogation room and into another." he said.

After repeated questioning, police told him they had an identification of him as the man who had committed two robberies. They said they would drop the robbery charges if he could confess to the kidnap-rape.

"So I made the statement," Miranda said.

But when he got to court he was told he was still charged with robbery. He said he repeatedly asked for a lawyer but was refused. Two weeks later, at a preliminary hearing, he was again denied a lawyer.

Finally, when he was arraigned, an attorney was appointed by the court—a 73-year-old attorney who had practiced virtually no criminal law for 16 years. He persuaded Miranda to plead guilty by reason of insanity.

Miranda was convicted of the robbery charge first and then of the kidnap-rape charges.

While in prison, his case caught the attention of the other lawyers. Phoenix attorney John J. Flynn argued Miranda's case before the U.S. Supreme Court, basing the appeal on the Fifth Amendment right to remain silent and the Sixth Amendment right to counsel. It was one of a number of similar cases before the court.

On June 13, 1966, the Supreme Court issued a 6–3 decision upholding the Fifth and Sixth amendment rights of prisoners.

By chance, Miranda's name was first on the list, so the decision became known as the Miranda decision.

In another case (*U.S.* v. *Mandujano*) the Supreme Court decided that a criminal suspect who appears before a grand jury need not be given the right to remain silent and the assistance of counsel during interrogation. They reasoned that the grand jury is a judicial inquiry, not a police interrogation. The Miranda rule applies to questioning in the police station. It does not apply to a grand jury proceeding, where a witness can invoke the Fifth Amendment's privilege against self-incrimination.

It has been said that the *Miranda Rule* figuratively handcuffs the police. Do you agree? Do you think it is necessary for every person taken into custody by the police to be read the *Miranda* rights and to be given the assistance of counsel? Is this a waste of public funds?

THE EXCLUSIONARY RULE: EXCLUDING ILLEGALLY SEIZED EVIDENCE FROM A TRIAL

Just as the *Miranda Rule* deals with abuses, such as intimidation and force, used to obtain confession the *Exclusionary Rule* deals with abuses used to obtain physical evidence. The framers of the Constitution were especially concerned about improper seizure of evidence because this abuse had been common prior to the American Revolution, when British soldiers had used general search warrants, called "writs of assistance," to search homes and businesses at all hours for smuggled goods. This invasion of privacy, which caused James Otis to invoke a famous English common law maxim: "A man's house is his castle," led to the Fourth Amendment's guarantee against government intrusion into one's home or place of business. The amendment declares:

The right of the people to be secure in their persons, houses, papers, and effects, against unreasonable searches and seizures, shall not be violated, and no warrants shall issue, but upon probable cause, supported by oath or affirmation, and particularly describing the place to be searched, and the persons or things to be seized.

This fundamental guarantee has given rise to many cases involving unreasonable searches and seizures. Although there are many court rulings relating to searches and seizures, there are few hard and fast rules defining probable cause to search and identifying the fine line between a reasonable and unreasonable search. When examining the reasonableness of searches, seizures, wiretapping, and eavesdropping, the following guidelines can be useful.

1. A search warrant based on an affidavit and signed by a magistrate or judge is generally necessary for a search and seizure of evidence. The warrant must be based on "probable cause" or reasonable grounds for suspicion.
2. The search warrant must describe the place to be searched and the specific articles that are being sought.
3. In using a search warrant, the police may seize any con-

traband or item connected with the crime which is "in plain view" in the place being searched.

4.   A search warrant is not necessry to search a moving vehicle, if the police officer has probable cause to believe that the car contains contraband or evidence of a crime.

5.   A person stopped by the police for speeding or for such traffic offenses as driving without a license can be asked to step out of the car. If the police have probable cause to suspect criminal activity, they can search the driver and the car.

There are also rules for obtaining warrants to eavesdrop (using electronic devices) and to engage in wiretaps.

In the now famous case of *Mapp* v. *Ohio* decided in 1961, the Supreme Court, divided six to three, ruled that the Fourth Amendment applies to state and local police officers, as well as to federal officers. (See Appendix A, pp. 248 to 254).

Justice Benjamin Cardozo of the Supreme Court raised an important question by his statement, in a 1926 case, that "The criminal is to go free because the constable has blundered." In other words, should an accused go free because a police officer in the course of his work has seized evidence illegally? Do you think this should be so? Or, should the evidence illegally seized be admitted into evidence against the accused? If you think so, should the police officer be censured and should the accused be given the right to sue the police for trespass?

---

6 DISORDER IN THE COURTROOM: DISRUPTING THE PLAY

Normally trials follow the script described in Chapter 5. But what happens when a defendant who decides that he or she cannot get a fair trial under the usual rules disrupts the course of the courtroom drama? The script that has been developed during the history of legal proceedings then becomes inadequate. If the players do not act on cue in their proper roles, another script must be presented. The following cases are important because they test due process procedure and demonstrate the way the courtroom drama can adapt to another script.

The following case of William Allen began in 1956 in Illinois; reached the U.S. Supreme Court on February 24, 1970; and was decided on March 31, 1970. The decision was handed down just five weeks after the attorneys had argued their case, which is unusual since the Court normally spends several months on a decision. The quick action by the high court and the nature of the case give special significance to this trial.

What measures can a judge take to control a disorderly defendant?

ILLINOIS v. ALLEN

Does the defendant have the right to be present during the trial?

William Allen was charged with taking $200 from a bartender at gunpoint after entering a tavern in Illinois and ordering a drink. After his indictment and during the pretrial stage, Allen refused court-appointed counsel and indicated to the trial court on several occasions that he wished to conduct his own defense. After considerable argument the trial judge told Allen, "I'll let you be your own lawyer, but I'll ask Mr. Kelly [court-appointed counsel] to sit in and protect the record for you, insofar as possible."

The trial began on September 9, 1956. While choosing the first juror, Allen examined him at such length that the trial judge interrupted Allen and requested that he confine his questions solely to matters relating to the juror's qualifications. At this point, Allen started to argue with the judge in a most abusive and disrespectful manner. In seeming desperation, the judge asked the appointed counsel to proceed with the examination of the jurors. Allen continued to talk, proclaiming that the appointed attorney was not going to act as his lawyer. He terminated his remarks by saying, "When I go out for lunchtime you're [the judge] going to be a corpse here."

At this point, Allen tore his attorney's file and threw the papers on the floor. The trial judge then told Allen, "One more outbreak of that sort and I'll remove you from the courtroom."

This warning had no effect on Allen. He continued to talk back to the judge, saying, "There's not going to be no trial either. I'm going to sit here and you're going to talk and you can bring your shackles out and straight jacket and put them on me and tape my mouth, but it will do no good because there's not going to be no trial."

Allen was then removed from the courtroom and the judge ordered the trial to proceed in his absence. The jury was then selected.

After the noon recess but before the jury had returned to the courtroom, Allen appeared before the judge and complained about the lack of fairness of the trial and his court-appointed attorney. He said that he wanted to be present in the court during his trial. The judge said that Allen would be permitted to remain in the courtroom if he behaved himself and did not interfere with the introduction of the case.

The jury was brought in and seated. Allen's counsel moved that witnesses be excluded from the courtroom. Allen protested this move and said, "There is going to be no proceeding. I'm going to start talking and I'm going to keep on talking all through the trial. There's not going to be no trial like this. I want my sister and my friends in court to testify for me."

Allen was removed a second time and remained out of the courtroom throughout the presentation of the state's case except for the several occasions at which he was brought in for identification. During one of these appearances, Allen responded to one of the judge's questions with vile and abusive language.

After the prosecution's case had been presented, the trial judge told Allen that he could return if he agreed to conduct himself properly. Allen gave his assurance and was conducted back into the courtroom by his court-appointed lawyer.

The jury found Allen guilty of armed robbery, and he was sentenced to serve ten to thirty years in the Illinois State Penitentiary.

You are his lawyer. Do you have grounds for appeal?

THE DEFENDANT'S ARGUMENTS

As Allen's lawyer, you would have to look at the United States Constitution to see whether you can find any provision that applies to your case. Get a copy of the Constitution and see what you can find. Before you read further in this book, try to find the key sentence or phrase that would be helpful in your appeal.

If you have found it, good for you. If you are having trouble, you may want to look at the Bill of Rights, Amendments I to X. What do you find there that will help your case?

The Sixth Amendment provides in part: "In all criminal prosecutions, the accused shall enjoy the right . . . to be confronted with the witnesses against him . . ." This is known as the confrontation clause. Does it apply to your case?

Remember that the Bill of Rights to the Constitution applies to federal government action, but the Allen case is a state prosecution, as you can see from its title, *Illinois* v. *Allen*. How could you argue that this provision applies to your client? See whether the Fourteenth Amendment helps you.

The Fourteenth Amendment provides that no state can deprive a person of life, liberty, and property without due process of law. Certainly you could argue that the Sixth Amendment confrontation clause is part of due process of law and that a defendant in a state case must be confronted with the witnesses against him or her. Without seeing the witnesses and hearing what they say, the accused could not refute the evidence and the testimony presented. The defense attorney may need to consult with the defendant about the accuracy of witnesses' statements in order to question and cross-examine them to test the truth of their testimony.

THE PROSECUTOR'S CASE

Assume that you are the prosecutor. How would you answer the defendant's powerful arguments? Would you say that the defendant is not entitled to confront the witnesses against him? Would you agree that the judge was correct in expelling Allen from the courtroom? What provisions in the Constitution can you find to support your side of the case?

THE ISSUE

The Supreme Court stated the issue as follows:

The question presented in this case is whether an accused can claim the benefit of this constitutional right to remain in the courtroom while at the same time he engages in speech and conduct which is so noisy, disorderly, and disruptive that it is exceedingly difficult or wholly impossible to carry on the trial.

THE SUPREME COURT'S DECISION AND OPINIONS

Because this case is so important, the following excerpts are presented to give a flavor of the Court's reasoning. Justice Black wrote the Court's opinion, which included this argument:

We explicitly hold today that a defendant can lose his right to be present at trial if, after he has been warned by the judge that he will be removed if he continues his disruptive behavior, he nevertheless insists on conducting himself *in a manner so disorderly, disruptive, and disrespectful of the court* that his trial cannot be carried on with him in the courtroom. Once lost, the right to be present can, of course, be reclaimed as soon as the defendant is willing to conduct himself consistently with the decorum and respect inherent in the concept of courts and judicial proceedings.

It is essential to the proper administration of criminal justice that dignity, order and decorum be the hallmarks of all court proceedings in our country. *The flagrant disregard in the courtroom of elementary standards of proper conduct should not and cannot be tolerated.* We believe trial judges confronted with disruptive, contumacious, stubbornly defiant defendants must be given sufficient discretion to meet the circumstances of each case. No one formula for maintaining the appropriate courtroom atmosphere will be best in all situations. *We think there are at least three constitutionally permissible ways for a trial judge to handle obstreperous defendants like Allen: (1) bind and gag him, thereby keeping him present; (2) cite him for contempt; (3) take him out of the courtroom until he promises to conduct himself properly.*

Which of these methods would you have used if you had been the judge? If you were a juror in a case in which the defendant had been bound and gagged, would you be affected by this sight?

It is not pleasant to hold that respondent Allen was properly banished from the court for a part of his own trial. *But our courts, palladiums of liberty as they are, cannot be treated disrespectfully with impunity.* Nor can the accused be permitted by his disruptive conduct indefinitely to avoid being tried on the charges brought against him. *It would degrade our country and our judicial system to permit our courts to be bullied, insulted, and humiliated and their orderly progress thwarted, and obstructed by defendants brought before them charged with crimes.* As guardians of the public welfare, our state and federal judicial systems strive to administer equal justice to the rich and the poor, the good and the bad, the native and foreign born of every race, nationality, and religion. Being manned by humans, the courts are not perfect and are bound to make some errors. But, if our courts are to remain what the Founders intended, the citadels of justice, their proceedings cannot and must not be infected with the sort of scurrilous, abusive language and conduct paraded before the Illinois trial judge in this case. The record shows that the Illinois judge at all times conducted himself with that dignity, decorum, and patience that befits a judge. Even in holding that the trial judge had erred, the Court of

Appeals praised his "commendable patience under severe provocation." We do not hold that removing this defendant from his own trial was the only way the Illinois judge could have constitutionally solved the problem he had.

We do hold, however, that there is nothing whatever in this record to show that the judge did not act completely within his discretion. Deplorable as it is to remove a man from his own trial, even for a short time, we hold that the judge did not commit legal error in doing what he did . . . [emphasis added]

Justice Brennan wrote a *concurring opinion*, that is, an opinion in which he agreed with the Court's decision but gave his own reasons in support of that decision.

As you read this excerpt from his opinion, can you state in your own words the message that he is trying to convey?

I would add only that when a defendant is excluded from his trial, the court should make reasonable efforts to enable him to communicate with his attorney and, if possible, to keep apprised of the progress of his trial. Once the court has removed the contumacious defendant, it is not weakness to mitigate the disadvantages of his expulsion as far as *technologically possible in the circumstances*. [emphasis added]

What Justice Brennan was probably referring to was the use of technology to make it possible for the defendant to communicate with his lawyer. Such methods as closed-circuit television and two-way telephone systems can be and have been used. The use of a bulletproof glass booth was used in the war crimes trial of Adolph Eichmann in Jerusalem. On that occasion, the booth was used to protect the prisoner from any attack, but it can be used to allow an accused to see and hear what is going on at the trial without being able to disrupt it.

Justice Douglas wrote a separate opinion in which he stated that the record seemed to show that Allen had a history of emotional disturbance. He concluded that the long period of time in which the case had rested in the courts (1956 to 1970) had made it a stale issue and suggested that the case be sent to a lower court to decide the issue of the defendant's mental health.

Because of the question of mental health, Justice Douglas questioned the use of this case to establish "guidelines for judicial control." He continued by saying, "The social compact has room for tolerance, patience, and restraint, but not for sabotge and violence. Trials involving that spectacle strike at the very heart of constitutional goverment."

Judge Harold R. Medina of the *Dennis* case (see page 52).

What did Douglas mean in the above paragraph?

The following two cases relate directly to the Allen case and have established principles for handling disruption by defendants during a courtroom proceeding.

DENNIS v. UNITED STATES

In 1949, eleven Communist leaders were tried in New York for conspiring to organize the Communist Party in order to teach and advocate the overthrow and destruction of the United States government by force and violence. The proceedings were marked by arguments, insults, and such delaying tactics as the endless reading of documents and innumerable objections by attorneys and charges that the judge was prejudiced. The trial ran on for ten months, and at its end the defendants were convicted. Judge Harold Medina held one defendant and five of the lawyers in contempt of court.

UNITED STATES v. DELLINGER ET AL.

UNITED STATES v. SEALE

The Chicago conspiracy trial of 1969-1970 has been described as "the most notorious disorderly trial in recent years." Eight leaders of the movement to oppose the Vietnam War were charged with conspiring, organizing, and inciting to riot during the 1968 Democratic National Convention in Chicago. The trial was marked by frequent confrontations between Judge Julius Hoffman and the defendants and their lawyers.

Much of the disorder at first centered around Bobby Seale. Seale had requested postponement of the trial until his lawyer, who was undergoing surgery, could represent him. When his request was denied, Seale demanded to represent himself. Judge Hoffman insisted that Seale was already represented by the attorneys for the other defendants. When Seale continued to disobey the judge's orders, particularly by trying to make statements on his own behalf and to examine witnesses, Judge Hoffman had him bound and gagged. This triggered further outbursts from the other defendants, their lawyers, and many of the members of the public who were observing the trial. Similar conflicts between defendants and their lawyers and the prosecution and the judge continued throughout the trial.

Six weeks after the trial opened, Judge Hoffman declared a mistrial for Seale and severed his case from that of the other defendants. At the same time, he adjudged Seale guilty of sixteen acts of contempt of court and sentenced him to three months for each.

Of the seven remaining defendants, all were found not guilty on the conspiracy charge; on the charge of crossing state lines with intent to incite to riot, five were found guilty and two were acquitted. In their case as well, Judge Hoffman handed down multiple contempt sentences at the end of the trial. Attorney William Kunstler received the longest sentence: four years for twenty-four separate contempt charges.

Bobby Seale as he was bound and gagged during the Chicago conspiracy trial.

Besides Bobby Seale, the other defendants in the Chicago conspiracy trial were Jerry Rubin (pounding his fist) and, *left to right*, John Froines, Abbie Hoffman, Lee Weiner, David Dellinger, Tom Hayden, and Rennie Davis.

Later the U.S. Court of Appeals overturned both the incitement to riot convictions and the contempt citations and ordered new hearings. The court also reversed the contempt citations against Bobby Seale and ordered the charges to be heard by a jury before a different judge. In this case the basis of the Court of Appeals' decision was the due process clause of the Fourteenth Amendment which has been interpreted by the Court to require that a defendant who may be deprived of liberty through a contempt proceeding be given a public hearing before a judge other than the one who brought the contempt charge. For the same judge who was the target of the alleged act of contempt to judge the defendant guilty and pass sentence would be like allowing a plaintiff to act as both judge and jury. In addition, the Court of Appeals stated that, by waiting until the end of the trials to issue the contempt citations, the judge had defeated the purpose of the contempt power. A charge of contempt is intended to discourage further acts of misconduct and to promote order in the courtroom. It cannot do this if it is delayed until the end of the trial.

In the cases involving the Communists and the Chicago protestors, the defendants insisted that they were being used as examples to repress dissent or criticism of government policies. The government argued, however, that the defendants had violated the laws of the country and had to suffer the consequences.

A BRIEF LOOK BACK AT THE ALLEN CASE

The *Allen* case, with which we began this chapter, was decided very quickly by the United States Supreme Court early in 1970. We asked the question, Why was this case decided with such unusual speed? The *Allen* decision was handed down while the Chicago conspiracy trial was in progress. Because of obvious parallels in the *Allen* and *Chicago Seven* (Bobby Seale) cases and the speed with which the *Allen* case was decided, many who followed the Supreme Court closely felt that the Court decided to use the *Allen* case to make known its views on court disruptions.

Explore the *Allen* opinions for possible references to the Chicago defendants and to Judge Hoffman.

Allen had demanded to act as his own lawyer. Seale also claimed the right to represent himself in the absence of his chosen counsel. While Allen had no apparent rational basis for wanting to represent himself, Seale had reasons of a political nature. His own attorney, who was in the hospital when the trial began, had special experience and skill in bringing out the political issues in a case. By insisting on representing himself, Seale called attention to the judge's refusal to postpone the trial until that attorney could be present.

Justice Black's opinion in *Allen* speaks of binding and gagging, of contempt citations as possible means of keeping a defendant quiet while allowing him to remain in the courtroom, and of removing the defendant from the room. Judge Hoffman had Seale bound and gagged and frequently threatened the defendants with contempts, although he did not actually issue contempt citations until the end of the trial. Justice Black seems to be saying that these means were permissible, if necessary, to allow the trial to proceed.

The majority opinion also notes that the trial record showed that the judge in the *Allen* case had conducted himself "with that dignity, decorum and patience that befit a judge." Is the Court telling the judge in the Chicago Seven trial that he was not conducting himself with such "commendable patience"?

Justice Douglas also included statements in his opinion which seem to refer to the trial of the Chicago Seven. He said that the *Allen* case should not be used as a basis for general "guidelines for judicial behavior," because it is too different from the political trials and the trials of minorities which may produce disorder. "There is time enough (to deal with such trials)," he added, "when a political trial reaches this Court for review."

At the same time, Justice Douglas warned that throughout history political defendants have deliberately provoked harsh and repressive measures against themselves in order to call attention to political issues. Perhaps he was suggesting that, in a political trial, a judge may need to act with greater dignity and patience than in an ordinary trial.

7 THE JURY HANDS DOWN A VERDICT

The members of the jury must observe the entire drama unfold before them, listening carefully to the lines, watching the faces of the players, and evaluating the credibility of the witnesses. On the basis of that drama they must determine whether the defendant is guilty.

The word, juror, comes from a Latin word meaning "to swear." In England, jurors were originally witnesses called by the king to testify about their neighbors, their property, and any crimes that might have been committed in their neighborhoods. It took hundreds of years for the system of trial by jury to replace the ordeals by fire, water, and battle and the trials by compurgation, which had been used to determine guilt or innocence. The present jury system represents a triumph of democracy, because it uses one's peers to determine guilt. Today jurors are expected to be unbiased and to swear or affirm that they will decide the case only on the evidence presented in court and not on any information that they may have picked up about the case from other sources such as TV, newspapers, or gossip.

Who should serve on a jury in a criminal case?

If you were being tried in a criminal proceeding, who would you want to judge you? You are entitled to a jury of your peers. Does that mean that teen-aged defendants should have teen-agers on the jury? Should Christians be tried by a jury of Christians, Jews by Jews, women by women, men by men, blacks by blacks, Chicanos by Chicanos, and so on?

The phrase "a jury of one's peers" has come to mean a jury of persons "representative of a cross-section of the community." Since the term "peers" does not appear in the constitutional provisions dealing with jury trials, the Supreme Court has interpreted a jury of peers to mean persons who can represent the conscience of the community—the good and common sense of the people.

Jurors are selected from voter registration lists or official tax lists of the county or community. The names of prospective jurors are placed in a metal container or wheel and are drawn out by the sheriff, the commissioner of jurors, or some other public official. Certain people may be excused from jury duty: doctors, lawyers, mothers who have to look after young children, or others for whom service would cause hardship.

Many people who are qualified for jury duty try to evade it by pleading hardship. Such hardships can include poor health, loss of income for those whose jobs pay more than the pay for jury duty,

The Jury in History

The origins of the present-day jury system are buried in the legends and history of the past. One source traces it to ancient Egypt, where, more than 4,000 years ago, workers in cemeteries were tried for minor offenses by juries of eight, four from each side of the Nile River. Another source traces the jury to the trial of a Greek god by a jury of twelve gods, whose split decision resulted in an acquittal. The first trial of a human in recorded Greek history was that of Orestes, accused of murdering his mother. Tried by a jury of twelve gods who split six to six, he was saved by Athena, Goddess of Wisdom, who interceded on his behalf and saved his life.

The most famous jury trial in Ancient Athens was that of Socrates. The jury of 501 men found him guilty by a majority of 60 and sentenced him to death. The size of Greek juries varied from 101 to 2001, depending on the importance of the case. The odd number was designed to break ties, while the large numbers probably prevented tampering with the jury through bribery, corruption, or exertion of influence.

Roman juries varied in size from fifty to seventy-five members. Known as *judices*, they decided both questions of fact and law, did the Greek jury. While a presiding officer or magistrate took charge of the proceedings of the Roman jury, a chairman presided over the informal Greek jury proceedings.

Historians trace early forms of jury decision-making to the Germanic tribes, the Scandinavians, and the Norse. More than 1,000 years ago, the Scandinavians had juries of twelve and the Norwegians had juries of thirty-six presided over by a law-man. The Scandinavian jury could arrive at decisions by a vote of seven. The Norwegian jury had to be unanimous. A non-unanimous decision could be overruled by the lawman and the king.

Unlike our present-day system, jurors in medieval England had to be *familiar with the facts in a case*. In reality, they were witnesses called together by the king's representatives to tell what they knew. Only many years later did jurors begin to resemble those of today—men and women who would swear to decide a case solely on the evidence presented in the court. Witnesses and jurors were eventually separated in court proceedings.

There is much speculation in the history of juries as to how the number twelve came to be accepted as the proper size. In medieval England, the number of juries varied from six to sixty-six, although the number twelve appears again and again. For example, twelve was the number associated with compurgation or wager of law. Alfred the Great (871–899) issued a decree that "If a royal thane be accused of homicide he shall purge himself with twelve thanes." In the reign of Henry II (1154–1189), a law provided that "The sheriff shall cause twelve legal men of the neighborhood . . . to take an oath in the presence of the bishop that they will declare the truth about it."

When the colonists settled this country, they brought with them the tradition of the jury trial. It became associated with the rights of Englishmen and was mentioned in many important documents, including the Declaration of Independence.

Sources: Lloyd E. Moore. The Jury: Tool of Kings, Palladium of Liberty. *Cincinnati: W. H. Anderson Company, 1973.*

Morris J. Bloomstein. Verdict: The Jury System. *Rev. ed. New York: Dodd, Mead & Co. 1972.*

and difficulty in finding and paying for child care. One possible solution for the problem of loss of income is that employers, as a public service, might pay employees the difference between their jury pay and their salary, or continue paying the salary while the jurors, in turn, give their jury pay to their employers. To help with the problem of child care, some day care centers might agree to take the children of jurors at a special reduced rate. Such cooperation between businesses and social agencies would encourage people to accept their responsibility of jury duty.

Before prospective jurors may serve on a jury, they must be questioned by the lawyers, the judge, or by both. Procedures differ among states and in the federal courts. The examination of prospective jurors is called *voir dire*, which is a French phrase freely interpreted to mean "to see and to say [the truth]." The lawyers and the judge try to determine whether the jurors are biased, whether they know or are related to the parties in the case, and whether they have made up their minds as to the guilt or innocence of the defendant. Our jury system requires jurors to be unbiased and willing to decide the case *only on the evidence and testimony presented in court*.

If you were a prosecutor or defense attorney, would you want unbiased jurors?

Since lawyers want to win their cases, it is reasonable to conclude that they would prefer jurors who are biased in their favor. For example, a prosecutor would prefer to have jurors who favor law and order and who are not easily moved by special circumstances. On the other hand, attorneys for minority defendants would prefer jurors who are sympathetic to minorities or who feel that those who are disadvantaged or have suffered discrimination should be given special consideration. Similarly, attorneys for wealthy defendants would want jurors who are sympathetic to people of their class.

Lawyers on either side may challenge a prospective juror and ask that he or she be excused from the case. A *challenge for cause* means that the lawyers have a good reason to suspect that the juror is not qualified. Such a challenge may be based on the juror's bias. For example, if the juror knows the facts in the case and has formed an opinion based on this knowledge or is related to one of the lawyers or parties in the case, he or she can be challenged for cause. There are unlimited challenges for cause. In addition, each side in the case has a limited number of *peremptory challenges* which allow them to ask that a juror be excused without giving any reason.

After the proper number of jurors has been selected, the jury is impanelled. The foreperson of the jury is either designated by the judge or elected by the jurors.

Some attorneys use psychologists and sociologists to help them select jurors likely to be sympathetic to their cases. These experts

THE SMALL SOCIETY

develop a profile of the kind of juror to be selected. They then suggest questions concerning such criteria as job; religion; education; preference in books, magazines, and TV programs; and style of hair-cut and clothing which will enable the lawyers to select jurors who fit the profile.

Opinions differ concerning the effectiveness of this procedure. Where trials in which this system was used ended in a hung jury or an acquittal, some observers have given credit to the selection process. Others claim that the selection process is not foolproof and may even be harmful to the defendant.

THE GRAND JURY

In addition to a jury that sits in a trial (known as a petit jury), there is a jury called a grand jury that is impanelled to decide whether or not to indict (charge) a defendant with a crime. These two juries emerged during the development of the justice system in England and were incorporated into the American system.

Grand juries are required by the Fifth Amendment, which states: "No person shall be held to answer for a capital, or otherwise in-famous, crime unless on a presentment or indictment of a grand jury." The grand jury has the power to hand down indictments or accusations against people in the community after the prosecutor has presented evidence to the grand jury to support probable cause that the accused has violated the law. As a rule, neither the accused nor the accused's lawyer has the right to appear before the grand jury. The prosecutor decides who will be called to testify under oath before the grand jury.

The grand jury has been criticized because the proceedings are secret and the accused is excluded. Those who defend the grand jury claim that secrecy is necessary to protect the innocent. They say that testimony may not be sufficient to accuse anyone and making the proceedings public would give a false impression about the people being investigated. They also point out that secrecy protects those who testify from reprisals.

What do you think? Would you rather have the grand jury sessions open for public attendance? If you were the accused, would you want to appear before the grand jury? Would you want the assistance of a lawyer?

Federal grand juries consist of twenty-three people chosen from the community who serve for a period of time. A majority of twelve is necessary to hand down a True Bill—an indictment or accusation. State grand juries consist of twenty-three or fewer people and each state can determine for itself the vote necessary for an indictment.

Do you know how many people are on the grand jury in your state and the vote necessary for an indictment?

THE PETIT JURY

We generally think of the petit jury as the twelve-person jury. How did the trial jury become a twelve-person jury? Why not use six, seven, or twenty-three people on the jury?

The number of people on the jury may have a biblical origin. The Bible speaks of twelve disciples, twelve tribes of Israel, and twelve judges in Solomon's temple. The number could have been a gradual development from the unwieldy juries of large numbers used originally to a more manageable size that allows individual jurors to feel a sense of responsibility for their judgment.

The Sixth Amendment declares that "in all criminal prosecutions, the accused shall enjoy the right to a speedy and public trial, by an impartial jury of the state and district wherein the crime shall have been committed." Note, however, that the Sixth Amendment makes no reference to the number of persons required to make up a jury.

In 1968 in *Duncan* v. *Louisiana*, the United States Supreme Court interpreted the due process clause of the Fourteenth Amendment to include the Sixth Amendment's right to trial by jury. This ruling extended the right to jury trials to people accused of crimes under state law. Before this decision, it was thought that under the Sixth Amendment a jury trial was required in federal cases only; the states at that time were free to make their own rules governing criminal trials.

Today, if you walk into a federal courthouse in which a criminal case is being tried, you will find a twelve-person jury. If you walk into a state or local courthouse in which a criminal trial is being held, you may find a six-person or a twelve-person jury. Since the right to jury trial is applicable today in both state and federal cases as a part of due process, why should due process not require the same number of jurors in both state and federal courts?

WILLIAMS v.
FLORIDA
Does the defendant get a fair trial with a six-person jury?

Johnny Williams was charged with robbery, tried, and found guilty in a Florida court. He was tried by a six-person jury. Williams appealed on the ground that the Fourteenth Amendment's due process of law clause required that Florida try him before the traditional twelve-person jury.

If you were a judge on the appellate court, how would you decide this issue? What would be your reasons?

The United States Supreme Court decided, with only Justice Thurgood Marshall dissenting, that the six-person jury was constitutional. Justice White, writing for the Court, said that the number twelve appeared to be an historical accident. He went on to say that the number of jurors is not important because there is no evidence to show that the twelve-person jury is more advantageous than a smaller number. Justice White stated:

To be sure, the number should probably be large enough to promote group deliberation, free from outside attempts at intimidation, and to provide a fair possibility for obtaining a representative cross-section of the community. But we find little reason to think that these goals are in any meaningful sense less likely to be achieved when the jury numbers six, than when it numbers twelve.

The majority of the Court decided that each state has the right to decide the number of jurors that would allow the defendant a fair hearing. This right rests with the states under the Tenth Amendment, which reserves to the states certain powers, one of which is the power to set up a system of criminal justice. In other words, a state must arrange its own jury system to give the defendant the due process of law required.

Once the Court had decided in the Williams case that six-person juries were constitutional, the question of the constitutionality of juries of less than six persons was inevitable. Georgia, Louisiana, and Virginia had created five-person juries for certain nonpetty criminal offenses. The Georgia law was the first to reach the Supreme Court.

BALLEW v. GEORGIA

Are five-person juries in criminal cases constitutional?

Claude Davis Ballew, the manager of the Paris Art Adult Theater in Atlanta, Georgia, was accused of showing an allegedly obscene film. Charged with distributing obscene material (a misdemeanor), he was tried before a five-person jury, which found him guilty after deliberating thirty-eight minutes. He was fined $2,000 and given a one-year prison sentence which would be suspended upon payment of the fine.

Ballew appealed on several grounds. One of his arguments was that a jury of five was "constitutionally inadequate" to assess the contemporary standards of the community. The Georgia statute stated that community standards were to be applied in determining obscenity. Supreme Court obscenity rulings also require the community standards measuring rod. A jury of twelve, Ballew argued, was better able than a jury of five to decide what was regarded as obscene in a community. The smaller jury was less likely to represent a cross-section of community attitudes.

Would you favor five-person jury trials in your community? What do you think of the argument that twelve individuals are better qualified to reach a verdict on obscenity than five persons?

The Supreme Court's decision was unanimous, but only one justice agreed with Justice Blackmun's opinion announcing the Court's decision. The other justices had their own reasons for reaching that decision.

The Court ruled that the five-person jury is unconstitutional. Referring to the case of *Williams* v. *Florida*, Justice Blackmun reaffirmed that the "purpose of the jury trial . . . is to prevent oppression by the Government." He went on to say that the right to be judged by a jury of one's peers gives the accused a safeguard against "the corrupt or over-zealous prosecutor and against the compliant, biased, or eccentric judge." The jury system makes it possible for the community to participate in the determination of guilt or innocence. In the jury, the common sense of the people of the community plays a critical role in the search for justice.

In the *Williams* case, the Court had decided that a six-person jury could fulfill the purpose of jury trials which the Sixth and Fourteenth Amendments intended. In the *Ballew* case, however, the Court ruled that the five-person jury could not fulfill the purpose of a jury trial for the following reasons:

1. Research studies show that "smaller juries are less likely to foster effective group deliberation." At some point, this decline in number leads to "inaccurate fact-finding and incorrect application of the common sense of the community to the facts." In larger juries, prejudices of individuals are more frequently counterbalanced.

Justice Harry Blackmun wrote the Supreme Court's decision in the *Ballew* case, which declared that the five-person jury is unconstitutional.

2. "Statistical studies suggest that the risk of convicting an innocent person . . . rises as the size of the jury diminishes."
3. As jury panels decrease in size, the number of hung juries decreases, representing a detriment to the defense.
4. Smaller juries may result in the exclusion of minority groups or minority viewpoints; the smaller the jury, the less it is truly representative of the community.
5. Verdict consistency must be considered. "When the case is close, and the guilt or innocence of the defendant is not readily apparent, a properly functioning jury system will insure evaluation by the common sense of the community and will also tend to insure accurate factfinding."

If all this is true, what is the actual difference between a five-person and a six-person jury? The Court agrees that there is not a clear line between the two, but it believes that a line has to be drawn somewhere. According to Justice Blackmun:

Because of the *fundamental importance* of the jury trial to the American system of criminal justice, any further reduction that promotes inaccurate and possibly biased decision making, that causes untoward differences in verdicts, and that prevents juries from truly representing their communities, attains constitutional significance. [emphasis added]

The Court then turns to the question, Why have states decided to decrease the number of jurors from the traditional twelve persons?

Can you think of any reasons why states have been using five- and six-person juries instead of twelve?

The answer seems obvious. Smaller juries cost less and are supposed to decide cases more quickly. The Court did not seem convinced that smaller juries save judicial time. Justice Blackmun concluded that Georgia had shown "little or no justification for its reduction to five members."

Justice White concurred with the observation that a five-person jury would fail "to represent the sense of the community" and would not satisfy the "fair cross-section requirement of the Sixth and Fourteenth Amendments."

Justice Powell, with Chief Justice Burger and Justice Rehnquist concurring, agreed with the judgment of the Court but expressed reservations concerning Justice Blackmun's use of "numerology," derived from statistical studies comparing jury sizes, which the court reviewed and cited in its opinion.

What number would you pick as being necessary for a fair trial? Do larger numbers of jurors necessarily mean greater fairness (due process) for the accused?

THE UNANIMOUS VERDICT RULE

The Constitution does not make any reference to a unanimous decision by the jury. However, a major principle of our legal system is that an accused is presumed innocent until proven guilty *beyond a reasonable doubt*. Proof beyond a reasonable doubt, although difficult to define, is generally understood to mean that the jurors are satisfied in their consciences and in their judgment that there is no real, substantial, or important reason to doubt the accused's guilt.

Since a person's life, liberty, or property (heavy fines may be imposed in addition to prison sentences) is at stake, proof beyond a reasonable doubt is an important protection for the innocent. The custom of a unanimous jury verdict developed as a part of the beyond-a-reasonable-doubt standard. If even one person disagreed, the accused had to be freed or tried again.

The laws in a number of states do not require a unanimous

verdict. Since the Constitution does not specifically state that a unanimous verdict is essential, the Supreme Court had to decide whether the due process clause should be interpreted to demand unanimity.

JOHNSON v.
LOUISIANA

APODACA v.
OREGON
Must a jury's verdict be unanimous?

The states of Louisiana and Oregon changed their laws dealing with jury verdicts. The Louisiana law reads as follows:

Cases in which punishment may be capital shall be tried by a jury of twelve jurors, all of whom must concur to render a verdict. Cases in which the punishment is necessarily at hard labor shall be tried by a jury of twelve jurors, nine of whom must concur to render a verdict. Cases in which the punishment may be imprisonment at hard labor, shall be composed of five jurors, all of whom must concur to render a verdict.

Frank Johnson was arrested for armed robbery in Louisiana and was tried by a twelve-person jury. He was convicted by a nine-to-three vote.

The Oregon law provided that:

In all criminal prosecutions, the accused shall have the right to public trial by an impartial jury in the county in which the offense shall have been committed . . . provided, however, that any accused person, in other than capital cases, and with the consent of the trial judge, may elect to waive trial by jury and consent to be tried by the judge of the court alone, such election to be in writing; provided, however, that in circuit court ten members of the jury may render a verdict of guilty or not guilty, save and except a verdict of guilty of first degree murder, which shall be found only by a unanimous verdict, and not otherwise . . .

Robert Apodaca, Henry Cooper, and James Madden were tried before separate Oregon juries for assault with a deadly weapon, burglary of a dwelling, and grand larceny, respectively. Apodaca and Madden were each convicted by a vote of eleven to one, Cooper by a vote of ten to two. Cooper and Madden joined Apodaca in appealing his case, and the three cases were consolidated for hearing in the Supreme Court.

The defendants in both the Louisiana and Oregon cases appealed their convictions to the U.S. Supreme Court on the grounds that the laws under which they had been tried were unconstitutional. They argued that the jury verdicts should have been unanimous.

Why do you think Louisiana and Oregon passed laws which permit nine-to-three and ten-to-two jury verdicts? What reasons would the state legislators have for allowing this?

Why do you think that the defendants in the Louisiana and Oregon cases protested the laws?

If you were a prosecutor, defense lawyer, juror, or member of the public, would you favor a nonunanimous verdict?

The Supreme Court found the issue difficult to resolve. Four justices agreed with Louisiana and Oregon that the state laws were constitutional. Four justices agreed with the defendants that the laws were unconstitutional. Justice Powell was the "swing" man whose vote decided the cases.

Justice Powell took the position that the states have the power to experiment with their systems of justice under the powers reserved to them by the Tenth Amendment. He cast his vote on the side of the states of Louisiana and Oregon. He also declared, however, that the federal court system must abide by the unanimous verdict rule because the federal government built its system on English common law which required a unanimous verdict.

In his concurring opinion, Justice Powell defended his conclusion in these words:

In an unbroken line of cases reaching back into the late 1800s, the Justices of this Court have recognized, virtually without dissent, that unanimity is one of the indispensable features of *federal* jury trial.

In these cases, the Court has presumed that unanimous verdicts are essential in federal jury trials, not because unanimity is necessarily *fundamental* to the function performed by the jury, but because that result is mandated by history. The reasoning that runs throughout this Court's Sixth Amendment precedents is that, in amending the Constitution to guarantee the right to jury trial, the framers of the Constitution desired to preserve the jury safeguard as it was known to them at common law. At the time the Bill of Rights was adopted, unanimity had long been established as one of the attributes of a jury conviction at common law. It therefore seems to me, in accord both with history and precedent, that the Sixth Amendment required a unanimous jury verdict to convict in a *federal* criminal trial.

But it is the Fourteenth Amendment, rather than the Sixth, which imposes upon the States the requirement that they provide jury trials to those accused of serious crimes. This Court has said . . . that due process does not require that the States apply the federal jury trial right with all its gloss. . . . [emphasis added]

Justice White, who wrote the opinion of the Court in both the *Johnson* and the *Apodaca* cases, stated that whatever the reasons that established the unanimity rule, they were not sufficient to bind the states at the present time. The Court declared that the important principle is that a jury determine the accused's guilt or innocence. A verdict of nine or ten of twelve is a lawful verdict.

In an interesting historical footnote, Justice White presented, in the Apodaca opinion, four possible explanations of the unanimity rule.

The origins of the unanimity rule are shrouded in obscurity, although it was only in the latter half of the fourteenth century that it became settled that a verdict must be unanimous. At least four explanations might be given for the development of unanimity. One theory is that unanimity developed to compensate for the lack of other rules insuring that a defendant received a fair trial. A second theory is that unanimity arose out of the practice in the ancient mode of trial by compurgation of adding to the original number of twelve compurgators until one party had twelve compurgators supporting his position; the argument is that when this technique of afforcement was abandoned, the requirement that one side obtain the votes of all twelve jurors remained. A third possibility is that unanimity developed because early juries, unlike juries today, personally had knowledge of the facts of a case; the medieval mind assumed there could be only one correct view of the facts, and, if either all the jurors or only a minority thereof declared the facts erroneously, they might be punished for perjury. Given a view that minority jurors were guilty of criminal perjury, the development of a practice of unanimity would not be surprising. The final explanation is that jury unanimity arose out of the medieval concept of consent. Indeed, "[t]he word consent (consensus) carried with it the idea of concordia or unanimity. . . ." Even in fourteenth century Parliament there is evidence that a majority vote was deemed insufficient to bind the community or individual members of the community to a legal decision; a unanimous decision was preferred. It was only in the fifteenth century that the decision-making process in Parliament became avowedly majoritarian. Four eighteenth-century state constitutions provided explicitly for unanimous jury verdicts in criminal cases . . . while other eighteenth-century state constitutions provided for trial by jury according to the course of the common law. Although unanimity had not been the invariable practice in seventeenth-century America, where majority verdicts were permitted in the Carolinas, Connecticut, and Pennsylvania . . . the explicity constitutional provisions, particularly of States such as North Carolina and Pennsylvania, the apparent change of practice in Connecticut, and the unquestioning acceptance of the unanimity rule by text writers such as St. George Tucker indicate that unanimity became the accepted rule during the eighteenth century, as Americans became more familar with the details of English common law and adopted those details in their own colonial legal systems.

But can it be said that a verdict where only nine or ten of twelve jurors agree that guilt beyond a reasonable doubt has been established? Justice White, writing for the majority, answered in this way:

But the fact remains that nine jurors—a substantial majority of the jury—were convinced by the evidence. In our view disagreement of three jurors does not alone establish reasonable doubt, particularly when such a heavy majority of the jury, after having considered the dissenter's views, remains convinced of guilt.

To discourage the numbers game (seven to five or eight to four), in state legislation however, Justice White warned that "a substantial majority" of the jury must be convinced.

Each of the four justices who dissented wrote a separate opinion. Justice Douglas' is the most sweeping in its attack on the majority. He wrote:

These civil rights—whether they concern speech, searches and seizures, self-incrimination, criminal prosecutions, bail, or cruel and unusual punishments—extend of course to everyone, but in cold reality touch mostly the lower castes in our society. I refer of course to the Blacks, the Chicanos, the one-mule farmers, the agricultural workers, the off-beat students, the victims of the ghetto. Are we giving the states the power to experiment in diluting their civil rights? It has long been thought that the Thou Shalt Nots in the Constitution and Bill of Rights protect everyone against governmental intrusion or overreaching. The idea has long been obnoxious that there are some who can be relegated to second-class citizenship. But if we construe the Bill of Rights and the Fourteenth Amendment to permit states to "experiment" with the basic rights of people we open a veritable Pandora's box. For hate and prejudice are versatile forces that can degrade the constitutional scheme.

Justice Douglas, as well as the other dissenting justices, was concerned that under the new rule the jurors who disagreed with the majority would not be heard. In other words, as soon as nine jurors agreed in a Louisiana case or ten in an Oregon case, the minority would not get a hearing. Justice Brennan put it this way:

When verdicts must be unanimous, no member of the jury may be ignored by the others. When less than unanimity is sufficient, consideration of minority views may become nothing more than a matter of majority graces. In my opinion, the right of all groups in this Nation to participate in the criminal process means the right to have their voices heard. A unanimous verdict indicates that right. Majority verdicts could destroy it.

Justice Marshall made the same point:

The juror whose dissenting voice is unheard may be a spokesman, not for any minority viewpoint, but simply for himself—and that, in my view, is enough. *The doubts of a single juror are in my view evidence that the government has failed to carry its burden of proving guilt beyond a reasonable doubt.* [emphasis added]

Justice Stewart voiced his concern in these words:

Under today's judgment, nine jurors can simply ignore the views of their fellow panel members of a different race or class. . . . The constitutional guarantee of an impartial system of jury selection in a state criminal case rests on the Due Process and Equal Protection

Clauses of the Fourteenth Amendment. . . . Today's decision grossly undermines those basic assurances. For only a unanimous jury so selected can serve to minimize the potential bigotry of those who might convict on inadequate evidence, or acquit when evidence of guilt was clear. . . . The requirements of unanimity and impartial selection thus complement each other in ensuring the fair performance of the vital functions of a criminal court jury.

Up to this point, we have seen that the Sixth Amendment's right to trial by jury is enmeshed in many complications. Sensitive to the historic role of the jury as "fundamental to the American sense of justice," as essential to due process of law, and as a "safeguard against the corrupt or overzealous prosecutor," as well as the "compliant, biased, or eccentric judge," the Justices have grappled with many issues. They accepted the six-person jury, they rejected the five-person jury, and they approved nonunanimous verdicts (nine of twelve and ten of twelve) in criminal cases.

In 1979, the Court was confronted with another puzzling issue about the number of jurors required to convict in a criminal case.

BURCH v. LOUISIANA

Is a nonunanimous verdict in a six-person jury trial constitutional?

The Louisiana Constitution provided that in certain criminal cases (nonpetty offenses) an accused shall be tried by "a jury of six, five of whom must concur to render a verdict." Of the two defendants charged with exhibiting allegedly obscene motion pictures, one was found guilty by a unanimous vote, while the other was adjudged guilty by a five to one vote. Both defendants appealed on the ground that the nonunanimous verdict law violated the due process clause of the Sixth and Fourteenth Amendments. The defendants lost in the Louisiana Supreme Court and, as is almost inevitable in complicated constitutional cases, the issue found its way to the United States Supreme Court.

How would you rule in this case, if you were a Justice? How would you weigh the State's economic and practical arguments on the scales of justice?

Writing the opinion of the Court, Justice Rehnquist admitted that the question presented was a "close one" and that it is not an easy matter to draw lines which will satisfy everyone. However, he declared, a line must be drawn somewhere if the substance of the jury trial is to be preserved.

Much the same reasons that led us in *Ballew* to decide that the use of a five-member jury threatened the fairness of the proceeding and the proper role of the jury, lead us to conclude now that conviction for a nonpetty offense by only five members of a six-person jury presents a similar threat to preservation of the substance of the jury

In the case of *Burch* v. *Louisiana*, Justice William ʌnquist wrote the Court's opinion declaring that ɔnunanimous verdicts by six-person juries are unconstitutional.

trial guarantee and justifies our requiring verdicts rendered by six-person juries to be unanimous. We are buttressed in this view by the current jury practices of the several States. It appears that of those States that utilize six-person juries in trials of nonpetty offenses, only two, including Louisiana, also allow nonunanimous verdicts. We think that this near-uniform practice of the Nation provides a useful guide in delimiting the line between those jury practices that are constitutionally permissible and those that are not.

As for the State's argument that this practice saves considerable time and money and reduces the number of hung juries, Justice Rehnquist responded that all this is speculative and the State's interest must yield when it threatens constitutional principles.

It is interesting to compare Justice Rehnquist's position here on the costs of justice with his remarks on the right to counsel in *Scott* v. *Illinois* (p. 19).

Justices Brennan, Stewart, and Marshall concurred with that part of the decision which declared the Louisiana law unconstitutional, but they dissented on several points. They felt the obscenity law under which the defendants had been found guilty should have been declared unconstitutional and that both defendants should have been freed. The majority had upheld the jury's unanimous verdict of one of the defendants and had ordered the second one retried.

SHOULD THE JURY SYSTEM BE ABOLISHED?

Some critics of the jury system have suggested that it be abolished, arguing that it is expensive and time-consuming. A minority of the jurors can delay a verdict and create a hung jury, which leads to a mistrial. In addition, the critics claim that many jurors are not capable of understanding the complex testimony and evidence in a case. Some jurors, they argue, decide cases on their feelings about the accused and can be swayed by the tactics of the attorneys who might put on such theatrics as pleading, crying, shouting, name calling, accusing, condemning, and objecting indignantly.

Do you think that any of these arguments is convincing? Would it be better for the drama to be played before one judge or several judges?

Other countries have made changes in the jury system. England, where our jury system originated, has abolished the grand jury and made changes in the petit jury in criminal cases. Although a unanimous verdict is still the goal for convictions, it is possible to have an acquittal by a majority vote of the jurors. When the jury retires, it is given two hours to reach a unanimous verdict. If it cannot do so, a less than unanimous verdict will be accepted. The effort to reach a unanimous verdict permits each juror to have a voice in the deliberations while the acceptability of a nonunanimous vote prevents an individual juror from creating a hung jury. If the jury consists of eleven members, ten must agree on a verdict. If the jury consists of ten members, nine must agree.

To help prevent jurors from being carried away by the eloquence of attorneys, the French have adopted a modification of the jury system. French juries consist of nine persons drawn by lot. The jury deliberates with the three professional judges assigned to the case. Each person has one vote, and a conviction requires a vote of eight out of twelve. Undecided votes count in favor of the accused.

Germany has developed two types of juries in criminal cases which are different from those in the United States or England. For the more serious crimes, two lay judges or jurors and three professional judges hear the case. Sitting as a bench, these five persons must determine by a 3 out of 5 vote the guilt of the accused, as well as the sentence. Less serious crimes are handled by assessor courts, which consist of a judge and two lay judges or jurors. A majority vote is necessary to decide such a case. Under German law, local authorities compile a list of nominees for lay judges every four years. The lay judges serve twelve days a year and are compensated for their work. Once a year a public drawing takes place and lay judges are assigned at random to particular courts for particular days. Dates may be swapped "so long as the cases to be decided in the session are not fixed."*

Compare the German jury system with the American and English systems in which jurors serve for just one short period. Which do you think is better in the interests of justice?

---

*This summary is based on John H. Langbein, Comparative Criminal Procedure: Germany. St. Paul, Minn.: West Publishing Company, 1977.

8 BEHIND THE SCENES: PLEA BARGAINING

Up to this point, the focus has been on the courtroom as theater and the drama that unfolds according to the script. Each player has his or her role, and when the curtain falls, the drama ends in the defendant's walking out as a free person or being sentenced.

An estimated one million serious crimes are committed each year in the United States, yet only 125,000 jury trials are conducted. What does this tell us? An obvious conclusion is that many criminals never go through a jury trial. What, then, is happening backstage, away from the courtroom drama? Let us go behind the scenes to study what happens to an alleged criminal if he or she does not go to court.

In most of the large cities and in many small cities in the United States, about ninety percent of the criminal cases are settled by a process known as *plea bargaining*. This procedure is very different from a trial with the due process procedural safeguards described in the earlier chapters. With plea bargaining, the set no longer is the courtroom; it can be the prosecutor's office, the corridors of the courthouse, or the judge's chambers. The cast still includes the judge, prosecuting attorney, defense attorney, and defendant, the jury, court personnel, witnesses, and public do not play a part in plea bargaining. Unlike a jury trial, plea bargaining casts the prosecuting attorney and defense attorney in starring roles; the judge does not play a starring role but enters the scene after most of the action has taken place.

Plea bargaining occurs in several ways. First, the prosecuting attorney must decide whether to plea bargain or to try a case. This decision is based on such factors as the availability of witnesses to testify, the sufficiency of evidence against the defendant, and, in many cases, the defendant's background, including whether he or she is a first offender. The defendant's attorney must also assess the evidence to determine whether the defendant is more likely to be found guilty than not guilty if tried.

In the next step, the defendant's attorney can seek out the prosecutor and offer to have the client plead guilty if the prosecutor will reduce the crime from a felony to a misdemeanor or from a more serious felony to one of a lesser degree, or if the prosecutor will recommend a more lenient sentence for the defendant. The prosecutor may take the initiative and bargain with the defendant's attorney, offering a less serious charge and a milder sentence in return for a guilty plea. Sometimes an accused waives counsel and simply accepts the prosecutor's offer, agreeing to plead guilty in return for an acceptable sentence. Occasionally during a pretrial hearing, the judge in the case may encourage plea bargaining negotiations.

After the prosecuting and defense attorneys have discussed the case, they may agree to negotiate. The defendant, as a rule, is not present during the plea bargaining. The defense attorney must present the plea bargain to the defendant. If the defendant refuses the bargain, the trial goes on. If the defendant decides to plead guilty, the plea bargain is presented to the judge for approval.

The judge is responsible for reviewing the facts of the case to determine two things: whether the facts support the charge against the defendant and whether the defendant is now making an intelligent and voluntary guilty plea. If satisfied on these points, the judge will approve the plea bargain and the defendant's guilty plea will be accepted by the court.

As a citizen, do you favor plea bargaining? What advantages and disadvantages do you see in this procedure?

PLEA BARGAINING VERSUS TRIAL—ADVANTAGES AND DISADVANTAGES

How did plea bargaining come to displace many of the traditional trials before a judge or jury? The answer involves certain developments in American society. While crimes have increased, the availability of courts, judges, and attorneys has not increased at the same rate; the criminal justice system cannot hold trials for all those accused in the six to seven million felonies and misdemeanors committed each year. Prosecuting attorneys are overwhelmed by the number of trials they must conduct. Attorneys for the poor (public defenders, legal aid, and court-appointed attorneys), like the prosecutors, find themselves swamped with cases which they cannot

Copyright 1973 Jules Feiffer. Reprinted by permission of Publishers—Hall Syndicate and the Village Voice.

prepare adequately. Confronted with such demands, the criminal justice system had to develop a method to handle all the cases. Plea bargaining provided a means. In many cases, it has replaced the traditional model of dealing with the accused—the trial.

In trials—especially jury trials—the procedures are slow, expensive, and deliberate. The plea bargaining method, on the other hand, is efficient and relatively inexpensive. It has been said that in plea bargaining justice moves along like an assembly line. Court calendars loaded with cases can be cleared quickly and with little expense to the community. If, however, we justify plea bargaining on the basis of our desire for efficiency and economy, are we forgetting something?

Suppose that you are a defendant. Would you favor having your case dealt with through plea bargaining by your lawyer? Think about this for a moment before you continue reading.

Your decision will depend, of course, on whether you are innocent or guilty. Your lawyer will probably tell you that if you plead not guilty and go on to trial, whether before a judge or a jury, the sentence you receive if convicted may be twice as severe as the one you would get under plea bargaining. This is one important consideration. If you are innocent but your lawyer feels that it would be difficult to make a strong defense, you might hesitate to go to trial and so would decide to plead guilty. But this is unjust. Or suppose you have been in jail for six months awaiting trial and the district attorney offers you a six-month sentence (the time served) in exchange for a guilty plea. Would you be tempted to accept the offer and go free? Or would you be willing to risk going to trial because you feel that your innocence would be established?

Plea bargaining raises many questions about justice, due process of law, the innocent who plead guilty, and the guilty who use the process to get lighter sentences. There are three important issues to consider in plea bargaining: fairness to the accused, fairness to the people of the state, and adherence to the ideals of a society which are expressed in its constitution.

SANTOBELLO v. NEW YORK

Can a prosecutor's plea bargaining promise to a defendant be broken?

Rudolph Santobello was indicted by the grand jury on two felony counts: promoting gambling in the first degree and possession of gambling records in the first degree. He pleaded not guilty on both counts. Later, after plea bargaining, the prosecuting attorney agreed to permit Santobello to plead guilty to a lesser offense: possession of gambling records in the second degree, which carries a maximum prison sentence of one year. The prosecutor promised to make no recommendation for the sentence, which meant that the judge could give the defendant any sentence within the one-year period—or even probation. Santobello then withdrew his plea of not guilty and entered a plea of guilty to a lesser offense. The judge accepted the plea and set a date for sentencing.

Then something happened. There was a delay of several months, and during this time some changes took place. A new attorney represented the defendant, a new prosecutor replaced the one who had made the plea bargain, and a new judge took over the case.

The new prosecutor recommended that the judge impose the maximum one-year sentence because of the defendant's criminal record and his alleged links with organized crime. The defense attorney objected on the ground that a promise had been made not to recommend sentence. Unmoved by this, the judge decided to impose the maximum sentence of one year.

Before sentencing, the defendant moved to withdraw his guilty plea because he had discovered that crucial evidence against him had been obtained by an illegal search and seizure. His motion to withdraw his plea was denied, and the sentence followed.

When the case reached the United States Supreme Court, a majority of the Justices decided to send the case back to the New York courts to determine whether the prosecutor should be required to live up to his predecessor's promise or whether the defendant should be permitted to withdraw his guilty plea. Chief Justice Burger delivered the opinion of the majority of the Court.

The disposition of criminal charges by agreement between the prosecutor and the accused, sometimes loosely called "plea bargaining," is an essential component of the administration of justice. Properly administered, it is to be encouraged. If every criminal charge were subjected to a full-scale trial, the States and the Federal Government would need to multiply by many times the number of judges and court facilities.

Disposition of charges after plea discussions is not only an essential part of the process but a highly desirable part for many reasons. It leads to prompt and largely final disposition of most criminal cases; it avoids much of the corrosive impact of enforced idleness during pretrial confinement for those who are denied release pending trial; it protects the public from those accused persons who are prone to continue criminal conduct even while on pretrial release; and by shortening the time between charge and disposition, it enhances

Chief Justice Warren Burger at work in his chambers.

whatever may be the rehabilitative prospects of the guilty when they are ultimately imprisoned.

However, all of these considerations presuppose fairness in securing agreement between an accused and a prosecutor . . . *when a plea rests in any significant degree on a promise or agreement of the prosecutor, so that it can be said to be part of the inducement or consideration, such promise must be fulfilled.* [emphasis added]

Justice Douglas wrote a concurring opinion in which he said that a defendant's preference in such cases should be the determining factor because it was his life and liberty that were at stake.

Do you think plea bargaining is fair if the defendant is guilty?

As this chapter has emphasized, the sheer number of crimes committed makes it impossible to consider a jury trial in every case. The traditional concept of due process fairness has undergone changes, as we have seen throughout this section. These changes have come about in part by a shift in our values but certainly also in large part because of the needs or requirements of our society. If the legal system is to continue to function well in its role in society, then it must inevitably accommodate changes in society, whether those changes are higher ideals of human dignity or just real, physical changes in the number of defendants the court system must handle. Plea bargaining, which represents a change in our notion of due process, must be evaluated in terms of fairness, not only to the accused but also to society and its needs.

Would you be willing to compromise your ideal of justice in the courtroom to meet the state's need to try large numbers of accused persons awaiting trial? If you refuse to compromise, what arguments can you make? If you agree to compromise, how far would you be willing to go?

SECTION II

The Courtroom as Theater:

The Curtain Falls

Excessive bail shall not be required, nor excessive fines imposed, nor cruel and unusual punishments inflicted.

Amendment VIII

. . . nor shall any state deprive any person of life . . . without due process of law . . .

Amendment XIV

The rack, the thumbscrew, the wheel, solitary confinement, protracted questioning and cross questioning, and other ingenious forms of entrapment of the helpless or unpopular had left their wake of mutilated bodies and shattered minds along the way to the cross, the guillotine, the stake and the hangman's noose. And they who have suffered most from secret and dictatorial proceedings have almost always been the poor, the ignorant, the numerically weak, the friendless, and the powerless.

Justice Hugo Black
Chambers v. Florida (1940)

79

INTRODUCTION

The history of civilization is strewn with bodies of men and women who were tortured, whipped, branded, mutilated, or executed by burning at the stake, hanging, beheading, shooting, or electrocution. Historical instruments of punishment, including the rack, the screw, the whip, and the pillory, were replaced by such modern techniques as electric shock, psychological torture, and drugs.

It was inevitable that the voices of men and women would be raised in condemnation of those practices. The spirit of such opposition was expressed by Robert Burns in a memorable couplet

> *Man's inhumanity to man*
> *Makes countless thousands mourn.*

The insistent and persistent cry that the punishment must fit the crime was not lost on policy makers, and in England and the American colonies steps were taken to moderate the cruel and inhuman treatment of the guilty. At first, greater progress was made in words than in deeds. For example, the English Bill of Rights of 1689 declared:

> *That excessive bail ought not to be required, nor excessive fines imposed, nor cruel and unusual punishments inflicted.*

Even before that, however, the Massachusetts Body of Liberties in 1641 reflected the new spirit in its provision

> *For bodilie punishments we allow amongst us none that are inhumane, barbarous or cruel.*

This same thought was later incorporated in the Delaware Declaration of Rights (1776), as well as in the colonial constitutions of Massachusetts, Virginia, Maryland, North Carolina, and New Hampshire. The Northwest Ordinance of 1787 provided that the newly created states in that region must adopt the following rights:

> *All persons shall be bailable, unless for capital offenses . . . All fines shall be moderate; and no cruel or unusual punishments shall be inflicted. . . .*

Despite these humane words, excessive bail and fines, as well as cruel and unusual punishments, continued to be the rule rather than the exception. Colonial Massachusetts, for example, provided that "a stubborn and rebellious son of sufficient understanding, sixteen years of age" who was disobedient to his parents could be put to death.

It took time and effort on the part of many reformers to moderate the excesses of the past. The framers of the Bill of Rights directed their attention to this issue: The result was the Eighth Amendment, which states:

> *Excessive bail shall not be required, nor excessive fines imposed, nor cruel and unusual punishments inflicted.* [emphasis added]

9 SENTENCING AND PUNISHMENT

This chapter examines the kinds of punishments which are prohibited by the Eighth Amendment. Again it must be noted, however, that this amendment does not specify the kind of punishment that is considered to be cruel and unusual. We must turn to Supreme Court decisions for interpretation and guidance in determining an appropriate punishment for a particular criminal act.

In recent years, the provision of the Eighth Amendment prohibiting infliction of cruel and unusual punishment has been used to attack not only sentences but also conditions in prison. For example, state courts have considered the issues of severe overcrowding, brutality by guards, lack of proper medical care, unhygienic conditions, solitary confinement, corporal punishment, and the use of tranquilizing drugs in the prisons. The discussion of the Eighth Amendment's prohibition of cruel and unusual punishment begins by examining the Supreme Court decisions interpreting this provision in the four cases which follow.

Analyze the issues in these four cases. What are the arguments on each side? How would you decide the cases? Support your decision with an opinion which justifies your conclusion. *(The decisions in these cases appear on pp. 84–88)*

FACTS

WEEMS v. UNITED STATES

In 1909 Paul Weems, an officer of the Bureau of the Coast Guard and Transportation of the United States Government of the Philippine Islands, was convicted in a Manila court for falsifying a public and official document. He was found guilty of falsely recording that he had paid 208 and 408 pesos in wages to employees of lighthouse services. Under Philippine law, he was sentenced to fifteen years in prison at hard labor and to be chained by the ankle and the wrists. His rights to vote and to hold office were taken away from him. This type of punishment was based on Spanish law, which preceded the American law instituted when the United States acquired the Philippines.

ISSUE

The Philippine law was attacked as being unconstitutional punishment under the Philippine and United States Bill of Rights.

> **What is your opinion? Does it make any difference to you that the punishment was Spanish in origin, although the Philippines were an American possession at the time of the case?**

FACTS

TROP v. DULLES

In May 1944 Albert Trop, a private in the United States army who was stationed in French Morocco, escaped from the stockade, where he had been confined for a breach of discipline. Although he was away less than a day and surrendered willingly, he was court-martialed, convicted of desertion, sentenced to three years at hard labor, and forfeiture of pay, and given a dishonorable discharge.

When he applied for a passport in 1952, his application was denied under the Nationality Act of 1940. The law provided that anyone convicted and dishonorably discharged for wartime desertion would lose his citizenship.

"Ninety-nine years. Justice triumphs again!"

ISSUE

Trop responded that this deprivation was cruel and unusual punishment, which was prohibited under the Eighth Amendment.

Do you agree with him? Keep in mind the fact that wartime desertion can be and has been punishable by death.

FACTS

ROBINSON v. CALIFORNIA

Lawrence Robinson was convicted under a California statute that made it a crime "to be addicted to the use of narcotics." The minimum punishment was ninety days and the maximum was one year. Even if the court decided to place the convicted person on probation, a mandatory ninety-day sentence had to be served.

ISSUE

Robinson denied the charges and claimed, on appeal, that the statute was unconstitutional under the cruel and unusual punishment provision of the Eighth Amendment.

Assume you are representing Robinson. Prepare your defense. What arguments do you anticipate from the state? How would you answer them?

FACTS

LOUISIANA EX REL. FRANCIS v. RESWEBER, SHERIFF

In September 1945 Willie Francis was convicted of murder and sentenced to be electrocuted. On May 3, 1946, he was placed in the electric chair and the switch was thrown. Because of some mechanical difficulty, he was not killed, although some current did pass through his body. He was removed from the chair and returned to his cell. A new death warrant for his execution was issued for May 9, 1946.

If you were his attorney, which provision of the Constitution would you invoke?

ISSUES

There are two possible constitutional violations here. The Fifth Amendment's double jeopardy clause says, " . . . nor shall any person be subject for the same offense to be twice put in jeopardy of life or limb. . . .'' Since this is a state case, does the Fourteenth Amendment's due process clause make the double jeopardy clause applicable to actions by the state? Or, is the Eighth Amendment's prohibition against cruel and unusual punishment a part of our concept of due process and therefore applicable to the states through the Fourteenth Amendment's due process clause? Francis's attorney argued for protection under the Fourteenth Amendment.

How do you think the Supreme Court treated these arguments? How would you, if you were a Justice?

THE DECISIONS

The Court concluded in its ruling that the punishment in the *Weems* Case was cruel and unusual and a violation of the Philippine and the United States Bill of Rights. The majority of the justices concluded that the punishment was one of "tormenting severity"; it was cruel in its excessiveness and unusual in its character.

In *Trop* v. *Dulles* Chief Justice Warren delivered the opinion of the Court, and only Justices Black, Douglas, and Whittaker joined in it. The Chief Justice focused on the meaning of the cruel and unusual punishment provision in the Constitution in the following words:

The exact scope of the constitutional phrase "cruel and unusual" has not been detailed by this Court. But the basic policy reflected in these words is firmly established in the Anglo-American tradition of criminal justice. The phrase in our Constitution was taken directly from the English Declaration of Rights in 1688, and the principle it represents can be traced back to the Magna Carta. *The basic concept underlying the Eighth Amendment is nothing less than the dignity of man.* While the State has the power to punish, the Amendment stands to assure that this power be exercised within the limits of civilized standards. Fines, imprisonment and even execution may be imposed depending upon the enormity of the crime, but any technique outside the bounds of these traditional penalties is constitutionally suspect. *This Court has had little occasion to give precise content to the Eighth Amendment, and, in an enlightened democracy such as ours, this is not surprising . . . . The Amendment must draw its meaning from the evolving standards of decency that mark the progress of a maturing society.* [Emphasis added]

What does the Chief Justice mean by the italicized words? Do you see merit in his thoughts?

Chief Justice Warren equated denationalization with cruel and unusual punishment. He pointed out that, while depriving an individual of citizenship entails no physical torture or mistreatment, it totally destroys the individual's status in society. Statelessness denies the political existence that took centuries to develop. Civilized nations of the world do not impose such a severe punishment. In short, "the Eighth Amendment forbids Congress to punish by taking away citizenship."

In their concurring opinions, Justices Black and Douglas agreed with the reasoning of the Chief Justice, but they made an additional point: Even if citizenship could be taken away, the military should not have that power.

Justices Frankfurter, Burton, Clark, and Harlan dissented on the ground that the Court should not interfere with the judgment of Congress, which passed the denationalization law.

Justice Stewart wrote the opinion for the Court in *Robinson v. California*.

It is unlikely that any State at this moment in history would attempt to make it a criminal offense for a person to be mentally ill, or a leper, or to be afflicted with a venereal disease. A State might determine that the general health and welfare require that the victims of these and other human afflictions be dealt with by compulsory treatment, involving quarantine, confinement, or sequestration. But, in the light of contemporary human knowledge, a law which made a criminal offense of such a disease would doubtless be universally thought to be an infliction of cruel and unusual punishment in violation of the Eighth and Fourteenth Amendments . . . narcotic addiction is an illness. Indeed it is apparently an illness which may be contracted innocently or involuntarily.

He then announced the holding of the majority—that is, the rule of law or the major principle underlying the decision—with the following words:

We hold that a state law which imprisons a person thus afflicted as a criminal, even though he has never touched any narcotic drug within the state or been guilty of any irregular behavior there, inflicts cruel and unusual punishment in violation of the Fourteenth Amendment. To be sure, imprisonment for ninety days is not, in the abstract, a punishment which is either cruel or unusual. But the question cannot be considered in the abstract. Even one day in prison would be cruel and unusual punishment for the "crime" of having a common cold.

Justice Douglas concurred.

A prosecution for addiction, with its resulting stigma and irreparable damage to the good name of the accused, cannot be justifiied as a means of protecting society, where a civil commitment would do as well. . . . This prosecution has no relationship to the curing of an illness. Indeed, it cannot, for the prosecution is aimed at penalizing an illness, rather than at providing medical care for it. We would forget

Justice Potter Stewart, author of the Supreme Court's decision in the *Robinson* case.

the teachings of the Eighth Amendment if we allowed sickness to be made a crime and permitted sick people to be punished for being sick. This age of enlightenment cannot tolerate such barbarous action.

Six Justices agreed that the California statute was unconstitutional. Justices Clark and White dissented, while Justice Frankfurter did not take part in the case. Justice Clark defended the power of the state to impose criminal penalties for drug addiction, arguing that narcotic addiction poses a threat of serious crime and that the law has recognized status offenses, such as drunkenness, and has imposed punishement.

Justice White considered this application of cruel and unusual punishment by the majority as:

. . . so novel that I suspect the Court was hard put to find a way to ascribe to the Framers of the Constitution the result reached today rather than to its own notions of ordered liberty. . . . I fail to see why the Court deems it more appropriate to write into the Constitution its own abstract notions of how best to handle the narcotics problem, for it obviously cannot match either the States or Congress in expert understanding.

Do you think society has the right to punish certain conditions, such as drunkenness or narcotics addiction, because of the conse-

quences to other members of society which may result from the effects of these illnesses? Why? Would you make a distinction between punishing individual instances of drunkenness or drug use and punishing the condition of being an alcoholic or an addict? Do you agree with Justice Stewart that the "crime" of narcotic addiction would be the same as the " 'crime' of having a common cold"?

In the *Francis* case, this issue, with human life at stake, sharply divided the Court. Four Justices saw it one way; four others saw it completely differently; the ninth Justice determined the fate of Francis.

Justice Reed wrote an opinion in which Chief Justice Vinson and Justices Jackson and Black concurred.

What do you think they decided?

Now read the following excerpts from their opinion.

First. Our minds rebel against permitting the same sovereignty to punish an accused twice for the same offense. . . . *we see no difference from a constitutional point of view between a new trial for error of law at the instance of the state that results in a death sentence . . . and an execution that follows a failure of equipment.* We find no double jeopardy here which can be said to amount to a denial of federal due process in the proposed execution.

Second. We find nothing in what took place here which amounts to cruel and unusual punishment in the constitutional sense. . . . The traditional humanity of modern Anglo-American law forbids the infliction of unnecessary pain in the execution of the death sentence. Prohibition against wanton infliction of pain has come into our law from the Bill of Rights of 1688. The identical words appear in our Eighth Amendment. *The Fourteenth would prohibit by its due process clause execution by a state in a cruel manner.*

Petitioner's suggestion is that because he once underwent the psychological strain of preparation for electrocution, now to require him to undergo this preparation again subjects him to a lingering or cruel and unusual punishment. . . . *The cruelty against which the Constitution protects a convicted man is cruelty inherent in the method of punishment, not the necessary suffering involved in any method employed to extinguish life humanely.* . . The situation of the unfortunate victim of this accident is just as though he had suffered the identical amount of mental anguish and physical pain in any other occurrence, such as, for example, a fire in the cell block. We cannot agree that the hardship imposed . . . rises to the level of hardship denounced as denial of due process because of cruelty. [emphasis added]

What do you think of this line of reasoning? Do you agree that the cruelty prohibited by the Constitution does not include the suffering involved in "humanely extinguishing" a life? What is meant by "humanely"?

Four Justices differed with this line of reasoning. Justice Burton wrote the dissenting opinion in which Justices Douglas, Murphy, and Rutledge concurred. Observe their reasoning:

It is unthinkable that any state legislature in modern times would enact a statute expressly authorizing capital punishment by repeated applications of an electric current separated by intervals of days or hours until finally death shall result. . . . In determining whether the proposed procedure is unconstitutional, we must measure it against a lawful electrocution. The contrast is that between instantaneous death and death by installments—caused by electric shocks administered after one or more intervening periods of complete consciousness of the victim. . . . The all-important consideration is that the execution shall be so instantaneous and substantially painless that the punishment shall be reduced, as nearly as possible, to no more than that of death itself. Electrocution has been approved only in a form that eliminates suffering.

The score thus stood four to four. Only Justice Frankfurter remained to be heard; his position would swing the decision. With whom would he side? Read what the swing Justice wrote.

The Court must abstain from interference with State action no matter how strong one's personal feeling of revulsion against a State's insistence on its pound of flesh. One must be on guard against finding in personal disapproval a reflection of more or less prevailing condemnation. . . . were I to hold that Louisiana would transgress the Due Process Clause if the State were allowed in the precise circumstances before us to carry out the death sentence, *I would be enforcing my private view rather than that consensus of society's opinion which, for purposes of due process, is the standard enjoined by the Constitution.* [emphasis added]

In the italicized sentence Justice Frankfurter draws a distinction between his private views and his public duty. What do you think of this distinction? He speaks of the consensus of society's opinion as the standard enjoined by the Constitution. How does he arrive at this conclusion? Do you agree with him? Why?

By this time you must be aware that Francis lost by a five to four vote. Undaunted, attorneys for Francis appealed for a rehearing, but the appeal was denied.

10 CAPITAL PUNISHMENT: CRUEL AND UNUSUAL?

This chapter focuses on the constitutionality of capital punishment. In reading the landmark decision in this chapter, the reader will observe the Justices of the Supreme Court grappling with legal, constitutional, and moral issues. The debate on the subject of capital punishment may be rooted in the provisions of the Constitution; but the voices of the past, the cries of the condemned, and the pleas of the compassionate echo through the minds of the Justices.

FURMAN v. GEORGIA

Is the death penalty prohibited by the Eighth Amendment?

In 1972, three cases (*Furman* v. *State of Georgia, Jackson* v. *State of Georgia,* and *Branch* v. *State of Texas*) in which capital punishment was imposed were consolidated on appeal and argued before the Supreme Court. These cases are known as the *Furman* decisions. William Henry Furman was convicted of murder and sentenced to death by the Georgia courts; Lucious Jackson, Jr., had been convicted of rape and was sentenced to death, also by the Georgia courts; Elmer Branch was convicted of rape and sentenced to death by the Texas courts. All three convicted men were black.

The men appealed their sentences on the ground that capital punishment is outlawed by the Eighth Amendment's prohibition against inflicting cruel and unusual punishment. The constitutional argument that the three appellants used was that under the Fourteenth Amendment a state cannot deprive a person of life without due process of law. Freedom from infliction of cruel and unusual punishment is necessary for due process. Therefore, if capital punishment is cruel and unusual, the Fourteenth Amendment prohibits states from using it to deprive a person of life.

The attorneys for the three convicted men were confronted with a series of obstacles to their position. Since the founding of our country, capital punishment has been used as an accepted penalty. The Constitution does not expressly prohibit capital punishment. At the time of the Furman case, forty of the fifty states, as well as the District of Columbia, had death penalty laws. The federal government also mandated the death sentence in cases involving air piracy and assassination of a president or a vice president. It could be argued that this mandate at the federal level along with capital punishment statutes in the majority of states is evidence that the majority of Americans approve of capital punishment.

If you were arguing *against* capital punishment, how would you respond to these facts?

Over the centuries, capital punishment has taken many forms such as burning at the stake, . . .

You might begin to counter these facts by saying that the meaning of the Bill of Rights in general and the Eighth Amendment in particular cannot be decided by popularity polls or by a majority vote of the community. The Bill of Rights was designed to protect the individual against capricious, arbitrary, and unreasonable acts of the government. Regardless of what the majority thinks, the constitutionality of capital punishment must be determined by the courts, not by the people through their legislatures.

beheading by a guillotine, and . . .

hanging.

If it were agreed that the Supreme Court should decide, the next question to be answered is, If capital punishment has been regarded as constitutional until 1972, why should the Supreme Court suddenly declare that practice to be unconstitutional?

How would you answer this question? Can you think of any reasons which would explain a shift in judicial thinking?

You could argue that the fact that forty-one states, the District of Columbia, and the federal government have legislated the death penalty in certain cases does not mean that it is constitutional. After all, by 1972 nine states and many nations had abolished or severely restricted the death penalty, which shows a change in moral and ethical standards.

Times have changed. We no longer behead people, crop ears, or burn people at the stake. Standards of human dignity and decency are constantly changing, as seen in the worldwide trend against capital punishment. Many legal scholars and religious and political leaders have condemned capital punishment. During the past forty years, fewer and fewer people have been executed, and the number of death sentences has decreased with relation to the number of cases in which it might have been imposed.

Another argument against capital punishment is that executing an innocent person is not an improbability, and such an act of finality can never be reversed. Is it worth taking this chance?

Those who favor the death penalty, however, could argue that the founding fathers approved of it; previous court rulings have upheld it; legislatures have enacted it; under our system of checks and balances, it is a legislative matter, not an issue for the courts to decide; and finally, it serves as a deterrent and satisfies society's desire for retribution.

If you find these arguments compelling, confusing, and distressing, do not be discouraged. The issue is one of life and death, and each of the nine Justices had to wrestle with it. So difficult was the task confronting them that each wrote his own opinion. The nine opinions total 116 pages. Excerpts from each opinion follow.

Can you figure out how the Justices voted and what the final decision was in this important case?

JUSTICE DOUGLAS'S OPINION

In the *Furman* case, Justice Douglas wrote:

It would seem to be incontestable that the death penalty inflicted on one defendant is "unusual" if it discriminates against him by reason of his race, religion, wealth, social position, or class, or if it is imposed under a procedure that gives room for the play of such prejudices. . . .

A study of capital cases in Texas from 1924 to 1968 reached the following conclusions:

"Application of the death penalty is unequal: most of those executed were poor, young, and ignorant. . . .

"Seventy-five of the 460 cases involved codefendants, who, under Texas law, were given separate trials. In several instances where a white and a Negro were codefendants, the white was sentenced to life imprisonment or a term of years, and the Negro was given the death penalty.

"Another ethnic disparity is found in the type of sentence imposed for rape. The Negro convicted of rape is far more likely to get the death penalty than a term sentence, whereas whites and Latins are far more likely to get a term sentence than the death penalty. . . ."

We cannot say from facts disclosed in these records that these defendants were sentenced to death because they were black. Yet our task is not restricted to an effort to divine what motives impelled these death penalties. *Rather, we deal with a system of law and of justice that leaves to the uncontrolled discretion of judges or juries the determination whether defendants committing these crimes should die or be imprisoned. Under these laws no standards govern the selection of the penalty. People live or die, dependent on the whim of one man or of 12.* . . .

He concluded that discretionary statutes which allow the sentencing jury or judge to choose between the death penalty and a less severe penalty are unconstitutional.

The high service rendered by the "cruel and unusual" punishment clause of the Eighth Amendment is to require legislatures to write *penal laws that are evenhanded, nonselective, and nonarbitrary, and to require judges to see to it that general laws are not applied sparsely, selectively, and spottily to unpopular groups. . . .* [emphasis added]

The points Justice Douglas made against discretionary statutes would not necessarily apply to all use of capital punishment. He concluded his opinion by saying that a statute which made the death sentence mandatory in specified situations might be constitutional if it could be employed in a nondiscriminatory way, but that issue was not raised in this case.

Imagine you are a legislator and you agree with Justice Douglas. Describe the provisions of a law which you would propose which would meet his standards or guidelines.

JUSTICE BRENNAN'S OPINION

Justice Brennan took the position that a punishment is cruel and unusual if it "does not comport with human dignity." He proposed four principles by which a court can determine whether or not a challenged punishment comports with human dignity.

If a punishment is unusually severe, if there is a strong probability that it is inflicted arbitrarily, if it is substantially rejected by contemporary society, and if there is no reason to believe that it serves any penal purpose more effectively than some less severe punishment then the continued infliction of that punishment violates the command of the Clause that the State may not inflict inhuman and uncivilized punishments upon those convicted of crimes.

Applying this four-part test to capital punishment he found first that it is uniquely severe and "uniquely degrading to human dignity."

The unusual severity of death is manifested most clearly in its finality and enormity. Death, in these respects, is in a class by itself. . . . Death is truly an awesome punishment. The calculated killing of a human being by the State involves, by its very nature, a denial of the executed person's humanity. The contrast with the plight of a person punished by imprisonment is evident. An individual in prison does not lose "the right to have rights."

Second, the death penalty is likely to be arbitrarily imposed. It is imposed in only a small percentage of the cases in which it is legally available; and that percentage has been declining since the 1930s. The conclusion is:

Furthermore, our procedures in death cases, rather than resulting in the selection of "extreme" cases for this punishment, actually sanction an arbitrary selection. For this Court has held that juries may, as they do, make the decision whether to impose a death sentence wholly unguided by standards governing that decision.

The third point, the social acceptance of capital punishment, was less clear-cut, but Justice Brennan suggested that opinion polls and the public's apparent willingness to retain capital punishment laws are not the most reliable indicators of society's attitudes.

The objective indicator of society's view of an unusually severe punishment is what society does with it, and today society will inflict death upon only a small sample of the eligible criminals. Rejection could hardly be more complete without becoming absolute. At the very least, I must conclude that contemporary society views this punishment with substantial doubt.

Fourth, available evidence indicates that the threat of death is no greater deterrent than the threat of imprisonment.

Turning from the constitutional question, Justice Brennan stated the fundamental issue, which, in his judgment, lies at the root of the controversy.

At bottom, the battle has been waged on moral grounds. The country has debated whether a society for which the dignity of the individual is the supreme value can, without a fundamental inconsistency, follow the practice of deliberately putting some of its members to death. In the United States, as in other nations of the western world, "the struggle about this punishment has been one between ancient and deeply rooted beliefs in retribution, atonement or vengeance on the one hand, and, on the other, beliefs in the personal value and dignity of the common man that were born of the democratic movement of the eighteenth century, as well as beliefs in the scientific approach to an understanding of the motive forces of human conduct, which are the result of the growth of the sciences of behavior during the nineteenth and twentieth centuries." *It is this essentially moral conflict that forms the backdrop for the past changes in and the present operation of our system of imposing death as a punishment for crime.* As the history of the punishment of death in this country shows, our society wishes to prevent crime; we have no desire to kill criminals simply to get even with them. [emphasis added]

As though it were necessary for him to reaffirm his position on this troublesome problem, Justice Brennan concluded with a final eloquent summary of his main points

In sum, the punishment of death is inconsistent with all four principles: *Death is an unusually severe and degrading punishment; there is a strong probability that it is inflicted arbitrarily; its rejection by contemporary society is virtually total; and there is no reason to believe that it serves any penal purpose more effectively than the less severe punishment of imprisonment.* The function of these principles is to enable a court to determine whether a punishment comports with human dignity. Death, quite simply, does not.

What does Justice Brennan mean when he says that "the battle has been waged on moral grounds"? Should Justices of the Supreme Court concern themselves with the morality of an issue? Is it not their responsibility to focus on the constitutionality of law? What similarities and differences do you see between the views of Justice Douglas and Justice Brennan?

JUSTICE STEWART'S OPINION

Justice Stewart emphasized the fact that the death penalty is unique because of its finality. His position is set forth in language that has been frequently quoted in subsequent decisions.

The penalty of death differs from all other forms of criminal punishment, not in degree but in kind. *It is unique in its total irrevocability. It is unique in its rejection of rehabilitation of the convict as a basic purpose of criminal justice. And it is unique, finally, in its absolute renunciation of all that is embodied in our concept of humanity.*

Looking at the sentences imposed in these cases, he said:

In the first place, it is clear that these sentences are "cruel" in the sense that they excessively go beyond, not in degree but in kind, the punishments that the state legislatures have determined to be necessary. In the second place, it is equally clear that these sentences are "unusual" in the sense that the penalty of death is infrequently imposed for murder, and that its imposition for rape is extraordinarily rare.

And finally, Stewart concluded that the death sentences imposed were cruel and unusual because they were "wantonly and freakishly" imposed.

JUSTICE WHITE'S OPINION

Justice White's opinion begins by asking what in his judgment is the central question.

The narrower question to which I address myself concerns the constitutionality of capital punishment statutes under which (1) the legislature authorizes the imposition of the death penalty for murder or rape; (2) the legislature does not itself mandate the penalty in any particular class or kind of case but delegates to judges or juries the decisions as to those cases, if any, in which the penalty will be utilized; and (3) *judges and juries have ordered the death penalty with such infrequency that the odds are now very much against imposition and execution of the penalty with respect to any convicted murderer or rapist.* It is in this context that we must consider whether the execution of these petitioners would violate the Eighth Amendment. [emphasis added]

Justice White answered the question in this way:

The imposition and execution of the death penalty are obviously cruel in the dictionary sense. But the penalty has not been considered cruel and unusual punishment in the constitutional sense because it was thought justified by the social ends it was deemed to serve. At the moment that it ceases realistically to further these purposes, however, the emerging question is whether its imposition in such circumstances would violate the Eighth Amendment. It is my view that it would, for its imposition would then be the pointless and needless extinction of life with only marginal contributions to any discernible social or public purposes. A penalty with such negligible returns to the State would be patently excessive and cruel and unusual punishment violative of the Eighth Amendment. . . .

But however that may be, I cannot avoid the conclusion that as the statutes before us are now administered, the penalty is so infrequently imposed that the threat of execution is too attenuated to be of substantial service to criminal justice.

What is the difference between the dictionary meaning and the constitutional meaning of the word "cruel"? On what grounds do Justices White and Stewart agree? What do you think of the argument that the death penalty is so seldom used as to be of little use to criminal justice?

JUSTICE MARSHALL'S OPINION

Justice Marshall's opinion covers many pages and many events. He examined the background of the Eighth Amendment in sixteenth and seventeenth century events, as well as its interpretation in the past decisions of the Supreme Court. His research led him to the following conclusion:

The cruel and unusual language "must draw its meaning from the evolving standards of decency that mark the progress of a maturing society." Thus, a penalty that was permissible at one time in our Nation's history is not necessarily permissible today.

The fact, therefore, that the Court, or individual Justices, may have in the past expressed an opinion that the death penalty is constitutional is not now binding on us.

Justice Marshall observed that recent studies indicate that "American citizens know almost nothing about capital punishment."

Justice Thurgood
Marshall has been a
continuing opponent of
capital punishment.

To make an informed judgment, he stated, one must know at least
that:

> . . . the death penalty is no more effective a deterrent than life im-
> prisonment, that convicted murderers are rarely executed, but are
> usually sentenced to a term in prison; that convicted murderers usually
> are model prisoners, and that they almost always become law-abiding
> citizens upon their release from prison; that the costs of executing
> a capital offender exceed the costs of imprisoning him for life; that
> while in prison, a convict under sentence of death performs none of
> the useful functions that life prisoners perform; that no attempt is made
> in the sentencing process to ferret out likely recidivists for execution;
> and that the death penalty may actually stimulate criminal activity.

First, he noted the apparent discriminatory effect. There are three
other facts to be considered, said Justice Marshall, in arriving at an
intelligent and informed judgment on the acceptability of capital
punishment.

Regarding *discrimination*, it has been said that "[i]t is usually the poor,
the illiterate, the underprivileged, the member of the minority group
— the man who, because he is without means, and is defended by
a court-appointed attorney — who becomes society's sacrificial lamb."
    It is the poor, and the members of minority groups who are least
able to voice their complaints against capital punishment. Their im-
potence leaves them victims of a sanction that the wealthier, better-
represented, just-as-guilty person can escape . . .

Second, he warned of the possibility of executing an innocent person.

Our "beyond a reasonable doubt" burden of proof in criminal cases is intended to protect the innocent, but we know it is not foolproof. Various studies have shown that people whose innocence is later convincingly established are convicted and sentenced to death.

Third, he pointed out the harmful effect on criminal justice system brought about by *sensationalism of a trial for life.*

While it is difficult to ascertain with certainty the degree to which the death penalty is discriminatorily imposed or the number of innocent persons sentenced to die, there is one conclusion about the penalty that is universally accepted — i.e., it *"tends to distort the course of the criminal law."*
The deleterious effects of the death penalty are also felt otherwise than at trial. For example, its very existence "inevitably sabotages a social or institutional program of reformation."

The opinion concludes with an appeal to our humanity. Recognizing that there is fear in our cities and that the average citizen is confronted daily with crime and crime statistics, Justice Marshall responded with an eloquent appeal.

At a time in our history when the streets of the Nation's cities inspire fear and despair, rather than pride and hope, it is difficult to maintain objectivity and concern for our fellow citizens. But, the measure of a country's greatness is its ability to retain compassion in time of crisis. No nation in the recorded history of man has a greater tradition of revering justice and fair treatment for all its citizens in times of turmoil, confusion, and tension than ours. This is a country which stands tallest in troubled times, a country which clings to fundamental principles, cherishes its constitutional heritage, and rejects simple solutions that compromise the values that lie at the roots of our democratic system.
In striking down capital punishment, this Court does not malign our system of government. On the contrary, it pays homage to it. Only in a free society could right triumph in difficult times, and could civilization record its magnificent advancement. In recognizing the humanity of our fellow human beings, we pay ourselves the highest tribute. We achieve "a major milestone in the long road up from barbarism" and join the approximately 70 other jurisdictions in the world which celebrate their regard for civilization and humanity by shunning capital punishment.

Is Justice Marshall correct when he says that informed Americans —those who are acquainted with the literature on capital punishment—oppose capital punishment? Would you consider yourself as informed on the subject of capital punishment? If not, would you be willing to read books and articles about it? To what extent are your opinions on this issue based on feelings; to what extent on evidence?

Chief Justice Burger dissented in the 1972 cases in which the Supreme Court struck down the capital punishment laws in 35 states.

CHIEF JUSTICE BURGER'S OPINION

Chief Justice Burger, apparently responding to the emotional appeal of Justice Marshall, began his opinion with the following observation:

Our constitutional inquiry, however, must be divorced from personal feelings as to the morality and efficacy of the death penalty, and be confined to the meaning and applicability of the uncertain language of the Eighth Amendment. There is no novelty in being called upon to interpret a constitutional provision that is less than self-defining, but, of all our fundamental guarantees, the ban on "cruel and unusual punishments" is one of the most difficult to translate into judicially manageable terms. The widely divergent views of the Amendment expressed in today's opinions reveal the haze that surrounds this constitutional command. *Yet it is essential to our role as a court that we not seize upon the enigmatic character of the guarantee as an invitation to enact our personal predilections into law.* [emphasis added]

What does the Chief Justice mean in the italicized sentences?

The Chief Justice stressed the importance of precedent. In the 180 years since the ratification of the Eighth Amendment, he said, "not a single decision of this Court has cast the slightest doubt on the constitutionality of capital punishment." Past decisions have denied that the death penalty is impermissibly "cruel."

In addition, Chief Justice Burger argued that in a democratic society the legislatures, not the courts, "are constituted to respond to the will and consequently the moral values of the people" and that "the legislative judgment is presumed to embody the basic standards of decency prevailing in the society." Noting that public opinion polls did not show widespread condemnation of capital punishment, he concluded that the legislatures were not out of touch with current social values when they enact capital punishment statutes.

Regarding the idea that capital punishment would deter people from committing crimes, the Chief Justice pointed out that it is hard to measure the effectiveness of any punishment as a deterrent. It is not proper "to put the states to the test of demonstrating the deterrent value of capital punishment." The Eighth Amendment was intended to guard against "torturous and inhuman punishments, not those of limited efficacy." It is not the province of the judiciary to intrude on legislative judgment in this matter, he concluded.

JUSTICE BLACKMUN'S OPINION

Justice Blackmun's opinion begins on a personal note, explaining the background of his own feelings about capital punishment.

I yield to no one in the depth of my distaste, antipathy, and, indeed, abhorrence, for the death penalty, with all its aspects of physical distress and fear and of moral judgment exercised by finite minds. That distaste is buttressed by a belief that capital punishment serves no useful purpose that can be demonstrated. For me, it violates childhood's training and life's experiences, and is not compatible with the philosophical convictions I have been able to develop. It is antagonistic to any sense of "reverence for life." Were I a legislator, I would vote against the death penalty for the policy reasons argued by counsel for the respective petitioners and expressed and adopted in the several opinions filed by the Justices who vote to reverse these judgments.

Justice Blackmun conceded that those who oppose the dealth penalty have powerful arguments. They point to "the progress of a maturing society" and appeal to "public opinion enlightened by human justice." But these arguments apply at the legislative level, where elected representatives have the responsibility of enacting laws which embody the standards of society. It is up to the legislature to decide the "moral" and the "right" thing to do. It is up to the judiciary to decide whether laws which are challenged are constitutional.

To reverse the judgments in these cases is, of course, the easy choice.

It is easier to strike the balance in favor of life and against death. It is comforting to relax in the thoughts—perhaps the rationalizations —that this is the compassionate decision for a maturing society; that this is the moral and the "right" thing to do; that thereby we convince ourselves that we are moving down the road toward human decency; that we value life even though that life has taken another or others or has grievously scarred another or others and their families; and that we are less barbaric than we were in 1879, or in 1890, or in 1910, or in 1947, or in 1958, or in 1963, or a year ago, in 1971, when *Wilkerson, Kemmler, Weems, Francis, Trop, Rudolph,* and *McGautha* were respectively decided.

This, for me, is good argument, and it makes some sense. But it is good argument and it makes sense only in a legislative and executive way and not as a judicial expedient. As I have said above, were I a legislator, I would do all I could to sponsor and to vote for legislation abolishing the death penalty. And were I the chief executive of a sovereign State, I would be sorely tempted to exercise executive clemency as Governor Rockefeller of Arkansas did recently just before he departed from office. There—on the Legislative Branch of the State or Federal Government, and secondarily, on the Executive Branch—is where the authority and responsibility for this kind of action lies. The authority should not be taken over by the judiciary in the modern guise of an Eighth Amendment issue.

In stressing the desirability of judicial restraint—that is, the desirability of leaving such matters to the legislative and the executive branches—Justice Blackmun points out that lawmakers have to deal with the "heinous and atrocious" nature of crimes, the misery of the victims and their families, and the terror and fear that stalk the cities. When they respond to these challenges with capital punishment, they are acting in accordance with their constitutional powers.

What do you think of Blackmun's reasoning? Should the judiciary defer to the judgment of the legislature in ruling on the death penalty?

JUSTICE POWELL'S OPINION

Justice Powell pointed out in his opinion that the Fifth Amendment makes three references to capital punishment.

No person shall be held to answer for a *capital* or otherwise infamous *crime*, unless on a presentment or indictment of a Grand Jury . . . ; nor shall any person be subject for the same offence to be twice put *in jeopardy of life* or limb; . . . nor be deprived of *life*, liberty, or property, without due process of law. . . . [emphasis added]

Since Justices Douglas and Marshall had focused their attention on the impact of capital punishment on the minorities, the poor, and the underprivileged, Justice Powell responded to their argument in the following manner:

Certainly the claim is justified that this criminal sanction falls more heavily on the relatively impoverished and underprivileged elements of society. The "have-nots" in every society always have been subject to greater pressure to commit crimes and to fewer constraints than their more affluent fellow citizens. *This is, indeed, a tragic byproduct of social and economic deprivation, but it is not an argument of constitutional proportions under the Eighth or Fourteenth Amendment. The same discriminatory impact argument could be made with equal force and logic with respect to those sentenced to prison terms.* The Due Process Clause admits of no distinction between the deprivation of "life" and the deprivation of "liberty." *If discriminatory impact renders capital punishment cruel and unusual, it likewise renders invalid most of the prescribed penalties for crimes of violence. The root causes of the higher incidence of criminal penalties on "minorities and the poor" will not be cured by abolishing the system of penalties.* Nor, indeed, could any society have a viable system of criminal justice if sanctions were abolished or ameliorated because most of those who commit crimes happen to be underprivileged. The basic problem results not from the penalties imposed for criminal conduct but from social and economic factors that have plagued humanity since the beginning of recorded history, frustrating all efforts to create in any country at any time the perfect society in which there are no "poor," no "minorities" and no "underprivileged." The causes underlying this problem are unrelated to the constitutional issue before the Court. [emphasis added]

Justice Powell also pointed out that neither the Eighth Amendment nor the Fourteenth Amendment, according to judicial interpretation, condemns capital punishment. Therefore, he concluded, for the Court to outlaw capital punishment would violate "the root principles of *stare decisis,* federalism, judicial restraint and — most importantly — separation of powers." Powell insisted that if the Court declared the death penalty unconstitutional, it would be overruling the legislatures of many states and several congressional enactments, including the Uniform Code of Military Justice.

Like Chief Justice Burger, Justice Powell was not convinced that most people were opposed to capital punishment.

Indeed, the weight of the evidence indicates that the public generally has not accepted either the morality or the social merit of the views so passionately advocated by the articulate spokesmen for abolition. But however one may assess the amorphous ebb and flow of public opinion generally on this volatile issue, this type of inquiry lies at the periphery — not the core — of the judicial process in constitutional cases. The assessment of popular opinion is essentially a legislative, not a judicial, function.

What is your reaction to Justice Powell's point that capital punishment should not be abolished simply because it is most likely to fall on the "have-nots"? Is Justice, as symbolized by the Goddess of Justice, blind to those who stand before her?

Retribution and *deterrence* are the two foundation stones on which the death penalty rests. As we have seen, some of the Justices regard these motives as unworthy of a civilized people. Justice Powell, however, described them as being useful to society.

Justice Powell felt that retribution expresses society's disapproval of especially shocking crimes, and is needed in a society where the criminal justice system requires public support. Powell called deterrence "a more appealing justification" for capital punishment than retribution, but acknowledged that there is disagreement over whether the death penalty really is an effective deterrent. He supported the right of states, however, to legislate punishments in an effort to deter crime.

Justice Rehnquist's opinion repeats the theme of judicial restraint. The nine Justices, he stated, have not been granted "a roving commission, either by the Founding Fathers or by the framers of the Fourteenth Amendment, to strike down laws that are based upon notions of policy or morality suddenly found unacceptable by a majority of the Court."

Based on your reading of the excerpts from the nine opinions, try to answer the following questions: What was the decision of the Court? How many of the Justices concluded that the death penalty was constitutional? How many disagreed? Analysts of this ruling have concluded that the Justices divided as follows: 1, 2, 2, 4. Can you solve this puzzle?

The Court handed down a *Per Curiam* opinion setting forth the decision in the case. This is an unsigned opinion on behalf of the Court and says in part:

Certiorari was granted limited to the following question: "Does the imposition and carrying out of the death penalty in these [cases] constitute cruel and unusual punishment in violation of the Eighth and Fourteenth Amendments?" . . . . The Court holds that the imposition and carrying out of the death penalty in these cases constitute cruel and unusual punishment in violation of the Eighth and Fourteenth Amendments. The judgment in each case is therefore reversed insofar as it leaves undisturbed the death sentence imposed, and the cases are remanded for further proceedings.

The Court decided by a vote of five to four that capital punishment as imposed in these cases was unconstitutional. The dissenters were Chief Justice Burger and Justices Powell, Blackmun, and Rehnquist.

Of the majority, two Justices (Brennan and Marshall) were unalterably opposed to capital punishment and concluded that it had no place in a civilized society. Justice Douglas did not go that far. He left unanswered the question of whether he might approve a mandatory death sentence if it could truly be imposed in a nondiscriminatory way. Justice Stewart found the present system of imposing death sentences "wanton" and "freakish." Justice White concluded that the death penalty was unconstitutional because, among other reasons, it was imposed infrequently. The Furman case was not the end, however, of the issue of whether capital punishment is constitutional.

11 DUE PROCESS GUIDELINES FOR IMPOSING THE DEATH PENALTY

The shock of the ruling in *Furman* v. *Georgia* reverberated throughout the halls of state legislatures. Thirty-five states rushed through new capital punishment legislation to conform to the principles stated in the Court's opinions. But what did that decision really say? The nine opinions had revealed a variety of points of view. Should the new laws mandate death in certain cases? Certainly this would remove the objection of wanton, capricious, freakish, and unpredictable behavior by judges and juries. How specific must the new legislation be to meet the objections of the Court?

Furman v. *Georgia* had been decided by a vote of five to four. Now there was a new Justice on the Supreme Court: Justice Stevens had replaced Justice Douglas, who had retired. Would this make a difference?

On July 2, 1976, the Court handed down five decisions in cases challenging recently-enacted capital punishment laws. The Justices upheld the laws of Georgia, Florida, and Texas while invalidating those of North Carolina and Louisiana. The judicial lineup now stood as follows: Justices Brennan and Marshall continued their attack on the constitutionality of capital punishment by dissenting in the three cases where capital punishment laws were upheld and joining Justices Stewart, Powell, and Stevens to make a majority in the other two cases. The latter three Justices sided with each other in all five cases, upholding three and condemning two of the state laws. Justices White and Rehnquist and Chief Justice Burger teamed up to support all five state laws. Justice Blackmun, standing on his dissent in the Furman case, also supported all five laws. The cases that so divided the Court follow.

GREGG v. GEORGIA

What procedures must be followed before imposing the death sentence?

Troy Leon Gregg and a companion were picked up by two drunk men. When their car broke down, one of the men purchased a new car, using part of a large roll of cash, which Gregg saw. Subsequently when the men stopped the car and got out to relieve themselves, Gregg also got out and shot the two as they returned to the car. Gregg then took $400 and the car from the men. When Gregg was asked why he shot them, he said, while in custody, "By God, I wanted them dead."

Gregg was convicted of armed robbery and murder and was sentenced to death. The Georgia Supreme Court affirmed the con-

The Legal Defense and Educational Fund for the National Association for the Advancement of Colored People, represented by Jack Greenberg, *left*, instituted the lawsuits that resulted in the 1976 death penalty cases. Anthony J. Amsterdam, *right*, argued them before the Court.

victions and upheld the death sentence for the murders but vacated the armed robbery sentences on the grounds that the death sentence had rarely been imposed for that offense.

The new Georgia law provided for a *bifurcated trial:* The jury first determines the guilt or innocence of the accused; then in another proceeding the same jury decides the sentence. In arriving at the guilty verdict and the death sentence, the jury had to consider aggravating and mitigating circumstances and find that at least one of the following aggravating circumstances existed beyond a reasonable doubt before the death penalty could be imposed:

(1) The offense of murder, rape, armed robbery, or kidnapping was committed by a person with a prior record of conviction for a capital felony, or the offense of murder was committed by a person who has a substantial history of serious assaultive criminal convictions.

(2) The offense of murder, rape, armed robbery, or kidnapping was committed while the offender was engaged in the commission of another capital felony or aggravated battery, or the offense of murder was committed while the offender was engaged in the commission of burglary or arson in the first degree.

(3) The offender by his act of murder, armed robbery, or kidnapping knowingly created a great risk of death to more than one person in a public place by means of a weapon or device which would normally be hazardous to the lives of more than one person.

(4) The offender committed the offense of murder for himself or another, for the purpose of receiving money or any other thing of monetary value.

(5) The murder (was) of a judicial officer, former judicial officer, district attorney or solicitor or former district attorney or solicitor during or because of the exercise of his official duty.

(6) The offender caused or directed another to commit murder or committed murder as an agent or employee of another person.

(7) The offense of murder, rape, armed robbery, or kidnapping was outrageously or wantonly vile, horrible or inhuman in that it involved torture, depravity of mind, or an aggravated battery to the victim.

(8) The offense of murder was committed against any peace officer, corrections employee or fireman while engaged in the performance of his official duties.

(9) The offense of murder was committed by a person in, or who has escaped from, the lawful custody of a peace officer or place of lawful confinement.

(10) The murder was committed for the purpose of avoiding, interfering with, or preventing a lawful arrest or custody in a place of lawful confinement, of himself or another.

In this case, the jury found that Gregg's criminal conduct (armed robbery and murder) included two of the above listed aggravating circumstances: sections (2) and (4).

In deciding whether to impose the death sentence, the jury may consider any mitigating circumstances that would make them judge the defendant less harshly. Although the Georgia statute did not specify mitigating circumstances, those factors that are usually considered mitigating circumstances are the defendant's age, prior record, emotional state at the time of the crime, and willingness to cooperate with the police.

To make certain that the judge and jury do not act unreasonably or with prejudice, the Georgia statute requires an automatic appeal to the Georgia Supreme Court, where the sentence is examined against the following three criteria: 1. Whether the sentence was imposed on the basis of prejudice or any other arbitrary factor. 2. Whether the evidence supported a finding of an aggravating circumstance. 3. Whether the penalty in the case was excessive compared to penalties which had been imposed in similar cases.

The Georgia Supreme Court affirmed the death sentence in Gregg's case. Gregg based his appeal of that decision on a number of grounds, including the claim that the death penalty is cruel and unusual punishment. Justice Stewart announced the judgment of the Court and wrote the opinion in which only Justices Powell and Stevens concurred. Although this represents a plurality opinion, four other Justices joined in the judgment to make it a seven to two ruling.

Justice Stewart, who had condemned the imposition of capital punishment as "wanton" and "freakish" in the *Furman* case, found the new statute constitutional. The Georgia law, he concluded, is carefully drawn, provides specific instructions to judge and jury, and mandates an automatic appeal to the state's highest court. The death penalty, he stated, is not necessarily cruel and unusual punishment. In this case, he concluded that the penalty for the murders cannot be considered excessive.

What Justice Stewart found especially relevant in influencing his change of mind on the death penalty were the events that followed the *Furman* ruling.

The most marked indication of society's endorsement of the death penalty for murder is the legislative response to *Furman*. The legislatures of at least 35 States have enacted new statutes that provide for the death penalty for at least some crimes that result in the death of another person. And, the Congress of the United States, in 1974, enacted a statute providing the death penalty for aircraft piracy that results in death. These recently adopted statutes have attempted to address the concerns expressed by the Court in *Furman* primarily (i) by specifying the factors to be weighed and the procedures to be followed in deciding when to impose a capital sentence, or (ii) by making the death penalty mandatory for specified crimes. But all of the post-*Furman* statutes make clear that capital punishment itself has not been rejected by the elected representatives of the people.

In the only statewide referendum occurring since *Furman* and brought to our attention, the people of California adopted a constitutional amendment that authorized capital punishment, in effect negating a prior ruling by the Supreme Court of California.

There is a saying which states that the Supreme Court follows the election returns. Do you think Justice Stewart was basing his decision on popular opinion rather than constitutional principles?

Justice Stewart summarized his position as follows:

In sum, we cannot say that the judgment of the Georgia Legislature that capital punishment may be necessary in some cases is clearly wrong. Considerations of federalism, as well as respect for the ability of a legislature to evaluate, in terms of its particular State, the moral consensus concerning the death penalty and its social utility as a sanction, require us to conclude, in the absence of more convincing evidence, that the infliction of death as a punishment for murder is not without justification and thus is not unconstitutionally severe.

Justice White, speaking for Chief Justice Burger and Justice Rehnquist, agreed with the decision, saying that Georgia law meets the criticism he and Justices Stewart and Douglas had expressed in the *Furman* case. The new arrangement prevents the imposition of the death penalty in a "discriminatory, standardless, or rare fashion."

Justice Blackmun, standing on his *Furman* dissent, concurred in the judgment. The dissenting opinions of Justices Brennan and Marshall appear on pp. 111–112.

JUREK v. TEXAS

Does the Texas law provide for adequate procedures to assure the constitutionality of imposing the death penalty?

Jerry Lane Jurek was found guilty of killing a ten-year-old girl, while attempting to kidnap and forcibly rape her, he strangled her and threw her unconscious body in a river. The issue was the constitutionality of the death penalty imposed on him by the jury.

After the decision in *Branch* v. *Texas,* decided with *Furman,* the Texas legislature rewrote its laws relating to capital punishment. The new law limited capital punishment to five situations: murder of a peace officer or fireman; murder committed in the course of kid-napping, burglary, robbery, forcible rape, or arson; murder committed for hire; murder committed while escaping or attempting to escape from prison; and murder committed by an inmate when the victim is a prison employee.

As in Georgia, the trial is bifurcated, with the jury first determining guilt and then, in a separate proceeding, deciding the sentence. In the second proceeding in which the jury decides whether the death sentence should be imposed, they are required to answer three questions:

1. Whether the defendant's conduct was committed deliberately and with reasonable expectation that death would result.
2. Whether there was a probability that the defendant would commit acts of criminal violence that would constitute a continuing threat to society.
3. Whether the defendant's conduct in killing the victim was unreasonable in response to provocation, if any, by the victim.

In the Jurek case, only the first two questions were regarded as relevant, and the jury answered each in the affirmative.

The issue here is whether the Texas law provides for the jury's consideration of aggravating and mitigating circumstances, as well as for appellate review to rule out arbitrary and capricious sentencing. Here the Court was confronted with a problem. Unlike the Georgia statute, the Texas law made no mention of mitigating circumstances.

Justice Stevens delivered the judgment and opinion of the Court, in which Justices Powell and Stewart joined. The opinion concluded that the aggravating circumstances could be inferred in the five crimes that were designated as capital offenses. Similarly, although mitigating circumstances are not stated, the three questions which the jury must consider before imposing the death sentence permit the defendant to bring before the members of the jury such relevant data as age, prior record, employment, duress, mental or emotional pressure, psychiatric records, and remorse. In addition, the Texas law, like the Georgia statute, provides for prompt review of the jury's verdict by a court of statewide jurisdiction. This allows for the Texas Court of Criminal Appeals to focus on the matter of mitigating circumstances in reviewing the case.

Jurek had argued that the second of the three questions which the jury had to answer was so vague that a lay person could not possibly handle it. How can the average juror, the defense counsel asked, predict the future behavior of a convicted person? Justice Stevens answered that "any sentencing authority must predict a convicted person's probable future conduct." A jury, he said, can make a reasonable prediction when presented with all possible relevant information. Texas law assured the presentation of such evidence.

Justices White and Rehnquist, joined by Chief Justice Burger, concurred in the decision. Justice White repeated his view that the Eighth Amendment does not forbid the death penalty. He also agreed that the new Texas statute eliminated the discretion of the Court, jury, and law enforcement officers, so that the death penalty would not be "seldom" or "arbitrarily" imposed. Justices Brennan and Marshall dissented. (See pp. 111–112).

PROFFITT v. FLORIDA

Can the judge decide whether the death sentence should be imposed?

The third capital punishment case was somewhat different from the first two and raised an interesting issue. Under the new Florida law, after the jury's verdict, a separate hearing is required to determine whether a death sentence or life imprisonment should be imposed. This responsibility rests with the judge, rather than with the jury as in the Georgia and Texas procedures. In arriving at his judgment, the judge has to determine whether statutory mitigating circumstances outweigh statutory aggravating circumstances. These circumstances are set forth in Florida law.

The aggravating circumstances are:

(a) The capital felony was committed by a person under sentence of imprisonment.

(b) The defendant was previously convicted of another capital felony or of a felony involving the use or threat of violence to the person.

(c) The defendant knowingly created a great risk of death to many persons.

(d) The capital felony was committed while the defendant was engaged, or was an accomplice, in the commission of, or an attempt to commit, or flight after committing or attempting to commit, any robbery, rape, arson, burglary, kidnapping, or aircraft piracy or the unlawful throwing, placing, or discharging of a destructive device or bomb.

(e) The capital felony was committed for the purpose of avoiding or preventing a lawful arrest or effecting an escape from custody.

(f) The capital felony was committed for pecuniary gain.

(g) The capital felony was committed to disrupt or hinder the lawful exercise of any governmental function or the enforcement of laws.

(h) The capital felony was especially heinous, atrocious, or cruel.

The mitigating circumstances are:

(a) The defendant has no significant history of prior criminal activity.

(b) The capital felony was committed while the defendant was under the influence of extreme mental or emotional disturbance.

(c) The victim was a participant in the defendant's conduct or consented to the act.

(d) The defendant was an accomplice in the capital felony committed by another person and his participation was relatively minor.

(e) The defendant acted under extreme duress or under the substantial domination of another person.

(f) The capacity of the defendant to appreciate the criminality of his conduct or to conform his conduct to the requirements of law was substantially impaired.

(g) The age of the defendant at the time of the crime.

Charles William Proffitt was tried and found guilty of first degree murder. After weighing the relevant aggravating and mitigating circumstances, the judge imposed the death sentence. The Florida law also required an automatic review by the state Supreme Court, and that court affirmed the death sentence.

This case raised the issue of whether sentencing by the judge rather than by the jury makes a critical difference.

What do you think? Would you prefer the sentencing authority to be the judge or the jury?

Justice Powell spoke for the Court, with the concurrence of only Justices Stevens and Stewart. They stated that the Florida law is constitutional because it clearly specifies mitigating and aggravating circumstances as well as automatic appeals. Judges are given specific and detailed guidance in deciding on the sentence. If they impose the death penalty they must state in writing the facts on which they based their decision. Justice Powell saw a possible advantage in having judges do the sentencing because:

. . . judicial sentencing should lead, if anything, to even greater consistency in the imposition at the trial court level of capital punishment, since a trial judge is more experienced in sentencing than a jury, and therefore is better able to impose sentences similar to those imposed in analogous cases.

Once again, Justice White spoke for Chief Justice Burger and Justice Rehnquist in an opinion concurring with the judgment of the Court. He reaffirmed his position that the death penalty is constitutional when it is imposed under procedures which regularize the deliberations of judge and jury. Justice Blackmun concurred in the judgment, citing his dissenting opinion in *Furman*.

THE DISSENTING OPINIONS OF JUSTICES BRENNAN AND MARSHALL

Justices Brennan and Marshall, whose opposition to capital punishment had put them on the side of the majority in the *Furman* case, now found themselves the only dissenters. They disagreed with the majority in the *Gregg*, *Jurek*, and *Proffitt* cases and each wrote a dissenting opinion in which he addressed all three cases together. In these dissents they continued their assault on the constitutionality of capital punishment as cruel and unusual.

Justice Brennan accused the majority of being more concerned with the procedures employed by the states to impose death than with the very essence of the penalty. He declared that the court, as the ultimate arbiter of the meaning of the Constitution, has the duty to speak out when punishments are "no longer morally tolerable in our civilized society." He stated that the death penalty is "degrading to human dignity," treats individuals as "nonhumans," and borders on "official murder."

Justice Marshall repeated two arguments he had made in his *Furman* opinion: that the death penalty is excessive and the American people if "fully informed as to the purposes of the death penalty and its liabilities," would reject it as "morally unacceptable;" and that retribution and deterrence do not justify a punishment that degrades the victim and violates the substance and spirit of the Eighth Amendment.

WOODSON v. NORTH CAROLINA

Is a law mandating the death penalty for certain crimes constitutional?

Different issues and a Court divided along different lines appear in the fourth and fifth cases which follow. Some of the states, in enacting new capital punishment laws to conform with the suggestions mentioned in the *Furman* opinions, made obvious attempts to escape any criticism that their new laws might be discriminatory or wantonly, freakishly, and infrequently imposed. To overcome these conditions, North Carolina enacted the following statute:

Murder in the first and second degree defined; punishment. — A murder which shall be perpetrated by means of poison, lying in wait, imprisonment, starving, torture, or by any other kind of willful, deliberate and premeditated killing, or which shall be committed in the perpetration or attempt to perpetrate any arson, rape, robbery, kidnapping, burglary or other felony, *shall be deemed to be murder in the first degree and shall be punished with death.* All other kinds of murder shall be deemed murder in the second degree, and shall be punished by imprisonment for a term of not less than two years nor more than than life imprisonment in the State's prison. [emphasis added]

Prior to the *Furman* decision, North Carolina had allowed the jury to choose whether or not to impose capital punishment for first-degree murder.

James Tyrone Woodson and Luby Waxton were convicted of first-degree murder and sentenced to death. The statute required the death penalty in all first-degree murder cases. The Supreme Court stated the issue which was raised in the case as follows:

The Court now addresses for the first time the question whether a death sentence returned pursuant to a law imposing a mandatory death penalty for a broad category of homicidal offenses constitutes cruel and unusual punishment within the meaning of the Eighth and Fourteenth Amendments.

Do you think that it is fair to require the death penalty for certain crimes such as first degree murder? It puts everyone in the state on notice that courts and juries have no choice in the matter. It does away with the "unbridled discretion" which makes it possible for juries to give some defendants life imprisonment, while others are put to death. If you were a Supreme Court Justice who had participated in the Court rulings up to this time, what would be your decision?

The judgment of the Court was delivered in an opinion announced by Justice Stewart and concurred in by Justices Stevens and Powell. The opinion began by tracing the history of mandatory punishment in this country.

In order to provide a frame for assessing the relevancy of these factors in this case we begin by sketching the history of mandatory death penalty statutes in the United States. At the time the Eighth Amendment was adopted in 1791, the States uniformly followed the common-law practice of making death the exclusive and mandatory sentence for certain specified offenses. Although the range of capital offenses in the American Colonies was quite limited in comparison to the more than 200 offenses then punishable by death in England, the Colonies at the time of the Revolution imposed death sentences on all persons convicted of any of a considerable number of crimes, typically including at a minimum, murder, treason, piracy, arson, rape, robbery, burglary, and sodomy. As at common law, all homicides that were not involuntary, provoked, justified, or excused constituted murder and were automatically punished by death. Almost from the outset jurors reacted unfavorably to the harshness of mandatory death sentences.

The reluctance of juries to return verdicts in mandatory death sentence cases led states to grant juries discretion in capital cases. The first states to abandon mandatory death sentences in favor of discretionary death sentences were Tennessee, in 1838, Alabama, in 1841, and Louisiana, in 1846. Congress acted in this area in 1897.

If you were a member of a jury in a mandatory death sentence case, would you feel comfortable with a situation in which your only choice was guilty or not guilty? Why do juries seem to be reluctant to impose mandatory death sentences?

The Court found that two criticisms of mandatory death sentences are that they are "unduly harsh and unworkably rigid." In the eyes of Justice Stewart and his two colleagues, the reluctance of juries to sentence and the legislative approval of discretionary jury sentencing by Congress and many of the states are evidence of "contemporary standards of justice" which the Court cannot disregard. And, in their view, it is the jury which remains the link between "contemporary community values and the penal system." It is for this very reason that the Justices concluded that the North Carolina law must be struck down.

North Carolina's mandatory death penalty statute for first-degree murder departs markedly from contemporary standards respecting the imposition of the punishment of death and thus cannot be applied consistently with the Eighth and Fourteenth Amendments' requirement that the State's power to punish "be exercised within the limits of civilized standards."

The opinion also cites the lack of standards to guide sentencing in the statute, the lack of a procedure for appellate review, and the failure of the statute to provide for consideration of individual circumstances surrounding the crime as reasons for finding that the North Carolina law violated the Eighth and Fourteenth Amendments. Another reason is given in the opinion for striking down the North Carolina law.

A third constitutional shortcoming of the North Carolina statute is its *failure to allow the particularized consideration of relevant aspects of the character and record of each convicted defendant before the imposition upon him of a sentence of death.* . . . A process that accords no significance to relevant facets of the character and record of the individual offender or the circumstances of the particular offense excludes from consideration in fixing the ultimate punishment of death the possibility of compassionate or mitigating factors stemming from the diverse frailties of humankind. It treats all persons convicted of a designated offense not as uniquely individual human beings, but as members of a faceless, undifferentiated mass to be subjected to the blind infliction of the penalty of death. . . . we believe that in capital cases the fundamental respect for humanity underlying the Eighth Amendment. . . . requires consideration of the character and record of the individual offender and the circumstances of the particular offense as a constitutionally indispensable part of the process of inflicting the penalty of death. [emphasis added]

Justices Brennan and Marshall joined Justices Stewart, Stevens, and Powell in the Court's decision but not in the reasoning of the Court's opinion. They reaffirmed their opposition to capital punishment and therefore found the North Carolina law unconstitutional.

The four dissenters were Chief Justice Burger and Justices White, Blackmun, and Rehnquist. Justice Rehnquist wrote a separate dissenting opinion in which he disagreed with practically everything in the Court's opinion. He concluded that there was little difference between the North Carolina statute, which the Court condemned, and the Texas and Georgia laws, which the Court approved.

Lousiana also enacted a new capital punishment law designed

to meet the objections voiced by the Court in the *Furman* case. The statute at that time read:

First degree murder

First degree murder is the killing of a human being:

(1) When the offender has a specific intent to kill or to inflict great bodily harm and is engaged in the perpetration or attempted perpetration of aggravated kidnapping, aggravated rape or armed robbery; or

(2) When the offender has a specific intent to kill, or to inflict great bodily harm upon, a fireman or a peace officer who was engaged in the performance of his lawful duties; or

(3) Where the offender has a specific intent to kill or to inflict great bodily harm and has previously been convicted of an unrelated murder or is serving a life sentence; or

(4) When the offender has a specific intent to kill or to inflict great bodily harm upon more than one person; [or]

(5) When the offender has specific intent to commit murder and has been offered or has received anything of value for committing the murder.

For the purposes of Paragraph (2) herein, the term peace officer shall be defined and include any constable, sheriff, deputy sheriff, local or state policeman, game warden, federal law enforcement officer, jail or prison guard, parole officer, probation officer, judge, district attorney, assistant district attorney or district attorneys' investigator.

Whoever commits the crime of first degree murder shall be punished by death.

(In 1975, (1) was amended to add the crime of aggravated burglary as a predicate felony for first-degree murder.)

ROBERTS v. LOUISIANA

Must aggravating and mitigating circumstances be considered where the death penalty is mandatory?

Stanislaus Roberts was found guilty of first-degree murder, and the death sentence was imposed under the new Louisiana law. He appealed on the grounds that capital punishment was cruel and unusual under the Eighth and Fourteenth Amendments and that the Louisiana law was similar to the legislation condemned in the *Furman* case.

Again there was a five to four decision, and again it was announced in an opinion by Justice Stevens and concurred in by Justices Stewart and Powell. They found the mandatory death penalty as dictated by Louisiana law unconstitutional under the Eighth and Fourteenth Amendments because it lacked a "meaningful opportunity for consideration of mitigating factors presented by the circumstances of the particular crime or by the attributes of the individual offender."

The Court compared the North Carolina and Louisiana statutes.

The Louisiana statute thus suffers from constitutional deficiencies similar to those identified in the North Carolina statute in *Woodson* v. *North Carolina*. . . . As in North Carolina, *there are no standards*

Justice John Paul Stevens, the Supreme Court's newest member, wrote the majority opinion in the 1976 case of *Roberts* v. *Louisiana*.

provided to guide the jury in the exercise of its power to select those first-degree murderers who will receive death sentences, and *there is no meaningful appellate review of the jury's decision.* As in North Carolina, death sentences are mandatory upon conviction for first-degree murder. *Louisiana's mandatory death sentence law employs a procedure that was rejected by that State's legislature 130 years ago and that subsequently has been renounced by legislatures and juries in every jurisdiction in this Nation.* . . . The Eighth Amendment, which draws much of its meaning from "the evolving standards of decency that mark the progress of a maturing society". . . . simply cannot tolerate the reintroduction of a practice so thoroughly discredited.

Accordingly, we find that the death sentence imposed upon the petitioner under Louisiana's mandatory death sentence statute violates the Eighth and Fourteenth Amendments and must be set aside. [emphasis added]

Observe that the opinion again emphasizes *standards* for guiding the jury and a procedure for *appellate* review of the decision to impose the death sentence.

As could be expected, Justices Brennan and Marshall joined in the judgment of the Court, but their reasoning differed from that of the opinion of the Court because they consistently maintained that capital punishment *per se* was a violation of the Eighth and Fourteenth Amendments.

Justices White, Rehnquist, and Blackmun and Chief Justice Burger dissented. Justice White's dissenting opinion again emphasized that contemporary community standards, to which the Court's opinion continually refers, seem to accept capital punishment, for at least some offenses.

Since the judgment in *Furman*, Congress and 35 state legislatures re-enacted the death penalty for one or more crimes. All of these States authorize the death penalty for murder of one kind or another. With these profound developments in mind, I cannot say that capital punishment has been rejected by or is offensive to the prevailing attitudes and moral presuppositions in the United States or that it is always an excessively cruel or severe punishment or always a disproportionate punishment for any crime for which it might be imposed. These grounds for invalidating the death penalty are foreclosed by recent events, which this Court must accept as demonstrating the capital punishment is acceptable to the contemporary community as just punishment for at least some intentional killings.

And, the dissenters were saying in their opinion, that the Louisiana law brought certainty into an area previously dominated by capricious, arbitrary, and freakish jury judgments, by eliminating the "guilty without capital punishment" verdict provision which had existed in the prior Louisiana statute, and making a verdict of "guilty of first degree murder" carry a mandatory death sentence. Justice White made it clear that he did not think it a proper exercise of the court's power of review to overturn the conclusions of Congress and 35 state legislatures, who found that there are circumstances in which the death penalty can serve as a deterrent of crime. Justice White rebuked the Justices, showing his annoyance with their reasoning.

Indeed, the more fundamental objection than the plurality's muddled reasoning is that in *Gregg* v. *Georgia*. . . . it lectures us at length about the role and place of the judiciary and then proceeds to ignore its own advice, the net effect being to suggest that observers of this institution should pay more attention to what we do than what we say. The plurality claims that it has not forgotten what the past has taught about the limits of judicial review; but I fear that it has again surrendered to the temptation to make policy for and to attempt to govern the country through a misuse of the powers given this court under the Constitution.

One might have thought that the capital punishment controversy had been resolved by the Court's prior rulings. But this was not so. In 1978, two cases reached the Court from the State of Ohio, and the issues posed brought forth a new ruling which divided the Justices again and in different ways.

LOCKETT v. OHIO
What mitigating circumstances must be considered?

Sandra Lockett was accused of driving the getaway car for a robbery during which the victim was killed. She was charged with aggravated robbery and aggravated murder, convicted, and sentenced to death under the Ohio capital punishment statute. The individual who actually committed the murder turned state's evidence and testified against her. Under Ohio law at the time, the death sentence was mandatory in this type of case unless the judge, considering "the nature and circumstances of the offense and the history, character, and conditions of the offender," determines that at least one of the following *mitigating* circumstances is established by a preponderance of the evidence:

1. The victim of the offense induced or facilitated it.
2. It is unlikely that the offense would have been committed but for the fact that the offender was under duress, coercion, or strong provocation.
3. The offense was primarily the product of the offender's psychosis or mental deficiency, though such condition is insufficient to establish the defense of insanity.

In accordance with Ohio law, the judge requested a presentence report, as well as psychiatric and psychological tests. The reports concluded that Lockett did not suffer from any psychoses and was not mentally deficient. Without specifically addressing the first two mitigating circumstances, the judge declared that he had "no alternative whether [he] like[d] the law or not" but to impose the death sentence.

Lockett challenged the trial and sentence on various grounds. The one which the Court considered crucial was her contention that her death sentence was invalid because the Ohio statute did not permit the judge to consider as mitigating circumstances such matters as age, character, prior record, her minor role in the crime, and the absence of specific intent to cause death.

What do you think of Lockett's argument? Does it seem to be based on the North Carolina and Louisiana cases? How would you expect the Justices to divide on this issue?

Chief Justice Burger delivered the opinion of the Court, and Justices Stewart, Powell, and Stevens agreed with his conclusion that the Ohio law was unconstitutional. Acknowledging that the prior opinions of the Court had been anything but crystal clear, the Chief Justice reassured the states that an attempt would be made in this opinion to clarify the Court's position, stating:

In the last decade, many of the States have been obliged to revise their death penalty statutes in response to the various opinions supporting judgments in *Furman* . . . and its companion cases. *The signals from this Court have not, however, always been easy to decipher. The States now deserve the clearest guidance that the Court can provide; we have an obligation to reconcile previously differing views in order to provide that guidance.* [emphasis added]

The Chief Justice then announced the principle that would serve as the guide.

We conclude that the Eighth and Fourteenth Amendments require that the sentencer, in all but the rarest kind of capital cases, not be precluded from considering *as a mitigating factor* [emphasis in original], any aspect of a defendant's character or record and any of the circumstances of the offense that the defendant proffers as a basis for a sentence less than death. . . . Given that the imposition of death by public authority is so profoundly different from all other penalties, we cannot avoid the conclusion that an individualized decision is essential in capital cases. . . .

. . . . There is no perfect procedure for deciding in which cases governmental authority should be used to impose death. *But a statute that prevents the sentencer in all capital cases from giving independent mitigating weight to aspects of the defendant's character and record and to circumstances of the offense proffered in mitigation creates the risk that the death penalty will be imposed in spite of factors which may call for a less severe penalty. When the choice is between life and death, that risk is unacceptable and incompatible with the commands of the Eighth and Fourteenth Amendments.* [emphasis added]

Since the Ohio statute did not permit "individualized consideration of mitigating factors," it failed to meet the standards required by the Eighth and Fourteenth Amendments in capital cases and was held unconstitutional.

Justice Brennan did not take part in the case. While Justice Marshall repeated his position that the Eighth and Fourteenth Amendments outlaw capital punishment.

Justice Blackmun agreed that the law was unconstitutional, but he offered two reasons which were not considered by the Court's ruling. He pointed out that the Ohio law provides the death penalty for a defendant who aids and abets a murder without allowing the sentencing authority to consider the extent of the defendant's actual involvement. His second objection was that while the Ohio law gave the sentencing judge full discretion to impose less than the death sentence on a defendant who pleaded guilty or no contest, it required the death penalty for one who insists on the right to a trial and is found guilty. It was this provision that had allowed the defendant who pulled the trigger to avoid the death sentence by pleading guilty, while Lockett, who was less involved in the crime, was sentenced to death.

Justice White also concurred in the Court's ruling but differed in his reasoning. Justice Rehnquist concurred in part and dissented in part. He responded to the principle of law announced in the Court's opinion with the warning:

If a defendant as a matter of constitutional law is to be permitted to offer as evidence in the sentencing hearing any fact, however bizarre, which he wishes, even though the most sympathetically disposed trial judge could conceive of no basis upon which the jury might take it into account in imposing a sentence, the new constitutional doctrine will not eliminate arbitrariness or freakishness in the impostion of sentences, but will codify and institutionalize it. By encouraging defendants in capital cases, and presumably sentencing judges and juries, to take into consideration anything under the sun as a "mitigating circumstance," it will not guide sentencing discretion but will totally unleash it. . . . I do not think Ohio was required to receive any sort of mitigating evidence which an accused or his lawyer wishes to offer.

BELL v. OHIO

Sixteen-year-old Willie Lee Bell was charged with aggravated murder which occurred in the course of a kidnapping. He waived his right to trial by jury and was convicted before a three-judge panel. In his statement to the police, Bell denied he had done the actual killing. He said his companion, eighteen-year-old Samuel Hall, had pulled the trigger and that he had not been aware of Hall's intention. Under Ohio law, the judges ordered a presentence investigation and psychiatric examination of Bell. The report of the psychiatrist concluded that none of the three mitigating factors mentioned in the statute were present in Bell's case (Refer to the *Lockett* case beginning on page 118 for the three factors). The presentence report supplied the judges with information regarding the offense, as well as Bell's background, intelligence, prior record, character, and habits. It described his intellectual capacity as low average or dull normal and noted that he had allegedly been using mescaline on the night of the crime.

Before sentencing, Bell's attorney was permitted to present evidence that Bell had a drug problem, that he regarded his accomplice as a "big brother" and had followed his instructions because he was afraid, and that he was emotionally unstable and mentally deficient. The lawyer brought out the facts that Bell had cooperated with the police and that there was a lack of proof that he had participated in the actual killing.

After considering the reports and the evidence, the judges first decided that none of the three mitigating factors defined by Ohio law were present and then imposed the death sentence. The Ohio supreme court held that the evidence that Bell had aided and abetted was enough to sustain the conviction and the death penalty because under Ohio law, an aider and abettor could be prosecuted as if he or she were the principal offender.

Chief Justice Burger again delivered the opinion of the Court in which Justices Stewart, Powell, and Stevens concurred. The opinion repeated the position taken by the four Justices in the *Lockett* case: The Eighth and Fourteenth Amendments require that sentencing judges and juries take into consideration *all* mitigating circumstances relating to the defendant's character, record, and any other evidence that the defendant wants to offer. Since the Ohio law did not permit "individualized consideration of mitigating factors," it was declared unconstitutional.

Justice Brennan did not take part in the case. Justice Marshall concurred but repeated his position stated in *Furman* that the death penalty is under all circumstances cruel and unusual punishment. Justice Rehnquist stood on his dissent in the *Lockett* case. Justice White concurred in the judgment of the Court that the Ohio law was unconstitutional but dissented from the reasoning of the Court's opinion. In an opinion dissenting in part from the Court's opinion in both *Lockett* and *Bell*, he said that the death sentences in both cases should be set aside because there was no finding that the defendants engaged in conduct "with the conscious purpose of producing death." Without a finding that a defendant possesses a purpose to cause the death of a victim, he said, the imposition of the death penalty violates the Eighth Amendment.

Do you think that the fact that Lockett was a woman and Bell a sixteen-year-old black youth influenced the court's holding which insisted on *individualized* consideration of mitigating circumstances?

---

12 CONCLUDING THOUGHTS ON CAPITAL PUNISHMENT

If, after reading the 1972, 1976, 1978 capital punishment cases, you are somewhat confused as to whether capital punishment is cruel and unusual, you are not alone. The subject is fraught with emotional overtones, historical references, sociological data, values conflicts, moral dilemmas, and constitutional principles.

Hanging over the debates and discussions "like a brooding omnipresence in the sky" is the finality of the death sentence and its relationship to the idea of justice. The Fourteenth Amendment commands that *no person shall be deprived of life without due process of law.* But what constitutes due process before a life may be taken? Or, as Justices Marshall and Brennan maintain, is the death sentence itself a violation of due process?

Why cannot the Justices agree on some principle which would clarify when the death sentence is or is not constitutional? Suppose you formulate a clear and simple rule such as: Anyone who kills another person must be put to death. Any objections? What would you do with the exceptions such as self-defense, insanity, mental incompetence, provocation, and other considerations?

Let us briefly review the positions of the Justices in the cases discussed. In the 1972 *Furman* decision, Justices Brennan and Marshall took the position that capital punishment was cruel and unusual and was thus prohibited by the Eighth Amendment and by the Fourteenth Amendment's due process clause. They maintained this position in all cases.

Justices Douglas, Stewart, and White agreed that the death penalty in the *Furman* case was unconstitutional, but each supported his position by different reasoning. Douglas found the discretionary sentencing permitted under the Georgia and Texas laws discriminatory. Stewart concluded that in both states the death sentence was "wantonly" and "freakishly" imposed. White concluded that, as the Georgia and Texas statutes were administered, the death penalty was so infrequently imposed that the threat of execution could not be of any substantial service to criminal justice as a means to deter others from crime. The result in this case was five to four against the Georgia and Texas laws. The majority consisted of Justices Brennan, Stewart, White, Marshall, and Douglas; The dissenters were Chief Justice Burger and Justices Blackmun, Powell, and Rehnquist.

Four years later, when the five 1976 cases were heard, Justice Douglas had resigned and Justice Stevens had replaced him. Justices Brennan and Marshall remained firm in their position that the Eighth and Fourteenth Amendments prohibited capital punishment. Chief Justice Burger and Justices Blackmun, Rehnquist, and White maintained that all five statutes (Georgia, Texas, Florida, North Carolina, and Lousiana) complied with the Constitution. The three swing justices, Stewart, Powell, and Stevens, determined the outcome in all five cases. Their opinions are referred to as *plurality opinions*, since a majority of the Court did not accept their reasoning, although they agreed with the decision. In this way, the laws of Georgia, Texas, and Florida were upheld by seven to two votes, while the laws of North Carolina and Louisiana were found unconstitutional by five to four votes.

The 1976 cases clarifed in some ways the position of a majority of the Court. To be constitutional, a capital punishment law must present to the sentencing authority (judges or juries) aggravating and mitigating circumstances, as well as a process of appellate review. Mandatory death sentence laws will not be approved, since they fail to limit and direct the discretion of juries. In deciding to inflict capital punishment, a jury must consider "the character and record of the individual offender and the circumstances of the particular offense." To be constitutional, the death penalty must be imposed in a consistent and rational manner so that there would be a "meaningful basis for distinguishing the cases . . . in which it is imposed from . . . the many cases in which it is not." Individualized consideration should be the rule in deciding whether or not to impose the death penalty.

In 1978 in the Lockett case, the Chief Justice promised to clarify the Court's position on the constitutionality of capital punishment statutes. His opinion, concurred in by Justices Stewart, Stevens, and Powell, found the Ohio law unconstitutional because it did not permit individualized consideration of all factors which the defendant considered relevant to submit to the judge or jury before sentencing.

Although Justice Brennan did not take part in the case, Justice Marshall did; and he agreed with the decision but not with the reasoning. Justices Blackmun and White also agreed with the ruling, but not with the reasoning. This meant that seven Justices agreed that the Ohio law was unconstitutional, but only four of the seven agreed with the reasoning of the Court's opinion. Justice Rehnquist dissented, saying that the Ohio law was constitutional.

In short, what we have are plurality opinions of the Court which provide the following guidelines telling us when capital punishment statutes will be ruled constitutional: if the statutes list aggravating circumstances to be considered and provide the opportunity for the defendant to present mitigating circumstances he or she wishes to present, and if the statute has a procedure for an effective and automatic system of appellate review to make sure that the death sentence was not imposed arbitrarily. If these guidelines are met, according to the plurality opinions, there is some assurance that capital punishment will not be imposed discriminatorily or arbitrarily and thus will not violate the commands of the Eighth Amendment and the due process clause of the Fourteenth Amendment.

It is reasonable to conclude that the drama of capital punishment will continue to be presented in the courts. When human life is at stake, the voice of justice insists on being heard.

13 THE CRITICS REVIEW THE PLAY

Since the courtroom is in many ways a theater in which a play takes place, it is not surprising to find that the play is reviewed regularly by critics. This is especially so when the play is a spectacular with prominent lawyers and well-known defendants. Journalists, magazine writers, and TV commentators generally have a great deal to say about the personalities and the procedure in such cases.

Apart from these daily critics who review the show for the media are the researchers and the scholars who devote years to studying the meaning of it all. Focusing on the process of justice rather than on sensational cases, they have made recommendations that deserve our attention if we are truly interested in understanding and improving the justice system in this country.*

In earlier chapters we considered some of the criticisms of the jury system and plea bargaining. In addition, critics argue that the traditional trial process is too slow, costly, and inefficient. On the other hand, attempts to speed up the justice process through such methods as plea bargaining can produce "assembly-line" proceedings in which important rights may neglected.

Jury trials take several days and sometimes weeks or even months. Often the defendants have been waiting in jail for many months before trial if they cannot afford bail. Even if they are out on bail, the cloud of the upcoming trial hangs over their heads. It may take a long time to select a jury. After it is finally chosen, there is not telling how the jury will react to the facts in the case. Will they be swayed by the eloquence of the attorneys? Will they feel sorry for the defendant or will they feel that the defendant should be punished as an object lesson to future offenders, even though the crime may have involved extenuating circumstances?

Juries add to the expense of a trial. Although the daily fee for jury duty is not large, when multiplied by the number of jurors and the days of the trial it becomes a significant amount. Lawyers also cost money, and the state has to assign one or two prosecutors to each case, depending on its difficulty. In addition, when the state uses expert witnesses, it has to pay them or take them away from their jobs, possibly for several days, in order to testify.

So critics ask: are the jury system and the adversary system the best ways of arriving at the truth? Could we develop a simple, less formal procedure, in which the accused can appear before a judge

*The criticisms which follow are taken in part from The Right to Counsel in Criminal Cases: The Mandate of Argersinger v. Hamlin (Executive Summary). National Institute of Law Enforcement and Criminal Justice and Law Enforcement Assistance Administration, U.S. Department of Justice (1976).

and explain the situation? This, some critics say, would be cheaper, quicker, and fairer.

As we have seen, only a small percentage of criminal cases receive a full-scale trial by jury. Most of the non-felony cases tried in this country—perhaps 90%—are heard in the lower (trial) courts. Critics have called these courts "sausage factories" or "assembly-line" hearings where the accused are offered "instant justice." One study has shown that in many of these courts judges tend to encourage waiver of counsel. Where counsel is appointed, indigency standards are vague and are not applied uniformly, so that a person who might be assigned a public defender in one court might be denied one in another court. A court-appointed attorney may be assigned to a case shortly before or during the trial when there is no time to prepare an adequate defense. In many of these courts, the lofty language of the Constitution and the landmark interpretations of the Supreme Court do not seem to be heard.

The response to these charges is that the sheer numbers of defendants have swamped the judicial facilities, making it impossible to abide by Supreme Court decisions on the right to counsel. Thus some critics suggest that the crisis in our criminal justice system can be resolved only by providing more courtroom facilities and more judges and public defenders.

Another recommendation is to reduce the demands on the courts by decriminalizing "victimless crimes," such as public drunkenness, prostitution, gambling, insignificant drug use, and nonharmful disorderly conduct. Those who recommend decriminalization wish to unclutter the courts so that judges, prosecutors, and defense attorneys will have time to apply the procedural safeguards required by the Constitution and Supreme Court decisions. They advocate diverting these cases from the courts to other agencies. Those in opposition argue that such action would lead to the further decline of moral standards and would encourage other criminal conduct.

Another criticism of our system of justice is that there is one law for the rich, another law for the poor, and still another law for the middle class in this country. Is there a price tag on American justice? Many critics say "Yes." The rich can choose from among lawyers highly experienced in the kind of case at hand; the poor must rely on lawyers assigned to them; the middle class must hire their own lawyers, though many people in the middle income group find it hard to pay legal fees. So, the argument goes, American justice costs money—and the more you have, the more justice you get.

In an attempt to make legal expenses more manageable, certain organizations, such as unions, have developed prepaid legal service programs. These programs, once referred to as "judicare," contract with law firms to provide their members with certain legal services. The members pay a small monthly premium into a general fund which is used to pay the attorneys. They are then entitled to a certain amount of legal advice and a limited number of court appearances.

The debate over the merits of the criminal justice system crosses over many subjects: the police, corrections, and capital punishment. Some contend that strict regulations are necessary to prevent the police from violating the rights of suspects, while their opponents argue that the courts have "handcuffed" the police in their crime detection work. Critics of the corrections system say that our prisons are often human warehouses and schools of crime, where conditions work against, rather than for, rehabilitation. Others, emphasizing punishment rather than rehabilitation, respond that criminals should expect to suffer for their crimes. Opponents of capital punishment continue their campaign to outlaw the death penalty. Defenders insist that the death penalty is an effective deterrent and should be kept as a warning to those who may be considering murder or other capital crimes.

Critics continue to challenge what they consider weaknesses in the system, pointing to discrepancies between our ideals and our practices. Defenders remind us that our system, despite its weaknesses, compares favorably with those of many countries which have no Bill of Rights and no Supreme Court to interpret the meaning of those rights. While the debate continues, the system still functions. Changes will come as the people, through their representatives in the state legislatures and Congress or the courts by interpreting constitutional rights try to resolve the moral and ethical dilemmas which constantly confront a democratic society.

SECTION III

Justice in the Juvenile Courts

. . . Neither the Fourteenth Amendment nor the Bill of Rights is for adults alone.

Justice Abe Fortas in
In Re Gault, 387 US 1(1967)

Neither man nor child can be allowed to stand condemned by methods which flout constitutional requirements of due process of law.

Justice William Douglas in
Haley v. Ohio, 332 US 596 (1948)

INTRODUCTION

Juvenile crime has reached epidemic proportions in recent years, and statistics disclose that most violent crimes are now committed by teenagers and people in their early twenties. Murder, robbery, burglary, and rape have created terror in some neighborhoods. Vandalism, assaults, and muggings in the schools have interfered with education. Experts seem to be at a loss as to what to do about this serious situation.

The response to the challenge of juvenile crime has taken several forms. There are those who want to return to the "good old days," when children accused of criminal acts were treated in the same way as adult criminals. Their argument is that children today mature very quickly and become sophisticated in a world in which television brings news and shows featuring crime and violence into nearly every home. Others believe that children are the victims of their environment, and argue that improving the environment and adjusting education to the needs of different personalities and abilities might make the difference between criminal and noncriminal conduct. Treat juveniles like criminals and throw them into the criminal courts and they will fulfill our expectations of their criminality, these people warn.

This debate takes place against the background of an interesting history of juvenile justice. For hundreds of years juveniles accused of crimes were tried in the same courts and imprisoned in the same institutions as adults. Seven was considered the age of reason—the dividing line after which children could be held accountable for their conduct. This was based on the belief of the church in medieval England that children under seven were not guilty of sin because they could not be aware of the nature and consequences of their acts. This position became incorporated into the English common law, and children under seven were not regarded as capable of committing criminal acts. Once they reached their seventh birthday, however, they were placed in the same category as adults so far as criminal conduct was concerned. In seventeenth-century England, children, as well as adults, were punished by public whippings and hangings. There were thirty-three crimes for which children and adults could be executed.

In time reformers protested against such practices, calling them cruel and inhuman. They warned that to place children in the same prisons as adults was to school them in a life of crime, and they offered proposals to differentiate between the treatment of children and that of adult criminals. This reform movement found many supporters in the United States. Perhaps the most significant achievement in this country took place in Chicago, where in 1899 the first juvenile court was established. Its influence ultimately was felt in every state of the union.

Juvenile Justice in the Past

Juvenile delinquency as it is known today did not exist in the early colonial days. The Puritan settlers considered the young an important and vital part of the labor force. Most of their children worked by the age of 12, and many at an even younger age. Puritan children also were apprenticed and indentured, because their parents believed that it was healthy for a child to work outside the home.

The Virginia company valued child labor and in 1619 sought to import children from London, which seized the opportunity as a way to rid its city streets, jails and poor houses of vagrants, paupers, petty thieves, and unwanted orphans.

An English Act of 1620 permitted the deportation of children with or without the child's approval, and it led to the abduction of children from every part of London. Upon arrival in the New World the children were apprenticed until they reached 21 years of age, at which age they were freed and given public land with cattle and corn. Mistreatment by masters and no guarantees that they would comply with their agreements once the children reached the end of their service were common problems.

Punishable offenses for youths in colonial days were running away from masters, incorrigibility, lying, swearing, fighting, stealing, and cheating—offenses for the most part not punishable if committed by adults.

Until the Revolution Americans lived under English common law, which held a child accountable for its acts after the seventh birthday. Prior to that age a child was considered incapable of possessing the ability to understand the nature of criminal behavior. Judges determined culpability of children between the ages of seven and fourteen years. But the maximum sentence—death by hanging—was the same as for the adult.

Capital punishment was common for children in seventeenth century England, where there were thirty-three offenses for which the sentence applied. In America it was less likely to be imposed. Instead, corporal punishment or incarceration was often used, although one eight-year-old was convicted and hanged for burning a barn with "malice, revenge, craft and cunning." From the seventeenth century to the early part of the eighteenth century children were sentenced to public whippings and to long-term prison sentences. Prisons in those days held a conglomeration of men, women, and children under the same roof. Physical conditions were inhumane . . .

The 1870s and 1880s brought a new wave of social interest in society's young criminals. The child-saving movement began. The child-savers were mostly women, well educated, politically oriented, with genteel backgrounds. By 1895 the Chicago Women's Club, one of the leaders in the child-saving movement, had a bill drafted providing for the formation of a separate court for juveniles. The bill failed, but it had aroused public interest. Illinois enacted a subsequent bill, entitled "an act to regulate the treatment and control of dependent, neglected, and delinquent children," in 1899, making the state the first to establish a separate Juvenile Court System. The city of Denver and the state of Rhode Island also passed juvenile court legislation that same year.

Source: Law Enforcement Assistance Administration, "Juvenile Justice and Delinquency Prevention," in Two Hundred Years of American Criminal Justice, An LEAA Bicentennial Study. Washington, D.C.: U.S. Department of Justice, 1976, pp. 62–70.

The purpose of that first juvenile court was to change the attitude of the Court toward the juvenile law-breaker by focusing on truth, love, and understanding. This ideal was reflected in these words of Julian Mack, the first judge of Chicago's juvenile court.

Seated at a desk, with the child at his side, where he can, on occasion, put his arm around the shoulder and draw the lad to him, the judge, while losing none of his judicial dignity, will gain immensely in the effectiveness of his work.

Today these idealistic thoughts of eighty years ago seem antiquated.

The reformer's plan was to appoint a kindly judge who would have the assistance of medical, psychological, psychiatric, and social specialists. Some studies show, however, that for many years the judges were not so well trained in this field as the reformers had hoped. In addition, most judges did not get the assistance needed from the specialists. As the number of cases of juvenile delinquency grew, juvenile courts lacked the time and personnel necessary to give individualized attention to each case.

At this point we might ask, What were the legal grounds on which the juvenile courts were established? What were the consequences of this new type of court for the juvenile?

There is an important legal expression *parens patriae*, which means that the state is the parent of the country. Freely translated, it makes the state the guardian of those children in need. The child is regarded as the ward of the state; and the juvenile court, acting for the state, is the child's guardian. The purpose of taking juveniles out of the criminal courts and placing them in special juvenile courts was to make juvenile proceedings *civil* or *administrative* matters and to eliminate the adversary process under which lawyers contend for their

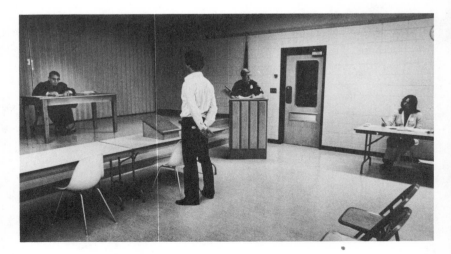

Although this juvenile court lacks the furnishings usually associated with a courtroom, its bare essentials of judge, juvenile offender, bailiff (uniformed officer), and court reporter, *right*, are all that is needed for hearing a case.

The Origin of the Denver Juvenile Court

Judge Ben B. Lindsey

He brought in a boy, whom I shall call "Tony Costello,"* and arraigned him before the court. The Clerk read the indictment; a railroad detective gave his testimony; the boy was accused of stealing coal from the tracks, and he had no defence. Frightened and silent, he stood looking from me to the jury, from the jury to the attorney, and from the attorney back to me—big-eyed and trembling—a helpless infant, trying to follow in our faces what was going on. The case was clear. There was nothing for me to do under the law but to find him guilty and sentence him to a term in the State Reform School. I did it—and prepared to go back to the affair of the second-hand furniture.

There had been sitting at the back of the courtroom an old woman with a shawl on her head, huddled up like a squaw, wooden-faced, and incredibly wrinkled. She waddled down the aisle toward the bench, while papers of commitment were being made out against the boy, and began to talk to the court interpreter in an excited gabble which I did not understand. I signed to the counsel for the warehouse-man to proceed with his case; he rose—and he was greeted with the most soul-piercing scream of agony that I ever heard from a human throat. The old woman stood there, clutching her shawl to her breast, her toothless mouth open, her face

Judge Benjamin B. Lindsey in 1934.

as contorted as if she were being torn limb from limb, shrieking horribly. They dragged her out into the hall, but through the closed door I could still hear her shrieking—shrieking terribly. I adjourned the court and retreated to my chambers, very much shaken and unnerved; but I still heard her, in the hall, wailing and sobbing, and every now and then screaming as if her heart was being torn out of her.

I did not know what to do. I thought I had no power, under the law, to do anything but what I *had* done. The boy was guilty. The law required that I should sentence him. The mother might scream herself dumb, but I was unable to help her.

She continued to scream. Two reporters, attracted by the uproar, came to ask

*This name, and those of all other children brought before the court, are disguised in order to protect the families from the consequences of publicity.

Reprinted from Ben B. Lindsey and Harvey J. O'Higgins. The Beast. Seattle: University of Washington Press, 1970, pp. 80–82. Reproduced by permission.

me if I could not do something for her. I telephoned the District Attorney and asked him whether I could not change my order against the boy—make it a suspended sentence—and let me look into the case myself. He was doubtful—as I was—about my right to do such a thing, but I accepted the responsibility of the act and he consented to it. After what seemed an hour to me—during which I could still hear the miserable woman wailing—the boy was returned to her and she was quieted.

Then I took the first step toward the founding of the Juvenile Court of Denver. I got an officer who knew Tony, and I went with him, at night, to the boy's home in the Italian quarter of North Denver. I need not describe the miserable conditions in which I found the Costellos living—in two rooms, in a filthy shack, with the father sick in bed, and the whole family struggling against starvation. I talked with Tony, and found him not a criminal, not a bad boy, but merely a boy. He had seen that his father and his mother and the baby were suffering from cold, and he had brought home fuel from the railroad tracks to keep them warm. I gave him a little lecture on the necessity of obeying the laws, and put him "on probation." The mother kissed my hands. The neighbours came in to salute me and to rejoice with the Costellos. I left them. But I carried away with me what must have been something of their view of my court and my absurd handling of their boy; and I began to think over this business of punishing infants as if they were adults and of maiming young lives by trying to make the gristle of their unformed characters carry the weight of our iron laws and heavy penalties.

clients. All proceedings would be informal, without the usual rules of evidence: Everything which would help in arriving at a just decision would be admitted without fear of objections by lawyers. Finally the goal was the rehabilitation rather than the punishment of the child.

Taking juvenile cases out of the criminal court system, however, brought certain legal consequences. In the interest of an informal quest for justice and the goal of saving a child's future, the constitutional safeguards of due process were no longer relevant. There would be no lawyers, no juries, no cross-examination of witnesses in the traditional sense, and no privilege against self-incrimination.

The discussion of the cases which follow will clarify what happened to the idea of juvenile justice. Before proceeding to these important rulings, a brief commentary is necessary on the nature of the cases which find their way into the juvenile justice system. There are two types of people involved in juvenile cases: persons in need of supervision (PINS) or children in need of supervision (CHINS) and juvenile delinquents. The former are not regarded as having committed criminal acts and are described as the incorrigibles, the neglected, the homeless, and the truants. The juvenile delinquents are those who commit acts which, if committed by adults, would be crimes under the laws of the state. The age range of juvenile court differs among the states. The general range is from seven to sixteen, although in some states it extends from seven to eighteen.

14 DUE PROCESS RIGHTS OF A JUVENILE

IN RE GAULT
Should an accused juvenile be granted due process protection in juvenile court?

On a Monday morning in June 1964, fifteen-year-old Gerald Gault and Ronald Lewis were taken into custory by a sheriff in a county in Arizona. They were accused of having made an obscene telephone call to a Mrs. Cook. Gault's parents were not notified, and when they returned home from work were told by the Lewis family what had happened. They went to the detention home where Gerald was being held and where they learned about the episode.

The following day a hearing was held. Gerald's mother attended, but Mrs. Cook, the complainant, was not present. No record was made, and no one was sworn in before testifying. At this hearing Gerald admitted that he had dialed Mrs. Cook's number but said that his friend had spoken to her. Since there was no record of what was said at the hearing, there was some conflict later as to what actually had happened. At the conclusion of the hearing, the judge said he would give the matter some thought.

Six days later, a second hearing was held. Gerald and his parents, as well as Ronald Lewis and his father, were present. Once again, the complainant was not present. The judge denied Mrs. Gault's request that Mrs. Cook be at the hearing.

The charge against the boys was making lewd phone calls. At the time that Gerald had been taken into custody, he was on six months probation for being found in the company of a boy who had stolen a wallet. The judge ruled that, on the basis of the testimony, Gerald was a juvenile delinquent and sentenced him to the State Industrial School "for a period of his minority, [that is, until age twenty-one] unless sooner discharged by due process of law." Under Arizona law, if Gerald had been an adult accused of this crime, his penalty would have been from $5 to $50 or imprisonment for not more than two months. Arizona law permitted no appeal from juvenile delinquency decisions.

What could Gerald or his parents do about this situation? If he couldn't appeal this ruling, does that mean that his case is over? Is this fair? Is there anything in the law which would permit the reopening of the case?

The way out of this dilemma is through the writ of habeas corpus, often referred to as The Great Writ. Gault and his parents, as well as the American people, have the English Parliament to thank for this writ. In its disputes with the English kings, Parliament passed a number of important laws defining and protecting the rights of Englishmen. In 1679 the Habeas Corpus Act was passed to prevent arbitrary arrests and imprisonments. Under this law those who regard their arrest, detention, or imprisonment as illegal can obtain a writ of habeas corpus (literally, you have the body) from a court. The writ commands a judge to hear the case and to determine whether the petitioner is being detained legally. If he is not, he must be released.

Gault's lawyers tried to obtain a writ of habeas corpus from the Arizona courts, but they lost their case all the way to the highest court in Arizona. They then decided to take the case to the federal courts.

On what grounds could Gault's case be heard on appeal to the Supreme Court of the United States?

The Fourteenth Amendment provides that no state shall deprive a person of liberty without due process of law. Is a juvenile accused of a crime "a person" in this sense? Assuming that juveniles are "persons" within the meaning of the amendment, is a juvenile court proceeding not fairer to the child than the formal procedure of a criminal court?

If you were arguing on behalf of Arizona, what points could you make in defense of the juvenile court procedure and ruling? If you were representing Gault, how would you answer your opponent?

Those representing Arizona could argue that two hearings had been held and that testimony had been taken. Gault did admit his participation in the episode, and he was on probation at the time it occurred. On that basis he was judged a juvenile delinquent. His parents could have had legal assistance, if they had requested it. Appeals were not permitted under Arizona law because juvenile proceedings were confidential.

Gault's lawyers could respond that the entire episode shows the weaknesses of the juvenile court system. Gault's parents had not been adequately notified of the charges. The hearings showed how all-powerful the judge can be in deciding, without any restraints, the fate of a child: anything the judge decides becomes the law. If lawyers had been present they could have put up a reasonable defense for Gault. The failure to cross-examine the state's chief witness was a fatal defect in the judicial process. Unless due process of law procedures were introduced in juvenile hearings, the judge would have no restraints on his power. Also, without the right to appeal, injustices could not be challenged.

At the time the Supreme Court decided his case, Gerald Gault, *center*, was on probation and working in the Job Corps learning automotive and heavy equipment operation.

How would you decide?

Justice Fortas wrote the opinion for the Court, with one Justice dissenting and one justice dissenting in part. He began by summarizing the reasons for the establishment of the juvenile justice system. He observed, however, that the "highest motives and most enlightened impulses" have not prevented "unfairness to individuals and inadequate or inaccurate findings of fact and unfortunate prescriptions of remedy." Although sympathic to the ideals upon which the juvenile court system was built, he concluded that the only safeguard against arbitrariness, loose procedures, and high-handed methods is due process of law. He summarized his thinking in the following passage:

Due process of law is the primary and indispensable foundation of individual freedom. *It is the basic and essential term in the social compact which defines the rights of the individual and delimits the powers which the state may exercise.* As Mr. Justice Frankfurter has said: *"The history of American freedom is, in no small measure, the history of procedure."* But in addition, the procedural rules which have been fashioned from the generality of due process are our best instruments for the distillation and evaluation of essential facts from the conflicting welter of data that life and our adversary methods present. It is these instruments of due process which enhance the possibility that truth will emerge from the confrontation of opposing versions and conflicting data. *"Procedure is to law what 'scientific method' is to science."* [emphasis added]

It might be worthwhile to stop at this point and ask, What do the italicized statements mean, and what is their connection with the *Gault* case?

Would the requirement of due process of law safeguards change the juvenile hearing from an informal proceeding into a trial with all the trappings of a criminal case? Justice Fortas did not think so. Rather, the introduction of due process requirements would build upon the informal procedures, provide some regularity, and ensure that the accused would receive a fair hearing. After all, he pointed out, to send young persons to a detention center is, in effect, to jail them.

Ultimately, however, we confront the reality of that portion of the Juvenile Court process with which we deal in this case. A boy is charged with misconduct. The boy is committed to an institution where he may be restrained of liberty for years. It is of no constitutional consequence—and of limited practical meaning—that the institution to which he is committed is called an Industrial School. The fact of the matter is that, however euphemistic the title, a "receiving home" or an "industrial school" for juveniles is an institution of confinement in which the child is incarcerated for a greater or lesser time. His world becomes "a building with whitewashed walls, regimented routine and institutional hours." Instead of mother and father and sisters and brothers and friends and classmates, his world is peopled by guards, custodians, state employees, and "delinquents" confined with him for anything from waywardness to rape and homicide.

In view of this, it would be extraordinary if our Constitution did not require the procedural regularity and the exercise of care implied in the phrase "due process." *Under our Constitution, the condition of being a boy does not justify a kangaroo court.* [Emphasis added]

What does Justice Fortas mean by the italicized sentence?

If Gerald Gault had been an adult, he would have been entitled to substantial procedural rights, such as specific notice of charges; time to prepare his defense; and the right to counsel at state expense if he was indigent, to confront witnesses against him, and to cross-examine. There is no reason, the majority opinion states, why an accused juvenile should be denied those procedures which guarantee a fair trial.

Justice Fortas then enumerated the due process rights to which a juvenile is entitled at an adjudicatory hearing—that is, the hearing at which guilt or innocence is to be determined. These were:

1. Notice of charges
2. Right to counsel

3. Privilege against self-incrimination
4. Confrontation and cross-examination of witnesses

Justice Fortas explained what kind of notice was required.

Notice, to comply with due process requirements, must be given sufficiently in advance of scheduled court proceedings so that reasonable opportunity to prepare will be afforded, and it must "set forth the alleged misconduct with particularity."

Due process of law requires notice of the sort we have described—that is, notice which would be deemed constitutionally adequate in a civil or criminal proceeding. It does not allow a hearing to be held in which a youth's freedom and his parent's right to custody are at stake without giving them timely notice, in advance of the hearing, of the specific issues that they must meet.

The second due process right, that of counsel was necessary, in Fortas' view because

The probation officer cannot act as counsel for the child. His role in the adjudicatory hearing, by statute and in fact, is as arresting officer and witness against the child. Nor can the judge represent the child. There is no material difference in this respect between adult and juvenile proceedings of the sort here involved. . . . A proceeding where the issue is whether the child will be found to be "delinquent" and subjected to the loss of his liberty for years is comparable in seriousness to a felony prosecution. The juvenile needs the assistance of counsel to cope with problems of law, to make skilled inquiry into the facts, to insist upon regularity of the proceedings, and to ascertain whether he has a defense and to prepare and submit it. The child "requires the guiding hand of counsel at every step in the proceedings against him." . . .

We conclude that *the Due Process Clause of the Fourteenth Amendment requires that in respect of proceedings to determine delinquency which may result in commitment to an institution in which the juvenile's freedom is curtailed,* the child and his parents must be notified of the child's right to be represented by counsel retained by them, or if they are unable to afford counsel, that counsel be appointed to represent the child. [emphasis added]

Note the italicized portion. At which hearing must attorneys be present?

In considering the third right, remember that Gerald Gault made certain admissions at the juvenile court hearings. He said that he had dialed Mrs. Cook's number. The juvenile court judge said that Gerald also said that he had made "some of the lewd statements." This amounted to a confession. At no time did the judge advise

Gerald or his parents that he did not have to testify or make a statement.

Is a juvenile entitled to the privilege against self-incrimination at a juvenile court hearing? Must the judge warn the accused that he has the right to remain silent?

The Supreme Court held that:

The privilege against self-incrimination is, of course, related to the question of the safeguards necessary to assure that admissions or confessions are reasonably trustworthy, that they are not the mere fruits of fear or coercion, but are reliable expressions of the truth . . . One of its purposes is to prevent the state, whether by force or by psychological domination, from overcoming the mind and will of the person under investigation and depriving him of the freedom to decide whether to assist the state in securing his conviction. It would indeed be surprising if the privilege against self-incrimination were available to hardened criminals but not to children.

Justice Fortas went on to say that the language of the Fifth Amendment ("nor shall be compelled, in any criminal case, to be a witness against himself") is applicable to the states under the Fourteenth Amendment due process clause.

Does the privilege against self-incrimination apply only in criminal cases? Since a juvenile court proceeding is not criminal in nature, why should this privilege be available to juveniles?

On this question the Court held that:

It is true that the statement of the privilege in the Fifth Amendment, which is applicable to the States by reason of the Fourteenth Amendment, is that no person "shall be compelled in any *criminal case* to be a witness against himself." *However, it is also clear that the availability of the privilege does not turn upon the type of proceeding in which its protection is invoked, but upon the nature of the statement or admission and the exposure which it invites.* The privilege may, for example, be claimed in a civil or administrative proceeding, if the statement is or may be inculpatory [incriminating].

It would be entirely unrealistic to carve out of the Fifth Amendment all statements by juveniles on the ground that these cannot lead to "criminal" involvement. In the first place, juvenile proceedings to determine "delinquency," which may lead to commitment to a state institution, must be regarded as "criminal" for purposes of the privilege against self-incrimination. . . . Commitment is a deprivation of liberty.

It is incarceration against one's will, whether it is called "criminal" or "civil." And our Constitution guarantees that no person shall be "compelled" to be a witness against himself when he is threatened with deprivation of his liberty—a command which this Court has broadly applied and generously implemented in accordance with the teaching of the history of the privilege and its great office in mankind's battle for freedom.

In addition, . . . the fact of the matter is that there is little or no assurance in Arizona, as in most if not all of the States, that a juvenile apprehended and interrogated by the police or even by the Juvenile Court itself will remain outside of the reach of adult courts as a consequence of the offense for which he has been taken into custody. . . .

Further, authoritative opinion has cast formidable doubt upon the reliability and trustworthiness of "confessions" by children. [emphasis added]

Based on this reasoning, the Court concluded:

. . . That the constitutional privilege against self-incrimination is applicable in the case of juveniles as it is with respect to adults. We appreciate that special problems may arise with respect to waiver of the privilege by or on behalf of children, and that there may well be some differences in technique—but not in principle—depending upon the age of the child and the presence and competence of parents. The participation of counsel will, of course, assist the police, Juvenile Courts and appellate tribunals in administering the privilege. If counsel was not present for some permissible reason when an admission was obtained, the greatest care must be taken to assure that the admission was voluntary, in the sense not only that it was not coerced or suggested, but also that it was not the product of ignorance of rights or of adolescent fantasy, fright, or despair.

The fourth due process right enumerated in the opinion, consisting of the rights to confront hostile witnesses and the right to cross-examine them, is essential to fairness in any proceeding. These rights were not present in the *Gault* hearings, because the intent was to keep the atmosphere in juvenile courts informal and non-threatening. Justice Fortas, speaking for the majority, concluded that these rights are essential to justice in the juvenile system.

We now hold that, absent a valid confession, a determination of delinquency and an order of commitment to a state institution cannot be sustained in the absence of sworn testimony subjected to the opportunity for cross-examination in accordance with our law and constitutional requirements.

In addition to raising issues involving these four rights, Gault's appeal argued that the due process clause entitled juveniles to the rights of appeal and to a transcript of the proceedings.

Arizona had argued that there was no right of appeal from a juvenile court order because the proceedings were confidential. Nor was a transcript of the proceedings kept, because the record had to be destroyed after a period of time. Although the majority decided not to rule on these two issues, they did include a warning.

As the present case illustrates, the consequences of failure to provide an appeal, to record the proceedings, or to make findings or state the grounds for the juvenile court's conclusion may be to throw a burden upon the machinery for habeas corpus, to saddle the reviewing process with the burden of attempting to reconstruct a record, and to impose upon the Juvenile Judge the unseemly duty of testifying under cross-examination as to the events that transpired in the hearings before him.

Justice Black's concurring opinion is based on the premise that Arizona had violated the Fifth (privilege against self-incrimination) and Sixth (notice, counsel, and right of confrontation) Amendments of the Bill of Rights. Justice White's concurring opinion concluded that it was unnecessary for the majority to have taken positions on the issues of self-incrimination, confrontation, and cross-examination.

Justice Harlan agreed with the majority that the Fourteenth Amendment's due process clause requires that timely notice, counsel for indigent juveniles, and a written record should be incorporated into the juvenile justice system. He felt, however, that the court should show judicial restraint in imposing on states the additional requirements of the privilege against self-incrimination, confrontation, and cross-examination, which he believed were not necessary at that time "to guarantee the fundamental fairness of juvenile proceedings."

Justice Stewart's dissenting opinion is short and to the point. The majority, he declared, is using an obscure Arizona case as a basis for transforming the juvenile court system of the fifty states. He felt that bringing the adversary system into the juvenile court would turn the clock back to the prejuvenile court days when juveniles were treated like common criminals.

In the last 70 years many dedicated men and women have devoted their professional lives to the enlightened task of bringing us out of the dark world of Charles Dickens in meeting our responsibilities to the child in our society. The result has been the creation in this century of a system of juvenile and family courts in each of the 50 States. There can be no denying that in many areas the performance of these agencies has fallen disappointingly short of the hopes and dreams of the courageous pioneers who first conceived them. For a variety of reasons, the reality has sometimes not even approached the ideal, and much remains to be accomplished in the administration of public juvenile and family agencies—in personnel, in planning, in financing, perhaps in the formulation of wholly new approaches. . . .

The inflexible restrictions that the Constitution so wisely made applicable to adversary criminal trials have no inevitable place in the proceedings of those public social agencies known as juvenile or family courts. And to impose the Court's long catalog of requirements upon juvenile proceedings in every area of the country is to invite a long step backwards into the nineteenth century. In that era there were no juvenile proceedings, and a child was tried in a conventional criminal court with all the trappings of a conventional criminal trial. So it was that a 12-year-old boy named James Guild was tried in New Jersey for killing Catherine Beakes. A jury found him guilty of murder, and he was sentenced to death by hanging. The sentence was executed. It was all very constitutional. [emphasis added]

He went on to say that a state must accord every person due process of law. This does not mean, however, that a juvenile proceeding must conform to "all the technical niceties" of a criminal case. For example, timely notice must be given, but the privilege against self-incrimination is not necessary or desirable, except in cases of a "brutually coerced confession."

He pointed out the Arizona Supreme Court's findings that Gault's parents knew the exact nature of the charges and were aware of their right to counsel and to subpoena and cross-examine witnesses. This, he said, met the necesary due process requirements. He concluded that the privilege against self-incrimination was really not an issue in the case.

15 THE NATURE OF PROOF IN A DELINQUENCY PROCEEDING

IN RE WINSHIP
How much evidence is necessary to prove that an accused is a juvenile delinquent?

Less than three years after the *Gault* case, the Court was confronted with another issue arising out of juvenile proceeding. Samuel Winship, a twelve-year-old boy, was accused of entering a locker and stealing $112 from a woman's pocketbook. The New York State Family Court Act defined a juvenile delinquent as "a person over seven and less than sixteen years of age who does any act which, if done by an adult, would constitute a crime." The petition in the juvenile court which charged Winship stated that this particular act, if committed by an adult, would be the crime of larceny.

The Family Court Act also provided that a decision relating to a juvenile's delinquency must be based on the evidence rule for burden of proof that is used in civil cases, such as breach of contract or negligence. According to this rule, the party which proves its side of the case by a *fair preponderance of the evidence* is entitled to a verdict. In criminal cases, however, the evidence rule for burden of proof requires proof *beyond a reasonable doubt*. Because in a criminal trial a person is innocent until proven guilty, the burden of proof is on the prosecution to present evidence sufficient to prove the defendant guilty beyond a reasonable doubt. Winship's lawyer argued that the same rule should apply in juvenile delinquency cases. The judge in the case had to decide whether the evidentiary rule for criminal trials should be applied to determine Winship's guilt or innocence. Although the judge conceded that the evidence against Winship was not beyond a reasonable doubt, he pointed out that he was directed by the Family Court Act to decide the case by a fair preponderance of the evidence—a less demanding rule. He found Winship to be a delinquent and sentenced him to a training school for eighteen months, subject to annual extensions until his eighteenth birthday, a possible term of up to six years.

On what grounds could Winship's lawyers appeal?

The Fourteenth Amendment provides that the state cannot deprive a person of liberty without due process of law. Is declaring a juvenile to be a delinquent by a fair preponderance of the evidence a denial of due process of law? If adults are tried under the rule of proof beyond a reasonable doubt in criminal trials, does due process of law demand the same treatment for juveniles? The Fourteenth Amendment also requires the states to extend to their inhabitants the equal protection of the law. Is it a denial of equal protection to apply one rule of evidence to adults and another to juveniles?

How could the state of New York answer these arguments?

The state could argue that juvenile proceedings are not criminal cases. They are civil proceedings and as such should be subject to the rules of evidence for civil cases. If you decide that the rule of "guilt beyond a reasonable doubt" should apply, it would be necessary to apply all other procedures and rules of criminal cases. This would defeat the purpose of the reformers who, in developing the juvenile justice system, hoped to avoid the atmosphere of a criminal trial.

How would you resolve this issue? Is there anything in the *Gault* case which could help you decide this case?

In arriving at its decision, the Supreme Court was divided six to three. Writing for the majority, Justice Brennan began with a discussion of the *Gault* case. In that ruling, he pointed out, the Fourteenth Amendment had been applied to adjudicatory hearings in juvenile proceedings. The rule of law announced in that case was that "the essentials of due process and fair treatment" must be applied in a hearing which determines whether a juvenile is a delinquent. This means that when the judge is deciding whether the

In the *Gault* case, Justice William Brennan wrote the majority opinion for the Supreme Court.

juvenile is guilty of the charges against him or her, the following
due process of law procedures must apply:

1. Notice of charges
2. Right to counsel
3. Right to confront and cross-examine witnesses
4. Privilege against self-incrimination

**Should the Court add to these important due process rights the
requirement that guilt be established beyond a reasonable doubt?**

An important principle of English common law which has been
included in our law since the early years of our nation is that when
a person's life or liberty is at stake, it is necessary to reduce the risk
of convicting someone because of a mistake in facts presented at the
trial. The reasonable-doubt standard of proof seeks to accomplish
this end. In the words of Justice Brennan's majority opinion:

> The requirement of proof beyond a reasonable doubt has this vital
> role in our criminal procedure for cogent reasons. The accused during
> a criminal prosecution has at stake interest of immense importance,
> both because of the possibility that he may lose his liberty upon
> conviction and because of the certainty that he would be stigmatized
> by the conviction. *Accordingly, a society that values the good name
> and freedom of every individual should not condemn a man for com-
> mission of a crime when there is reasonable doubt about his guilt.* . . .
> There is always in litigation a margin of error, representing error in
> factfinding, which both parties must take into account. Where one
> party has at stake an interest of transcending value—as a criminal
> defendant his liberty—this margin of error is reduced as to him by
> the process of placing on the other party the burden of . . . per-
> suading the factfinder at the conclusion of the trial of his guilt beyond
> a reasonable doubt. Due process commands that no man shall lose
> his liberty unless the Government has borne the burden of . . . con-
> vincing the factfinder of the guilt.

He went on to say that use of this standard was necessary to have
the respect and confidence of the community—so that people would
have the assurance that no one could be found guilty of a crime
unless the jury was convinced with utmost certainty.

> Lest there remain any doubt about the constitutional stature of the
> reasonable-doubt standard, *we explicitly hold that the Due Process
> Clause protects the accused against conviction except upon proof
> beyond a reasonable doubt of every fact necessary to constitute the
> crime with which he is charged.* [emphasis added]

In relating the reasonable-doubt standard to the *Winship* case,
Justice Brennan took into account the following points:

1. A juvenile proceeding is not a criminal case.
2. A delinquency adjudication is not a conviction.
3. A juvenile hearing is informal and flexible.
4. Juvenile proceedings are designed not to punish, but to save the child.

He concluded that applying the standard of proof beyond a reasonable doubt would not eliminate any of these benefits. It would, however, make sure that the judge had no reasonable doubt about the facts before him or her.

The following thoughts from Justice Harlan's concurring opinion summarize the principle that a person is innocent unless proven guilty beyond a reasonable doubt.

I view the requirement of proof beyond a reasonable doubt in a criminal case as bottomed on a fundamental value determination of our society that it is far worse to convict an innocent man than to let a guilty man go free. . . .

When one assesses the consequences of an erroneous factual determination in a juvenile delinquency proceeding in which a youth is accused of a crime, I think it must be concluded that, while the consequences are not identical to those in a criminal case, the differences will not support a distinction in the standard of proof. First, and of paramount importance, a factual error here, as in a criminal case, exposes the accused to a complete loss of his personal liberty through a state-imposed confinement away from his home, family, and friends. And, second, a delinquency determination, to some extent at least, stigmatizes a youth in that it is by definition bottomed on a finding that the accused committed a crime. Although there are no doubt costs to society (and possibly even to the youth himself) in letting a guilty youth go free, I think here, as in a criminal case, it is far worse to declare an innocent youth a delinquent. I therefore agree that a juvenile court judge should be no less convinced of the factual conclusion that the accused committed the criminal act with which he is charged than would be required in a criminal trial . . .

Today's decision simply requires a juvenile court judge to be more confident in his belief that the youth did the act with which he has been charged. [emphasis added]

Do you agree with the emphasized sentences? Why?

Three Justices wrote two dissenting opinions. Chief Justice Burger's dissenting opinion, with which Justice Stewart concurred, warned that interference by the Court with the right of states to design their own systems of juvenile justice could turn back the clock to the days when juveniles were treated in the same way as adult criminals. The atmosphere of informality and benevolence is being eroded by the majority's insistence on "the trappings of legal procedure and judicial formalism," he said. To survive its crises, the juvenile system needs "breathing room and flexibility."

Justice Black's dissenting opinion centered on the fact that the Constitution and Bill of Rights do not include "any statement that conviction of crime requires proof of guilt beyond a reasonable doubt."

I prefer to put my faith in the words of the written Constitution itself rather than to rely on the shifting day-to-day standards of fairness of individual judges.

To Justice Black, due process of law is not a judicial hunting license to go forth seeking "fundamental fairness" or the principles "implicit in the concept of orders liberty." It means that, in a government of limited powers, the government must proceed according to constitutional and statutory provisions. Governmental actions concerning life, liberty, and property must conform to the law of the land. The Supreme Court, according to the Justice, has often veered from this course and imposed its own sense of what is constitutional.

Justice Black concluded that, according to the law of the land, the states have the power to enact laws which are not prohibited by the United States Constitution or the Bill of Rights. For example, states have accepted the historic common law principle that an accused in a criminal case is innocent until proven guilty beyond a reasonable doubt. There is nothing in the Constitution to forbid such an act by state legislatures. Nor is there anything in the Constitution which prohibits a state from requiring juvenile courts to adjudge a juvenile a delinquent by a fair preponderance of the evidence. That is what New York State had done, and it was in accord with "the law of the land" that states could enact their sense of fairness and decency into law through the acts of the state legislature. Such laws may be unwise, but they are not unconstitutional unless they contravene a provision of the Constitution.

IVAN V. v. CITY OF NEW YORK
Should the reasonable doubt standard be applied to cases decided before *Winship*?

The Supreme Court decided unanimously (Chief Justice Burger did not participate in the case) that the Winship ruling of proof beyond a reasonable doubt had to be applied retroactively. In this case, since Ivan had been declared a delinquent on the basis of a fair preponderance of the evidence, the lower court was overruled. Ivan had to be retried on the basis of the "reasonable doubt" rule.

16 JURY TRIALS IN JUVENILE PROCEEDINGS

McKEIVER v.
PENNSYLVANIA

In re BURRUS

TERRY v.
PENNSYLVANIA

**Is an accused
juvenile entitled to a
jury trial?**

After the Gault case, it was inevitable that the Supreme Court would be confronted with the issue of jury trials in juvenile proceedings. The year after the Winship ruling, the Court dealt with this question.

Joseph McKeiver was sixteen years of age when he was arrested for having participated with twenty to thirty other young people in chasing three teenagers and taking twenty-five cents from them. He was charged with robbery, larceny, and receiving stolen goods as acts of juvenile delinquency. He had never been arrested before and had a record of gainful employment. His request for a jury trial was denied, and he was adjudged a delinquent. According to the court record, the testimony of two of the victims was inconsistent and weak.

Edward Terry, fifteen years of age, was charged with assault and battery for hitting a police officer with his fists and a stick when the officer tried to break up a fight which Terry and others were watching. Previously Terry had been adjudged a delinquent for an assault on a teacher. His request for a jury trial was denied, and he was committed to the Youth Development Center. Edward Terry's case was consolidated with McKeiver's on appeal in the Pennsylvania Supreme Court.

Barbara Burrus and forty-five other black children, ranging in age from eleven to fifteen, were tried in a North Carolina juvenile court. According to the testimony of highway patrolmen, the children and a number of black adults had on several occasions taken part in demonstrations protesting school assignments and school consolidations. The group had walked along Highway 64, "singing, shouting, clapping, and playing basketball." When asked to leave the highway, they refused. They were then taken into custody and charged with willfully impeding traffic, a misdemeanor.

A district judge sitting as a juvenile court tried the combined cases, and the same lawyer represented all the juveniles. A request for jury trial was denied, and in most cases the public was excluded from the hearings. The court adjudged all the juveniles to be delinquent. A custody order was entered committing them to the custody of the County Department of Public Welfare for placement in a suitable institution. The court suspended the commitments, however, and placed the juveniles on probation for either one or two years. In addition, each was ordered to be at home by 11 o'clock each night and to attend a school approved by the welfare director.

The Pennsylvania and North Carolina cases were combined for argument before the Supreme Court.

Using the principles of due process fairness developed in the *Gault* and *Winship* cases, prepare a statement arguing for the right to jury trials in juvenile proceedings. Using the same cases, prepare a statement against these arguments. In weighing the arguments for and against jury trials, which arguments do you find most persuasive? Why?

Those who would argue on behalf of jury trials could present the following arguments. In *Gault* and *Winship* the Supreme Court decided that juveniles are entitled to the protection of some of the rights associated with due process of law under the Fourteenth Amendment. These rights include appropriate notice of charges, counsel, confrontation and cross-examination of witnesses, the privilege against self-incrimination, and proof beyond a reasonable doubt before a juvenile can be adjudged a delinquent. It seems inconsistent to grant juveniles all these due process rights and yet deny them access to trial by jury, which is one of the foundations of the due process system.

Another line of argument might be that a juvenile proceeding is already similar to a criminal trial in many important ways. Plea bargaining may be used. An order committing a juvenile to a correctional institution has basically the same effect as a prison sentence for an adult convicted of a crime. In theory, juvenile proceedings are supposed to be protected from publicity, but sometimes the press and public are admitted. The stigma of having been adjudged delinquent can do lasting damage to the juvenile's reputation. In these ways jury trials would not change the nature of the juvenile proceeding. They could have the desirable effect of bringing to public attention some of the problems society must face in providing fair treatment for accused juveniles.

To counter the arguments for jury trial, opponents could say that a careful reading of the *Gault* and *Winship* cases does not say that juveniles are entitled to all the procedures in due process of law. They are entitled to the "essentials of due process and fairness," which does not include a jury trial. Opponents could emphasize the distinction between juvenile proceedings and criminal cases. To include juries in juvenile proceedings would make them more like criminal cases, bringing into the proceedings the adversary system—lawyer versus lawyer. In this atmosphere it would be easy to lose sight of the larger question of the child's welfare and future.

What is your position on the issue of whether juveniles have constitutional right to a jury trial in the adjudicatory hearing which determines delinquency?

How France Treats Children in Trouble

Paul A. Strasburg

An Overview

The age of civil and penal majority in France is eighteen. Law-breaking by juveniles is not thought to demand condemnation and punishment; it is taken as a signal that measures of "protection, assistance, supervision or education" are required. This principle is absolute for children younger than thirteen; under no circumstances may they be punished with confinement in locked institutions or with fines. For youths thirteen or older the law acknowledges that "the circumstances and personality of the delinquent" may sometimes require punitive responses, but these are clearly to be the exception, not the rule . . .

Sentences for youths thirteen to sixteen are limited to half the maximum adult term.[1] If the defendant is sixteen or older, the court may choose to disregard the mitigating circumstance of youth, and impose the full adult sentence.

Prison terms are the least common sanction applied. Other possible dispositions, roughly in order of their frequency, are simple warnings and counselling, "supervised liberty" (equivalent to probation), and placement in residential education institutions or *foyers* (group homes). In addition, services such as foster care or medical treatment may be ordered for children who need them. The duration of non-penal dispositions is set by the judge or

tribunal but may not extend beyond the juvenile's eighteenth birthday unless the youth himself requests it.

The Judge's Role

The linchpin of the French system is the juvenile judge, who, like all French judges, is a career civil servant with a law degree and at least three additional years of specialized training in law and human sciences. He conducts his work alone in chambers as well as on the bench in a juvenile tribunal. The choice of forum depends on several factors—the gravity of the offense, the penalty envisioned, and the kind of impression the judge wants to make on the delinquent.

Hearings in Chambers. The preferred course of action is a hearing in chambers with only the child, his parents, the judge and the judge's clerk present. (All accused juveniles are entitled to lawyers, either privately retained or publicly provided, but it is not considered essential—or even proper for them to take part in proceedings in chambers.) In this comparatively informal setting, the judge assumes the roles of investigator, psychologist, family counsellor and decision-maker all at once and attempts to determine the underlying causes of the child's behavior and the appropriate response to it. He is supported in this task by a permanent team of social workers who investigate the backgrounds of the children and their families and seek appropriate social services or placement openings. The judge also has access to

---

[1] A juvenile guilty of an offense that carries the death penalty or life in prison for an adult may receive ten to twenty years in prison.

Source: Adapted from Judicature, Vol. 61, No. 1 (June–July 1977): 23–26. Reprinted from Judicature, The journal of the American Judicature Society.

psychologists and doctors, and to observation centers and hospitals where more detailed diagnosis can be made if necessary.

The dispositions available to a judge acting alone in chambers are limited to warnings, foster care, or supervised liberty (probation). If placement or a criminal penalty is a possibility, the case must be heard before a juvenile tribunal. This reduces the risk of restricting a child's liberty on the basis of what he appears to be rather than what he has done, and without the benefit of due process of law.

Courtroom trials. Trials before the juvenile tribunal involve the full formality of criminal procedure, complete with defense attorneys, prosecutors, and witnesses. The juvenile judge is assisted by two lay "assessors," each with a vote equal to his own. Assessors are community residents over the age of thirty who are appointed for four-year renewable terms and serve without pay. They are selected on the basis of their "competence" and "the interest they bring to questions concerning youth." Often they are doctors, teachers or psychologists.

The juvenile tribunal is competent to hear any delinquency case the judge chooses to send there, with one exception. Cases involving youths sixteen or older charged with "crimes" (roughly speaking those offenses for which adults would spend five years or more in prison) must be tried before a special Court of Assizes for Minors. This court is similar to the adult criminal court in structure. It has a three-judge bench, one judge from the Court of Appeals and two juvenile judges, plus a jury of nine. . . .

Protection hearings. In addition to dealing with delinquency cases, French juvenile judges are also charged with the civil responsibility of protecting the welfare of children "in danger." This category includes victims of parental neglect and abuse as well as juvenile prostitutes, runaways and others for whom the danger is seen to be eventual delinquency. This latter group might be compared to status offenders under American juvenile law . . .

All protection cases are handled by the judge acting alone in chambers. In protection hearings, unlike delinquency hearings, the judge has the power to order placement in residential education centers without having to pass the case before the juvenile tribunal. It is asserted that many juvenile judges seeking to avoid formal, time-consuming tribunal hearings will sometimes close delinquency cases in chambers with a light disposition (perhaps a warning) and immediately open a civil protection case for the same juvenile leading to institutional placement.

On the surface, this procedure would seem to hold considerable potential for conflict with the rights of children. Yet this occurs less often than expected. The law instructs judges to seek the agreement of both parents and children to the solutions worked out, and it is said that judges commonly view themselves more as mediators than as judges in these situations. Although both parents and children have the right to counsel and to appeal in protection cases, less than one per cent of all decisions are appealed.

On June 21, 1971, the nine Justices of the Supreme Court filed five opinions in these three combined cases. This gives us an idea of how sensitive the issue was, as well as how difficult to resolve. While it is easy to say yes or no to the question at issue, it is quite difficult to reason through the implications of each position.

Justice Blackmun announced the judgment of the Court, but only the Chief Justice and Justices Stewart and White joined in the reasoning of the opinion. This makes it a plurality, not a majority opinion. Justice White also filed his own opinion, Justice Harlan wrote a concurring opinion, while Justice Brennan concurred in part and dissented in part. Justices Douglas, Black, and Marshall dissented. What all of this tells us is that there is not an easy solution to the problem.

Justice Blackmun announced the judgment of the Court, conceding that the dream of the early reformers has not been realized and that the juvenile court system has not lived up to their expectations. He referred to a study showing that half of the juvenile court judges had not received undergraduate degrees; one-fifth had received no college education at all; and one-fifth were not members of the bar. He said that this does not mean, however, that we ought to give up all hope for the system and jettison it.*

Justice Blackmun added that introducing the jury system would not necessarily help, and it could be harmful. The jury system would bring with it "the traditional delay, the formality, and clamor of the adversary system and, possibly, the public trial." Furthermore, if you introduce the jury system, you might just as well drop the juvenile system and try juveniles in the regular criminal courts.

Justice Blackmun pointed out that although ten states provide for a jury trial under certain circumstances in juvenile proceedings, twenty-eight states and the District of Columbia deny this right to juveniles. Other states make the question of whether to allow jury trials a matter of judicial discretion. The reason for this difference in practice is that the Constitution does not require jury trials in juvenile proceedings. The Sixth Amendment requires that "in all criminal prosecutions" the accused shall have the right to an impartial jury. This requirement has been extended to the states under the Fourteenth Amendment. Justice Blackmun concluded, however, that because juvenile proceedings are not defined as criminal trials, the constitutional requirement does not extend to them. In fact, even in adult criminal courts many cases are tried before judges without a jury. But, although there is no constitutional right to a trial by jury in juvenile proceedings, states are free to experiment with their juvenile courts. For example, there is nothing in the Constitution that prevents a state from creating advisory juries or instituting a regular jury system. The states, Justice Blackmun concluded, should have the option of introducing jury trials but should not be required to do so.

Justice White wrote a concurring opinion in which he agreed that a juvenile hearing is not a criminal trial, and therefore the Sixth Amendment's trial by jury does not apply. He also observed that a conscientious judge might do a better job than a jury in finding the facts of a case. He emphasized that a "substantial gulf" exists "between criminal guilt and delinquency." The consequences of

---

*Justice Blackmun drew extensively from material in the Task Force Report: Juvenile Delinquency and Youth Crime, 7–9 (1967), President's Commission on Law Enforcement and Administration of Justice, to support his conclusions.

being found guilty in a criminal proceeding are much greater than those of being adjudged delinquent. It is because of these severe consequences that the Sixth Amendment provides for jury trials in criminal proceedings. The "differences of substance between the criminal and the juvenile courts" convinced Justice White that juries are not required in the latter.

Justice Brennan's opinion focused on the fact that in the Pennsylvania cases the courtrooms were open to the public and the press. He felt that the presence of public and press at a juvenile proceeding has an effect similar to the involvement of a jury in a criminal trial. Both provide "an appeal to the community conscience" and a protection against abuses in the judicial process. In such cases public opinion can confront injustices. Where the general public is excluded however, only a jury trial could protect the juvenile against the "misuse of the judicial process." In the Pennsylvania cases the open courtroom was a safeguard to the "fundamental fairness" in factfinding required by the due process clause, and there was no need for jury trials. However, North Carolina either permits or requires exclusion of the general public from juvenile proceedings. The judge in the North Carolina case had ordered the public excluded although the petitioners had repeatedly requested a public hearing. Justice Brennan concluded that in the North Carolina case a jury trial was necessary to protect the due process rights of the juveniles.

Justice Harlan's very brief concurring opinion is based on his view that criminal jury trials are not required of the states under either the Sixth Amendment or the due process clause of the Fourteenth Amendment.

Justice Douglas's dissenting opinion was joined by Justices Black and Marshall, who took the position that the consequences in juvenile cases resemble closely those in criminal cases. Confinement can last until the juvenile reaches the age of majority. For a young child this could result in as much as ten years in an institution. No adult facing the possibility of a ten-year sentence could be denied a jury trial. The Fourteenth Amendment speaks of denial of rights to "any person," not "any adult person." A juvenile is a person, and any juvenile facing possible loss of liberty is entitled to the same constitutional protections—including trial by jury—as an adult.

Justice Douglas pointed to the negative effects of denying juveniles such procedural safeguards by quoting from an opinion of Judge DeCiantis of the Family Court of Providence, Rhode Island.

The child who feels that he has been dealt with fairly and not merely expediently or as speedily as possible will be a better prospect for rehabilitation. Many of the children who come before the court come from broken homes, from the ghettos; they often suffer from low self-esteem; and their behavior is frequently a symptom of their own feelings of inadequacy. Traumatic experiences of denial of basic rights only accentuate the past deprivation and contribute to the problem. Thus, a general societal attitude of acceptance of the juvenile as a person entitled to the same protection as an adult may be the true beginning of the rehabilitative process.

Judge DeCiantis went on to say that:

[t]rial by jury will provide the child with a safeguard against being prejudged by a judge who may well be prejudiced by reports already submitted to him by the police or caseworkers in the case. Indeed the child, the same as the adult, is in the category of those described in the Magna Carta: "No freeman may be . . . imprisoned . . . except by the lawful judgment of his peers, or by the law of the land."

Justice Douglas's dissenting opinion concluded that "these cases should be remanded for trial by jury on the criminal charges filed against these youngsters."

17 TRANSFER OF JUVENILE CASES TO CRIMINAL COURTS

When a juvenile court system feels it cannot handle an offender, the case can be transferred to the criminal courts. This procedure is referred to as a waiver of jurisdiction by the juvenile court. The transfer of a case from juvenile court to criminal court is a serious matter. While a juvenile can be punished as a delinquent by being confined for a period of time—sometimes up to the age of majority—a juvenile tried as an adult in a criminal proceeding can be sentenced to life imprisonment.

KENT v. U.S.
Should a juvenile transferred to adult criminal court for trial have a hearing before the transfer?

In 1959 a boy named Morris Kent, fourteen years of age, was apprehended for several housebreakings and attempted purse snatchings. He was placed on probation by the juvenile court of the District of Columbia. As part of his probation he was interviewed regularly, and the authorities accumulated a social service file describing his conduct. In 1961, while still on probation, he was taken into custody and charged with housebreaking, robbery, and rape.

He was initially in custody of the juvenile court, but his mother and his attorney were informed that the case might be transferred by waiver to the criminal court of the District of Columbia. His attorney objected and arranged for psychiatric examinations of the boy. On the basis of these examinations, a psychiatrist stated that Kent was "a victim of severe psychopathology" and recommended hospitalization for psychiatric observation. Kent's attorney then filed with the juvenile court an affidavit certifying this diagnosis and a motion for a hearing on the question of waiver. He also asked for the boy's social service file.

The juvenile court judge did not rule on these motions and did not hold a hearing. Without conferring with the boy's parents and counsel, he entered an order stating that after a "full investigation" he waived jurisdiction and directed that Kent be held for trial in the regular criminal court. (It should be noted that the social service file indicated that Kent was suffering from a mental illness.)

At the criminal trial, Kent was found guilty of six counts of housebreaking and robbery and was sentenced to serve five to fifteen years on each count, or a total of thirty to ninety years in prison. He was found not guilty of rape by reason of insanity.

Kent's attorney appealed on several grounds. He argued that:

1. The waiver was defective because no hearing was held.
2. The juvenile court gave no reasons for the waiver.
3. Counsel was denied access to the social service file.

The Supreme Court handed down a five to four decision. How do you think the Supreme Court ruled? Keep in mind that this case was decided in 1966, one year before the *Gault* case.

Speaking for the majority, Justice Fortas appeared shocked, saying, "There is no place in our system of law for reaching a result of such tremendous consequences without ceremony—without hearing, without effective assistance of counsel, without a statement of reasons." He pointed out the meaning of these consequences: In a juvenile proceeding Kent might have been confined until he was twenty-one—a total of five years—while in criminal court he might have received the death sentence. The majority opinion continued:

> Accordingly, we hold that it is incumbent upon the Juvenile Court to accompany its waiver order with a statement of the reasons or considerations therefore . . . we conclude that an opportunity for a hearing which may be informal, must be given the child prior to entry of a waiver order . . . the child is entitled to counsel in connection with a waiver proceeding, and . . . counsel is entitled to see the child's social records. These rights are meaningless—an illusion, a mockery—unless counsel is given an opportunity to function.
>
> The right to representation by counsel is not a formality. It is not a grudging gesture to a ritualistic requirement. It is of the essence of justice. Appointment of counsel without affording an opportunity for hearing on a "critically important" decision is tantamount to denial of counsel. . . . it was error to fail to grant a hearing.
>
> *We do not mean by this to indicate that the hearing to be held must conform with all the requirements of a criminal trial or even of the usual administrative hearing; but we do hold that the hearing must measure up to the essentials of due process and fair treatment.*
>
> With respect to access by the child's counsel to the social records of the child, we deem it obvious that since these are to be considered by the Juvenile Court in making its decision to waive, they must be made available to the child's counsel. [emphasis added]

Keeping in mind that the *Gault* case was decided the following year, what conclusion can you draw from the italicized paragraph? Can you recall who wrote the majority opinion in the *Gault* case?

The dissenting opinion, written by Justice Stewart and concurred in by Justices Black, Harlan, and White, noted that the Supreme Court's general practice is to leave undisturbed the decisions of the court of appeals of the District of Columbia on the application of laws governing District of Columbia affairs. However, since its decision in *Kent* the Court of Appeals had handed down two decisions which indicated it had modified its views of juvenile court procedures. The dissent concluded that the *Kent* case ought to be sent back to the appeals court for reconsideration in the light of those decisions.

If a juvenile court judge waives a case over to criminal court, does this violate the constitutional prohibition against double jeopardy?

Let us assume that a juvenile is taken into custody and charged with a serious offense. At the adjudicatory hearing, it is decided that he is a delinquent. Since the offense is serious, it is then decided that the juvenile should be transferred to the regular criminal court.

BREED v. JONES
Does the transfer of a juvenile case to an adult court violate the constitutional prohibition against double jeopardy?

This happened in 1971 to a young man named Gary Jones, seventeen years of age. At the time of the case, California law stated that any person under age twenty-one who violated the criminal law was subject to the juvenile court. (The age was subsequently lowered to eighteen.)

Charged with armed robbery, Jones was given a hearing and declared a delinquent. Two weeks later the juvenile court judge indicated that he was considering waiving the case to the criminal courts because he believed that Jones was "unfit for treatment as a juvenile." Taken by surprise, Jones's attorney protested that he did not know that the court was considering such action. Nevertheless, a week later the court ordered Jones to be tried as an adult. He was tried, found guilty, and committed to the California Youth Authority, which handles the cases of youths up to age twenty-five.

Jones's attorney petitioned for a writ of habeas corpus, arguing that Jones's second trial had placed him in double jeopardy and was therefore unconstitutional. The basis of this argument is included in the section of the Fifth Amendment which states:

. . . nor shall any person be subject for the same offense to be twice put in jeopardy of life or limb. . . .

This is known as the double jeopardy clause. It applies to all federal judicial procedures and is also applicable to state proceedings through the due process clause of the Fourteenth Amendment.

Do you think this constitutional provision applies to Jones? Was Jones being tried twice for the same crime?

The Supreme Court was unanimous in its decision in this case. Chief Justice Burger delivered the opinion of the Court. Once again, the

Court noted that it was troubled by the special status of the juvenile justice system. Since the double jeopardy clause applies only in criminal cases, how could it apply to the so-called civil proceedings of a juvenile court?

The Chief Justice answered this by emphasizing that the label "civil" as applied to juvenile cases is no longer appropriate. The consequences determine the nature of the case. When the consequence of a juvenile hearing may be conviction and loss of liberty, the juvenile is in jeopardy.

As we have observed, the risk to which the term jeopardy refers is that traditionally associated with "actions intended to authorize criminal punishment to vindicate public justice" . . . . Because of its purpose and potential consequences, and the nature and resources of the State, such a proceeding imposes heavy pressures and burdens—psychological, physical, and financial—on a person charged. The purpose of the Double Jeopardy Clause is to require that he be subject to the experience only once "for the same offence."

In *In re Gault*, . . . this Court concluded that, for purposes of the right to counsel, a "proceeding where the issue is whether the child will be found to be 'delinquent' and subjected to the loss of his liberty for years is comparable in seriousness to a felony prosecution." See *In re Winship*, . . . The Court stated that the term "delinquent" had "come to involve only slightly less stigma than the term 'criminal' applied to adults," *In re Gault*, . . . *In re Winship*, . . . and that, for purposes of the privilege against self-incrimination, "commitment is a deprivation of liberty. It is incarceration against one's will, whether it is called 'criminal' or 'civil.' "

Thus, in terms of potential consequences, there is little to distinguish an adjudicatory hearing such as was held in this case from a traditional criminal prosecution. For that reason, it engenders elements of "anxiety and insecurity" in a juvenile, and imposes a "heavy personal strain."

The Court concluded that Jones was placed in jeopardy at the adjudicatory hearing, when he was "put to trial before the trier of facts"—in this case, a judge. As soon as the juvenile court judge began to hear evidence against Jones, Jones's liberty was jeopardized. Since he was tried twice, Jones was "twice put to the task of marshalling his resources against those of the State, twice subjected to the 'heavy personal strain' which such an experience represents." This is unconstitutional.

To avoid this situation, the Court suggested that transfer hearings and decisions be made prior to adjudicatory hearings. Then if a transfer is rejected, a different judge should preside over the adjudicatory hearing to ensure fairness. The juvenile can, however, waive this right to another judge.

In this case, it has become more apparent that the Justices are beginning to regard juvenile proceedings as having most of the elements of a criminal case. The due process of law safeguards which they have held applicable to juvenile proceedings are designed to ensure that when a young person's liberty is in jeopardy the hearing will be fair and impartial rather than arbitrary and unreasonable.

18 COMPENSATING THE VICTIM

Critics of our criminal justice system have charged with considerable justification that while we are concerned about the rights of an accused, we generally neglect the victim. For example, when a young offender or an adult criminal commits larceny, rape, murder, or assault and battery, the Constitution and the Supreme Court rulings command a fair trial based on the principles set forth in the Fourth Fifth, Sixth, and Eighth Amendments. As a rule, however, little concern is shown for the victim, who may have been badly hurt or deprived of needed money or precious posessions or both.

In recent years a number of states have passed Victim Compensation Laws, which cover to some extent the medical bills and the loss of working time suffered by innocent victims of criminal action. Not all victims are eligible, however, and compensation is not always adequate to cover the loss or the hurt. A recent case raised the issue of compensation for those who were injured by young offenders.

DURST v. UNITED STATES

Should those who break the law be required to compensate their victims?

Rickey Lee Durst and four other youths pleaded guilty to a number of offenses. Durst and a youth named Rice pleaded guilty to obstruction of the mails, and the other three pleaded guilty to stealing United States government property valued at less than $100. They were all sentenced under the Federal Youth Corrections Act, which applies to young people between the ages of sixteen and twenty-two. Each was sentenced to probation and a suspended sentence of imprisonment. As a condition of probation, each was ordered to pay fines ranging from $50 to $100. Durst was additionally ordered to make restitution in the amount of $160.

Is this fair? Is it constitutional to single out one of the offenders and require him to repay the injured party?

The unanimous Court, with Justice Blackmun taking no part in the case, declared that fines and restitution were legal under the Youth Corrections Act. Justice Brennan's brief opinion pointed out that the federal statute provides that while on probation a defendant may be required:

1. To pay a fine in one of several sums and
2. To make restitution or reparation to aggrieved parties for actual damages or loss caused by the offense for which the conviction was had . . . .

The attorney for the youths argued that being placed on probation was sufficient punishment. Requiring fines and retribution in addition to this punishment contributed not to rehabilitation but to punishment. The response of Justice Brennan was that the Youth Corrections Act permitted all of these actions as part of the judicial procedure.

Observe that this decision applies to youthful offenders (sixteen to twenty-two years of age). Do you think that it ought to apply to juvenile offenders?

19 CONCLUDING THOUGHTS ON JUVENILE JUSTICE

The President's Commission of Law Enforcement and Administration of Justice (1967) produced a *Task Force Report on Juvenile Delinquency and Youth Crime.* Two excerpts from this report summarize the high hopes and the bitter disappointments associated with the juvenile court system.

What emerges then is this: In theory the juvenile court was to be helpful and rehabilitative rather than punitive. In fact the distinction often disappears, not only because of the absence of facilities and personnel but also because of the limits of knowledge and technique. In theory the court's action was to affix no stigmatizing label. In fact a delinquent is generally viewed by employers, schools, the armed services—society generally—as a criminal. In theory the court was to treat children guilty of criminal acts in noncriminal ways. In fact it labels truants and runaways as junior criminals.

In theory the court's operations could justifiably be informal, its findings and decisions made without observing ordinary procedural safeguards, because it would act only in the best interest of the child. In fact it frequently does nothing more nor less than deprive a child of liberty without due process of law—knowing not what else to do and needing, whether admittedly or not, to act in the community's interest even more imperatively than the child's. In theory it was to exercise its protective powers to bring an errant child back into the fold. In fact there is increasing reason to believe that its intervention reinforces the juvenile's unlawful impulses. In theory it was to concentrate on each case the best of current social science learning. In fact it has often become a vested interest in its turn, loathe to cooperate with innovative programs or "avail itself of forward-looking methods". . . .

Nevertheless, study of the juvenile courts does not necessarily lead to the conclusion that the time has come to jettison the experiment and remand the disposition of children charged with crime to the criminal courts of the country. As trying as are the problems of the juvenile courts, the problems of the criminal courts, particularly those of the lower courts, which would fall heir to much of the juvenile court jurisdiction, are even graver; and the ideal of separate treatment of children is still worth pursuing. What is required is rather a revised philosophy of the juvenile court based on the recognition that in the past our reach exceeded our grasp. The spirit that animated the juvenile court movement was fed in part by a humanitarian compassion for offenders who were children. That willingness to understand

and treat people who threaten public safety and security should be nurtured, not turned aside as hopeless sentimentality, both because it is civilized and because social protection itself demands constant search for alternatives to the crude and limited expedient of condemnation and punishment. But neither should it be allowed to outrun reality. The juvenile court is a court of law, charged like other agencies of criminal justice with protecting the community against threatening conduct. Rehabilitating offenders through individualized handling is one way of providing protection and appropriately the primary way in dealing with children. But the guiding consideration for a court of law that deals with threatening conduct is nonetheless protection of the community. The juvenile court, like other courts, is therefore obliged to employ all the means at hand, not excluding incapacitation, for achieving that protection. What should distinguish the juvenile from the criminal courts is greater emphasis on rehabilitation, not exclusive preoccupation with it.*

One effort designed to meet these criticisms of the juvenile court system was the Federal Youth Corrections Act, which was modeled after England's Borstal System, which aims at rehabilitation rather than punishment. Each of these programs incorporates three essential components in its rehabilitation program

1.   Separating youthful offenders from hardened criminals.
2.   Flexibility in treatment and availability of a variety of programs tailored to individual needs.
3.   Flexibility in determining the duration of commitment and of supervised release.

The Borstal System has been described as follows:

Among the 13 institutions, some are walled; others are open; and each has its own specialty. One has trade training in metal and woodwork; another is similar to a summer camp with out-of-door work and activities; a third is devoted to agriculture and stock raising; and a fourth graduates skilled workers in the building trades. The one thing all institutions have in common is concern for individual needs and the return of the young offenders to society as rehabilitated individuals.**

*This quotation originally appeared in McKeiver v. Pennsylvania, 91 S.Ct. 1975 (1971) at 1986–1987.

**This quotation originally appeared in the U.S. House of Representatives Report No. 2979, 81st Congress, 1st Session, 3(1950) and is quoted in the Court's opinion in Durst v. U.S., 98 S.Ct. 849 (1978) at 851.

Improving the Juvenile Justice System

Many people—judges, lawyers, parents, and young people—have criticized the juvenile justice system for its failure to measure up to the standards of justice which we associate with due process of law. While these complaints were being voiced, the Institute of Judicial Administration, a private, non-profit research and education organization, and the American Bar Association created a Joint-Commission on Juvenile Justice Standards. Between 1973 and 1979, this Commission produced seventeen volumes touching every aspect of juvenile justice from home and school to police conduct and court hearings.

Among the important recommendations of this Commission, which were approved by the House of Delegates of the American Bar Association in 1979 were:

1. The arresting officer must inform juveniles of their Miranda rights in "clearly understandable language" or in the accused's native language. If necessary, interpreters must be used.
2. Parents must be informed promptly of the arrest.
3. Within two hours of arrest, the juvenile must be taken to a juvenile facility or must be released.
4. Pending hearings, the juvenile should be released unconditionally, unless detention is necessary to protect the juvenile or society.
5. Written records must be kept at all stages of judical proceedings.
6. The juvenile must be granted the right to a private or court-appointed attorney *at every stage of the proceedings.*
7. The juvenile has the right to a public and speedy trial.
8. The juvenile has the right to demand a jury trial. The jury may consist of as few as six persons and the verdict should be unanimous.
9. A juvenile court adjudication of delinquency is not a conviction of crime and should not be viewed as an indication of criminality.
10. The juvenile is to be protected against double jeopardy.
11. Indigent juveniles who appeal their cases must have the benefit of counsel and a copy of the transcript of the adjudication and disposition hearings at public expense.
12. Due process of law should apply to juveniles in correctional institutions.
13. Use of adult jails for juveniles is to be prohibited.
14. Juveniles in detention centers should be afforded privacy, attorneys, and visitors.
15. Juvenile records should not be considered public records. They should be available only to a limited number of authorized persons.
16. There should be periodic destruction of juvenile records based on such criteria as death of the juvenile, age of the record, lack of usefulness, and harm to the juvenile, if improperly disseminated.
17. Third parties such as private and public employers and employment, credit, insurance, and educational institutions should be prohibited from inquiring or seeking information con-

cerning the arrest, adjudication, or sentencing of a juvenile.

18. Juveniles who are eighteen or over should be considered to be adults for all legal purposes.

Since these statements are recommendations, implementation of them can only come from the fifty state legislatures. They have the responsibility to pick and choose those recommendations which fit in with their philosophy of juvenile justice. The future of these ideas rests with those voters who are sensitive to the problems which plague the juvenile justice system and who would like to see the system improved.

With which of these recommendations do you agree? Disagree? Do you have any recommendations to offer for the improvement of the juvenile justice system?

SECTION IV

Justice in the Schools

Today, education is perhaps the most important function of state and local government. Compulsory school attendance laws and the great expenditures for education both demonstrate our recognition of the importance of education to our democratic society. . . . It is the very foundation of good citizenship.

Chief Justice Warren in Brown v.
Board of Education, *347 U.S. 483 (1954)*

Neither man nor child can be allowed to stand condemned by methods which flout constitutional requirements of due process of law.

Justice William Douglas
Haley *v.* **Ohio,** *332 U.S. 596*

INTRODUCTION

Our schools are often referred to as the "laboratories of democracy" and as the "showcase of democracy." These phrases imply that the schools educate students to become responsible leaders and intelligent followers in society. The purpose of the schools, according to these descriptions, is to train the young in ways of understanding, appreciating, and perpetuating the democratic way of life.

School systems are designed to move the young through programs of learning. If anyone interferes with the learning process or violates the rules of the school, those responsible for the educational process have the power to take steps to stop the intrusion and to punish the offenders. In other words, discipline in the school setting is necessary for effective teaching and learning. The discipline may be self-discipline in which students exercise self-control, or it may be discipline imposed by such means as detention of students after class, suspension from school or classes, expulsion, or corporal punishment.

In punishing students for misconduct, do school authorities have to follow certain procedures, or are they free to act as they think proper under the circumstances?

For many years the rule followed was that of *in loco parentis*. School officials were considered to stand *in the place of the parents* when dealing with students in the schools. When schools and classes were small, the *in loco parentis* rule made sense, because students and school authorities knew each other quite well. With the growth in the size of schools and classes, however, an impersonal relationship developed so that students and their teachers and principals often were strangers to each other. Inevitably the *in loco parentis* rule has had to be reconsidered.

In recent years the Supreme Court has heard a number of cases dealing with young people. Between 1967 and 1969 there were two landmark rulings. In the *Gault* case (1967), discussed on pages 137–145, the Justices concluded that certain procedures associated with due process of law must be incorporated into juvenile courts. Although *Gault* dealt with a delinquency proceeding, it did have implications for the schools. How far the Court would go in incorporating due process procedures into school disciplinary cases was a question for the future.

Two years after the Gault decision the Court, in *Tinker* v. *Des Moines Independent School District*, upheld the right of students to wear black armbands to express their opposition to the war in Vietnam. The majority of the Court held that students cannot be deprived of their First Amendment right to freedom of speech without due

When the Supreme Court handed down its decision in February 1969 on the *Tinker* case, Mary Beth, *right*, and her brother, *center*, wore black armbands to school to celebrate her victory. Their mother is on the left.

process of law, and that unless school administrators can reasonably predict that student conduct will materially and substantially interfere with school activities and learning, they cannot prohibit students' anticipated or ongoing conduct.

With the Court's emphasis on the importance of due process of law for young people, how would the Justices react to cases in which students in school were punished for violating school rules? Would they invoke the *in loco parentis* rule to support school officials, or would they insist that those accused of misconduct be accorded hearings complying with due process?

20 SUSPENSIONS AND EXPULSIONS

GOSS v. LOPEZ
Must school officials conform to due process of law procedures in suspending students from school or class?

The state of Ohio provides free public education to all children between the ages of six and twenty-one. At the time of the *Goss* case, Ohio law gave principals of Ohio public schools the power to suspend students for up to ten days or to expel them. A student's parents had to be notified within twenty-four hours and given the reasons for the action. Expelled students could appeal their punishment to the Board of Education, but suspended students had no such right of appeal. *There was no requirement that hearings be held prior to suspensions or expulsions.*

During the month of February and March 1971 there was a great deal of student unrest in the Columbus, Ohio, public schools, and a number of students were suspended without hearings. Nine of the suspended students initiated this case as a class action—a lawsuit brought on behalf of all the students who had been suspended.

According to the court record, six of the students had been disruptive or disobedient in the presence of the school administrator who ordered the suspensions. Of these, one had demonstrated in the school auditorium while a class was in session and another had physically attacked a policeman who was trying to remove the first. Dwight Lopez had been suspended for participating in a disturbance in the lunchroom; he said that he had been an innocent bystander. Betty Crone had attended a demonstration at another high school and had been arrested along with other young people, but had not been charged. Like the others, she had been suspended for ten days without a hearing. There was no record or testimony showing the reasons for the suspension of the ninth student. After the suspensions had taken place, the students and their parents had been offered an opportunity to attend a conference relating to the suspensions.

The students began a legal action in the United States District Court to have the Ohio law declared unconstitutional. Their suit charged that by failing to provide a hearing prior to a ten-day suspension the Ohio law violated the due process clause—that part of the Fourteenth Amendment which says that a state cannot deprive a person of life, liberty, or property without due process of law. The lawsuit also sought an injunction against school officials to prevent them from suspending any students under the law. Finally the students requested the court to remove all references to the suspensions from their files.

If you were one of the school administrators involved in this action, how would you defend yourself? After all, you had acted under a law enacted by the Ohio legislature. Try to think through your line of reasoning.

You could argue that one of the powers reserved to the states under the Tenth Amendment of the United States Constitution is power over education. Under this power the states have the option of establishing free public education. They are not required to do so. If they decide to establish public schools, the students who attend these schools are subject to the disciplinary rules set by the school authorities acting under state law. Since there is no constitutional right to an education, due process procedures do not apply in suspension cases.

You could also take the position that a ten-day suspension is not a very damaging punishment. Students suspended for a relatively short period do not suffer a serious loss of education.

Your third argument could very well be that education should be left to educators and that judges should refrain from interfering with disciplinary procedures in the schools. It is the educator who is on the front line; and it is the educator who understands best how to develop responsible citizens.

How would you, as a student, answer these arguments? If you insist that there must be a hearing before a ten-day suspension, how can you justify your position?

Take a look at that part of the Fourteenth Amendment which declares that the state cannot deprive any person of life, liberty, or property without due process of law. What connection can you see between the right to an education and the right to liberty? Is there any connection between the right to an education and the right to property? Is a ten-day suspension a trivial thing to a student? What kind of effect can it have on a student's future?

These were not easy questions for the students, for the educators, or for the Justices. After a three-judge district court declared that the students had been denied due process, several administrators of the school system challenged the court's decision with an appeal to the United States Supreme Court. The decision of the nine Justices was a close one, indicating that they, too, had a difficult time with the case. When their deliberations were over, a five to four decision on the issue emerged: does a ten-day suspension prior to a hearing violate the due process clause of the Fourteenth Amendment?

Justice White, speaking for the majority, began by agreeing with the school authorities that Ohio was not required by the Constitution to maintain a public school system. Once it had done so, however, it had to respect the constitutional rights of the students. He then proceeded to explain his reasoning.

The authority possessed by the State to prescribe and enforce standards of conduct in its schools although concededly very broad, must be exercised consistently with constitutional safeguards. Among other things, the State is constrained to recognize *a student's legitimate entitlement to a public education as a property interest which is protected by the Due Process Clause* and which may not be taken away for misconduct without adherence to the minimum procedures required by that Clause.

   The Due Process Clause also forbids arbitrary deprivations of liberty. "Where a person's good name, reputation, honor, or integrity is at stake because of what the government is doing to him," the minimal requirements of the Clause must be satisfied. . . . School authorities here suspended appellees from school for periods of up to 10 days based on charges of misconduct. If sustained and recorded, *those charges could seriously damage the students' standing with their fellow pupils and their teachers as well as interfere with later opportunities for higher education and employment.* It is apparent that the claimed right of the State to determine unilaterally and without process whether that misconduct has occurred immediately collides with the requirements of the Constitution. [emphasis added]

Explain the meaning of the emphasized portions. In what way is an education a "property interest"? In what ways could the charges damage a student's future opportunities?

According to the majority, students have property rights in education because the state has made it available to them and because higher education and employment depend on it. In addition, a student's right to liberty includes reputation, honor, integrity, and standing with teachers and other students. Would or could a suspension from school for no more than ten days really adversely affect a student's future? Is such a short-term suspension a deprivation of liberty and property rights? In law, this is referred to as the *de minimis* argument: The law does not concern itself with trivial or insignificant matters. Is a ten-day suspension sufficiently harmful to a student's future to raise a constitutional issue? Justice White answered as follows:

   A 10-day suspension from school is not *de minimis* in our view and may not be imposed in complete disregard of the Due Process Clause.

   A short suspension is, of course, a far milder deprivation than expulsion. But, "education is perhaps the most important function of state and local governments." *Brown* v. *Board of Education* . . . and the total exclusion from the educational process for more than a trivial period, and certainly if the suspension is for 10 days, is a serious event in the life of the suspended child. Neither the property interest in educational benefits temporarily denied nor the liberty interest in reputation, which is also implicated, is so insubstantial that suspensions may constitutionally be imposed by any procedure the school chooses, no matter how arbitrary.

Having decided that due process of law procedures apply to suspensions of up to ten days, the majority then set forth the rules that school administrators must follow before making a decision.

We do not believe that school authorities must be totally free from notice and hearing requirements if their schools are to operate with acceptable efficiency. Students facing temporary suspension have interests qualifying for protection of the Due Process Clause, *and due process requires, in connection with a suspension of 10 days or less, that the student be given oral or written notice of the charges against him and, if he denies them, an explanation of the evidence the authorities have and an opportunity to present his side of the story.* The Clause requires at least these rudimentary precautions against unfair or mistaken findings of misconduct and arbitrary exclusion from school.

There need be no delay between the time "notice" is given and the time of the hearing. In the great majority of cases the disciplinarian

Justice Byron R. White drafted the Supreme Court's ruling in the 1975 case of *Goss* v. *Lopez.*

may informally discuss the alleged misconduct with the student minutes after it has occurred. We hold only that, in being given an opportunity to explain his version of the facts at this discussion, the student first be told what he is accused of doing and what the basis of the accusation is. . . . Since the hearing may occur almost immediately following the misconduct, it follows that as a general rule notice and hearing should precede removal of the student from school. [emphasis added]

Suppose, however, that a student's conduct is so serious that he or she "poses a continuing danger to person or property or an ongoing threat of disrupting the academic process." In such cases, according to the majority opinion, the administrators have no choice but to remove the student immediately from the school. Such suspension must be followed by notice of charges and a hearing as soon as is practicable.

In holding a hearing involving the misconduct of a student, what are the specific due process rights of the students? Are they permitted to have an attorney present? Can they bring their own witnesses? Can they confront or cross-examine witnesses against them? The Court answered these questions as follows:

We stop short of construing the Due Process Clause to require, countrywide, that hearings in connection with short suspensions must afford the student the opportunity to secure counsel, to confront and cross-examine witnesses supporting the charge, or to call his own witnesses to verify his version of the incident. Brief disciplinary suspensions are almost countless. To impose in each such case even truncated trial-type procedures might well overwhelm administrative facilities in many places and, by diverting resources, cost more than it would save in educational effectiveness. Moreover, further formalizing the suspension process and escalating its formality and adversary nature may not only make it too costly as a regular disciplinary tool but also destroy its effectiveness as part of the teaching process.

On the other hand, requiring effective notice and informal hearing permitting the student to give his version of the events will provide a meaningful hedge against erroneous action. At least the disciplinarian will be alerted to the existence of disputes about facts and arguments about cause and effect. He may then determine himself to summon the accuser, permit cross-examination, and allow the student to present his own witnesses. In more difficult cases, he may permit counsel. In any event, his discretion will be more informed and we think the risk of error substantially reduced. [emphasis added]

In concluding the opinion for the majority, Justice White emphasized the need for a hearing, even where the disciplinarian has witnessed an infraction of the school rules. Since "things are not always as they seem to be," an informal give-and-take between student and school administrator offers the student an opportunity to explain the action that took place and enables the administrator to place it in its proper context.

There may be times, however, when the simple procedures out-lined by the Court may be inadequate.

We should also make it clear that we have addressed ourselves solely to the short suspension, not exceeding 10 days. Longer sus-pensions or expulsions for the remainder of the school term, or per-manently, may require more formal procedures. Nor do we put aside the possibility that in unusual situations, although involving only a short suspension, something more than the rudimentary procedures will be required. [emphasis added]

In this case, since there was no hearing either before or after the suspensions, each suspension was invalidated. The Ohio law was ruled unconstitutional because it permitted suspensions without no-tice or hearing.

The four dissenting Justices disagreed completely with the ma-jority ruling. Justice Powell's opinion for the dissenters began with a statement opposing judicial intervention in school disciplinary cases.

The decision unnecessarily opens avenues for judicial intervention in the operation of our public schools that may affect adversely the quality of education. The Court holds for the first time that the federal courts, rather than educational officials and state legislatures, have the authority to determine the rules applicable to routine classroom discipline of children and teenagers in the public schools. It justifies this unprecedented intrusion into the process of elementary and sec-ondary education by identifying a new constitutional right: the right of a student not to be suspended for as much as a single day without notice and a due process hearing either before or promptly following the suspension.

Justice Powell stated that we are dealing with an "insignificant infringement of education, since the Ohio law authorizes a maximum suspension of eight school days, less than 5% of the normal 180-day school year." Suspensions for so brief a period "rarely affect a pupil's opportunity to learn or his scholastic performance," he said. He noted that there was no data showing that any of the students had been "seriously damaged" by the suspensions. In cases of this type, he found no property or liberty interests, and not enough was at stake to justify a constitutional rule based on due process of law.

According to Justice Powell, there are differences between the rights and duties of children and adults. In criminal law and in civil law, as well as in the right to vote and hold office, adults have rights not available to minors. This applies especially in the school setting.

When Ohio established its public school system, it coupled the opportunity to attend school with the delegation of authority to school officials to use their discretion in maintaining proper discipline in those schools. It is for this reason, according to the dissenting opinion, that the power to suspend a student for a brief period rests properly with school officials and does not call for judicial intervention.

The State's interest, broadly put, is in the proper functioning of its public school system for the benefit of all pupils and the public generally. Few rulings would interfere more extensively in the daily functioning of schools than subjecting routine discipline to the formalities and judicial oversight of due process. Suspensions are one of the traditional means—ranging from keeping a student after class to permanent expulsion—used to maintain discipline in the schools. *It is common knowledge that maintaining order and reasonable decorum in school buildings and classrooms is a major educational problem and one which has increased significantly in magnitude in recent years. Often the teacher, in protecting the rights of other children to an education (if not his or their safety), is compelled to rely on the power to suspend.*

The facts leave little room for doubt as to the magnitude of the disciplinary problem in the public schools, or as to the extent of reliance upon the right to suspend. They also demonstrate that if hearings were required for a substantial percentage of short-term suspensions, school authorities would have time to do little else. [emphasis added]

What is your opinion of the position presented in the emphasized sentences? Is discipline a "major educational problem"? If so, why impose restrictions on those who must handle discipline problems?

In writing opinions dealing with educational matters, Supreme Court Justices often express concern for the state of the public schools. Justice Black's dissenting opinion in the *Tinker* case stressed the nature and extent of disciplinary problems in the schools. In a similar vein, Justice Powell said:

The State's generalized interest in maintaining an orderly school system is not incompatible with the individual interest of the student. *Education in any meaningful sense includes the inculcation of an understanding in each pupil of the necessity of rules and obedience thereto. This understanding is no less important than learning to read and write. One who does not comprehend the meaning and necessity of discipline is handicapped not merely in his education but throughout his subsequent life.* In an age when the home and church play a diminishing role in shaping the character and value judgments of the young, a heavier responsibility falls upon the schools. When an immature student merits censure for his conduct, he is rendered a disservice if appropriate sanctions are not applied or if procedures for their application are so formalized as to invite a challenge to the teacher's authority—an invitation which rebellious or even merely spirited teenagers are likely to accept.

The lesson of discipline is not merely a matter of the student's self-interest in the shaping of his own character and personality; it

Four Justices disagreed with the majority opinion in the *Goss* case. Justice Lewis F. Powell, Jr. wrote the dissenting opinion.

provides an early understanding of the relevance to the social compact of respect for the rights of others. The classroom is the laboratory in which this lesson of life is best learned. Mr. Justice Black summed it up:

> "School discipline, like parental discipline, is an integral and important part of training our children to be good citizens— to be better citizens."

Do you agree with Justice Powell's belief that there is a close relationship between discipline and the development of good character and good citizenship? How do you see this relationship? How do you think students can best develop self-discipline and respect for the rights of others?

The dissenting Justices pointed to what they saw as a major weakness of the majority opinion: It treats the normal teacher-student relationship as an adversary proceeding, subject to judicial supervision, and disregards "the commonality of interest of the state and pupils in the public school system."

One of the more disturbing aspects of today's decision is its indiscriminate reliance upon the judiciary, and the adversary process, as the means of resolving many of the most routine problems arising in the classroom. *In mandating due process procedures the Court misapprehends the reality of the normal teacher-pupil relationship. There is an ongoing relationship, one in which the teacher must occupy many roles—educator, adviser, friend, and, at times, parent-substitute.* It is rarely adversary in nature except with respect to the chronically disruptive or insubordinate pupil whom the teacher must be free to discipline without frustrating formalities.

The Ohio statute, providing as it does for due notice both to parents and the Board, is compatible with the teacher-pupil relationship and the informal resolution of mistaken disciplinary action. *We have relied for generations upon the experience, good faith and dedication of those who staff our public schools, and the nonadversary means of airing grievances that always have been available to pupils and their parents.* One would have thought before today's opinion that this informal method of resolving differences was more compatible with the interests of all concerned than resort to any constitutionalized procedure, however blandly it may be defined by the Court. [emphasis added]

What is your reaction to the emphasized sentences? What are the nonadversary means of airing grievances? Do you think the Court's decision changes the teacher-student relationship?

The dissenters concluded that the decision of the majority not only was unwise but set a dangerous precedent. If a brief suspension of a student now invokes a constitutionally protected right under due process of law, will the same right apply to students who fail courses or are assigned to classes or courses which they find unsatisfactory?

No one can foresee the ultimate frontiers of the new "thicket" the Court now enters. Today's ruling appears to sweep within the protected interest in education a multitude of discretionary decisions in the educational process. Teachers and other school authorities are required to make many decisions that may have serious consequences for the pupil. They must decide, for example, how to grade the student's work, whether a student passes or fails a course, whether he is to be promoted, whether he is required to take certain subjects, whether he may be excluded from interscholastic athletics or other extracurricular activities, whether he may be removed from one school and sent to another, whether he may be bused long distances when available schools are nearby, and whether he should be placed in a "general," "vocational," or "college-preparatory" track.

In these and many similar situations claims of impairment of one's educational entitlement identical in principle to those before the Court today can be asserted with equal or greater justification. . . .

If, as seems apparent, the Court will now require due process procedures whenever such routine school decisions are challenged, the impact upon public education will be serious indeed. The discretion and judgment of federal courts across the land often will be substituted for that of the 50 state legislatures, the 14,000 school boards, and the 2,000,000 teachers who heretofore have been responsible for the administration of the American public school system.

Do you think the alarm of the dissenters with the majority ruling is justified? Why or why not?

WOOD v.
STRICKLAND

Can school board members be sued for violating students' constitutional rights?

The ruling in *Goss* v. *Lopez* was handed down by the Court on January 22, 1975. One month later, on February 25, 1975, *Wood* v. *Strickland* was decided. While *Goss* dealt with hearings for students prior to suspensions, *Wood* raised the issue of the liability of school board members for denying hearings prior to expulsion.

The case began with a prank by three tenth-grade students at an Arkansas high school. Peggy Strickland, her friend Virginia Crain, and a third girl, Jo Wall, decided to spike the punch at an extracurricular school organization meeting attended by parents and students. Since the school was in a dry county, they crossed the state line into Oklahoma and purchased two 12-ounce bottles of Right Time, a malt liquor, and six bottles of a soft drink. They mixed the malt liquor and the soft drinks together in a milk carton, took the mixture to school, and added it to the punch. The punch was served, according to the report, "without apparent effect."

The teacher in charge of the extracurricular group learned of the episode. She told the girls that the principal would probably hear about what had happened and urged them to tell him themselves, before the story became "distorted." They confessed to the principal and he suspended them for two weeks pending a decision of the school board. The board met that evening, but neither the girls nor their parents attended the meeting. The teacher and the principal recommended leniency. While the meeting was going on, the teacher's husband phoned the superintendent of school, and told him that Jo Wall had been in a fight at a basketball game that evening. The principal and the teacher withdrew their request for leniency, and the school board voted to expel all three girls from school for the remainder of the semester, a period of three months. The students were adjudged guilty of violating the school regulation prohibiting the use or possession of intoxicating beverages at school or school-sponsored activities.

Two weeks later the board held a meeting at which the girls, their parents, and their attorney were present. The charges were read, and the girls admitted their part in the episode. The board refused to grant their request for leniency, and the expulsions were reaffirmed.

The girls took their case to federal court under an old, but very important, law enacted during the Reconstruction Period following the Civil War. During that period the federal government enacted legislation extending the rights of citizenship to former slaves. One of these laws, the Civil Rights Act of 1871, provided that anyone who, acting under color of any statute, causes any person, or citizen of the United States, to be deprived "of any rights, privileges, or immunities secured by the Constitution and the law" shall be liable to the party injured in any action at law, suit in equity, or other proper proceeding for redress. Under this law, the students sued the school board and two school administrators, contending that their constitutional due process rights had been violated. They asked for compensatory and punitive damages, for injunctive relief allowing them to return to classes, and for the removal of the expulsion from their records.

The jury failed to reach a verdict, and a mistrial was declared. The district court directed a verdict in favor of the school board and officials on the grounds that they were immune from damages in the absence of any malice or ill will toward the students. The court of appeals reversed the decision, and the case was then appealed to the Supreme Court.

The school board members presented a powerful defense. Under the common law, they argued, school board members were immune from damage lawsuits (civil actions) for their acts, so long as they acted in their official capacity. If it were otherwise, few people would want to serve in these positions, which offer little or no monetary compensation. To allow students to sue school board members in a civil action for damages for harm resulting from their decisions would create chaos in the school and would lead to an abdication of decision making for fear of lawsuits.

What do you think of this line of argument? How would you answer it?

If you are having difficulty thinking of an answer, do not be discouraged. The nine Justices of the Supreme Court also had a difficult time with this case.

Would you apply the ruling in *Goss* v. *Lopez* as a precedent? Are the cases the same, or do you see important differences?

Certainly school officials acting in good faith in pursuance of their official duties deserve consideration. They have to make important decisions based on the evidence brought before them. When a case reaches the courts, however, the judges have to evaluate the decisions of the school officials based on at least two guidelines: whether their decision in this case was made in good faith; and whether there was any malice present in the proceedings.

How would you have ruled, if you had been one of the Justices? What would have been your reasons?

Once again, the Court divided five to four, and the division was the same as in *Goss*. Again Justice White wrote the opinion for the majority and began by stating the rule of law.

Common-law tradition, recognized in our prior decisions, and strong public-policy reasons also lead to a construction of § 1983 [the 1871 Civil Rights law] extending a *qualified good-faith immunity* to school board members from liability for damages under that section. . . . State courts have generally recognized that *such officers should be protected from tort liability under state law for all good-faith, nonmalicious action taken to fulfill their official duties.* [emphasis added]

Observe carefully the wording of the preceding passage. School officials are entitled to a *qualified* immunity, not an *absolute* immunity from lawsuits. Yet some type of immunity for school officials is necessary.

We think there must be a degree of immunity if the work of the schools is to go forward; and, however worded, the immunity must be such that public school officials understand that action taken in the good-faith fulfillment of their responsibilities and within the bounds of reason under all the circumstances will not be punished and that they need not exercise their discretion with undue timidity.

What do you think the Court means by "good faith," "tort liability," "immunity," "nonmalicious," and "official duties"? [Keep these terms in mind as you read the excerpts from this opinion and the opinion in the *Carey v. Piphus* case on pp. 192–194.

Suppose, however, that a school official is acting in good faith, without malice, and yet makes a decision which violates a student's constitutional rights. Is there liability here? Justice White replied:

The official himself must be acting sincerely and with a belief that he is doing right, *but an act violating a student's constitutional rights can be no more justified by ignorance or disregard of settled, indisputable law on the part of one entrusted with supervision of students' daily lives than by the presence of actual malice.* . . . A school board member, who has voluntarily undertaken the task of supervising the operation of the school and the activities of the students, must be held to *a standard of conduct based not only on permissible intentions, but also on knowledge of the basic, unquestioned constitutional rights of his charges.* Such a standard neither imposes an unfair burden upon a person assuming a responsible public office requiring a high degree of intelligence and judgment for the proper fulfillment of its duties, nor an unwarranted burden in light of the value which civil rights have in our legal system. Any lesser standard would deny much of the promise of § 1983 [the 1871 Civil Rights law]. Therefore, in the specific context of school discipline, we hold that a school board member is not immune from liability for damages under § 1983 if *he knew or reasonably should have known that the action he took within his sphere of official responsibility would violate the constitutional rights of the student affected, or if he took the action with the malicious intention to cause a deprivation of constitutional rights or other injury to the student.* That is not to say that school board members are "charged with predicting the future course of constitutional law." . . . A compensatory award will be appropriate only if the school board member has acted with such an impermissible motivation or with such disregard of the student's clearly established constitutional rights that his action cannot reasonably be characterized as being in good faith. [emphasis added]

Since the lower court had not clearly decided the issue of whether there had been a violation of due process of law in the first or the second hearing, the case was sent back to the court of appeals to decide that issue. If such a violation had taken place, the 1871 Civil Rights Law had been infringed and the school board members could be held liable for money damages.

The four dissenting Justices were the same as in the *Goss* case, and once again Justice Powell answered Justice White and the majority. His dissenting opinion condemned the majority ruling because it punished school officials who acted in good faith, and equated ignorance of the law with actual malice. Good faith is no longer good enough to ensure immunity; what is now required of school officials is "knowledge of the basic, unquestioned constitutional rights" of the students. But, Justice Powell declared, this standard set by the majority is unreasonable, because not even Justices of the Supreme Court can agree on what is "settled, indisputable law." He used the following arguments to attack the majority ruling:

The Court states the standard of required knowledge in two cryptic phrases: "settled, indisputable law" and "unquestioned constitutional rights." Presumably these are intended to mean the same thing, although the meaning of neither phrase is likely to be self-evident to constitutional law scholars—much less the average school board member. One need only look to the decisions of this Court—to our reversals, our recognition of evolving concepts, and our five-to-four splits—to recognize the hazard of even informed prophecy as to what are "unquestioned constitutional rights." Consider, for example, the recent five-to-four decision in *Goss* v. *Lopez* . . . holding that a junior high school pupil routinely suspended for as much as a single day is entitled to due process. I suggest that most lawyers and judges would have thought, prior to that decision, that the law to the contrary was settled, indisputable, and unquestioned.

As in the *Goss* case, Justice Powell concluded with an observation concerning the practical implications of the new ruling for American education.

There are some 20,000 school boards, each with five or more members, and thousands of school superintendents and school principals. Most of the school board members are popularly elected, drawn from the citizenry at large, and possess no unique competency in divining the law. Few cities and counties provide any compensation for service on school boards, and often it is difficult to persuade qualified persons to assume the burdens of this important function in our society. Moreover, even if counsel's advice constitutes a defense, it may safely be assumed that few school boards and school officials have ready access to counsel or indeed have deemed it necessary to consult counsel on the countless decisions that necessarily must be made in the operation of our public schools.

In view of today's decision significantly enhancing the possibility of personal liability, one must wonder whether qualified persons will continue in the desired numbers to volunteer for service in public education. [emphasis added]

Once again the dissenters express alarm at the possible consequences of the majority ruling. What do you think of their criticism?

CAREY v. PIPHUS
Can a student suspended without due process collect damages from school officials?

Now that you have read and understood the rulings in *Goss* v. *Lopez* and *Wood* v. *Strickland*, you should be able to apply these two precedents to the following case. The events took place in Chicago during the 1973–74 school year.

Jarius Piphus, a high school student, and another student were standing outside the school on school property and were passing between them "an irregularly shaped cigarette." The principal approached them unnoticed and smelled what he believed to be the odor of marijuana. When the students saw the principal, they threw the cigarette away. The students were taken to the disciplinary office, where they were given the usual 20-day suspension for violating the school rule against the use of drugs. The students argued that they had not been smoking drugs. A meeting was subsequently arranged which was attended by Piphus's mother and sister, school officials, and a representative from a legal aid clinic. The purpose of this meeting was to explain the reason for the suspension, not to determine whether the boys had been smoking marijuana.

Silas Brisco, a sixth-grade student, came to school wearing one small earring. The principal of the school had issued a rule against the wearing of earrings by boys because he believed that this practice denoted gang membership and could be used to terrorize other students. Brisco maintained that the earring was a symbol of black pride, and he refused to remove it. He argued that the no-earring rule violated his freedom of expression guaranteed under the Fourteenth Amendment. His mother supported him, despite the threat by the school administrator to impose a twenty-day suspension. Brisco was suspended.

Both students, with their mothers acting as guardians for the purpose of the lawsuits, took their case to court. They sued the General Superintendent of Schools of Chicago and the members of the Chicago Board of Education.

On what grounds could they sue?

They brought their lawsuit under the old Civil Rights Act of 1871, which was also the basis of the *Wood* suit (pages 188–192). That law, as we have seen, sought to protect citizens from being deprived of the "rights, privileges, and immunities secured by the Constitution." Any citizen deprived of these rights could initiate a tort action against the person who had violated this law.

A tort action for a civil wrong (a wrongful act which is not a crime) generally asks for the payment of money damages for the injury caused by the act. Ordinarily people sue for compensatory damages; that is, they seek to recover for the actual harm done to them. They may also ask for punitive damages, a greater amount which serves as a punishment or warning that the wrong should not be committed again. In this case, the students sued for both compensatory and punitive damages: Piphus sued for $3,000 and Brisco for $5,000. In asking for punitive damages, they were requesting the court to punish the wrongdoers by imposing a severe penalty. In addition, they asked for an injunction [an order from the court commanding the superintendent and school board to lift the suspension] against the suspensions.

If you were the attorney for the students, how would you argue? What constitutional arguments would you present?

You could show that there had been no hearings in accordance with the due process of law requirement of the Fourteenth Amendment. Of course, it should be noted that the events in the *Piphus* and *Brisco* cases took place before the Court ruled on the *Goss* and *Wood* cases. But that does not excuse a violation of an individual's constitutional rights.

You could also develop the argument that the school officials should have known that a lengthy suspension without a hearing to determine the facts relating to guilt or innocence violates procedural due process, and that they are therefore not entitled to immunity.

Or you could take the position that the denial of a constitutional right, such as a due process hearing, causes harm to the individual and to society. You could also maintain that mental and emotional distress is the by-product of an unfair suspension.

If you were the attorney for the school officials, how would you answer these powerful arguments?

You might have to concede that there had been a violation of the due process rights of the students. Having agreed that a mistake had been made, however, where do you go from here? You could promise for your clients not to do it again. But how do you handle the matter of damages? You could ask the students to show or prove in court the actual damages that they have suffered.

On appeal in the United States District Court (remember, a federal issue—a constitutional right—is involved, so the case may be heard in federal court), the district court ruled that the students' rights had been violated but refused to award damages. The United States Court of Appeals decided that the students were entitled to "nonpunitive damages" even if the suspensions could be justified and even if they could not prove actual damages because of the denial of due process of law. The school officials then appealed to the Supreme Court.

Now let us look at the Supreme Court's unanimous opinion. This time Justice Powell spoke for a unanimous Court, with Justice Blackmun taking no part in the case. A suspension can be justified, said the Court, and yet at the same time it can involve a denial of due process of law because of the lack of a proper hearing. When this occurs, the person whose legal rights have been violated is entitled to damages for injuries. If the injured party has suffered mental or emotional distress because of the denial of due process of law, the remedy available is damages to compensate for suffering.

However—and here is the nub of the Court's ruling—the damages cannot be taken for granted. They must be proven in court. In this case, the students failed to show that they had suffered actual damages because of the school's failure to hold proper hearings. In such a case, the Court held, the students were entitled to recover nominal damages not to exceed one dollar.

What do you think of this judgment? Was it fair? Keep in mind that the decision was unanimous. How do you think this ruling will affect future actions against school officials?

---

21 CORPORAL PUNISHMENT

The Bible says that "foolishness is bound up in the heart of a child, but the rod of correction shall drive it far from him." Since before Biblical times, the "rod of correction" has been used to punish, discipline, and educate children. "Spare the rod and spoil the child" has been a popular maxim for parents and teachers.

So long as educators were considered to stand *in loco parentis* they had the authority to impose physical punishment on their students. The common law supported this practice, and today only Massachusetts and New Jersey prohibit it. All the other states either have laws permitting moderate corporal punishment or follow the common law rule.

It was inevitable, in view of the *Goss* and *Wood* opinions, that the Supreme Court would be confronted with this sensitive issue. On April 19, 1978, the decision was finally handed down.

INGRAHAM v. WRIGHT

Is corporal punishment cruel and unusual?

James Ingraham and Roosevelt Andrews were students at Drew Junior High School in Dade County, Florida. The state law, as well as the local school board regulation, permitted corporal punishment under certain conditions. It could not be "degrading or unduly severe"; it could not be inflicted before consulting the principal or teacher in charge; the paddling had to be on the buttocks; the paddle had to be less than two feet long, three to four inches wide, and about one-half inch thick; and the normal punishment consisted of one to five licks or blows. It was under this law that the boys were paddled.

Ingraham received more than twenty licks with the paddle for being slow in leaving the stage of the auditorium when ordered to do so by his teacher. The injury was so severe, according to the Court's account, that the boy required medical attention for the bruises on his body, and he remained out of school for eleven days.

Andrews had been paddled several times for such offenses as being late to class, making noise, fooling around, and not having his tennis shoes for gym class. On two occasions, according to the Court's opinion, he was struck on the arms; and at one time he lost the use of one arm for a week.

Other students also testified at the trial about beatings received and injuries suffered. Some said that they had received as many as fifty licks.

Through their parents, Ingraham and Andrews filed a complaint in the United States District Court on January 7, 1971. They sued Willie J. Wright, the principal of the school; two of his assistant principals; and the superintendent of schools of Dade County. They

In 1970 school officials in Florida disciplined James Ingraham, seen here in 1977, by swatting him with a wooden paddle. This action led to the case of *Ingraham* v. *Wright*.

asked the court to award them damages for their injuries and an injunction requiring the school officials to refrain from using corporal punishment on all students in Dade County.

On what grounds could the students sue the school officials? After all, corporal punishment was authorized by state law. Is there a constitutional issue involved here?

The student-plaintiffs based their case on violation of their constitutional rights, arguing that corporal punishment was cruel and unusual punishment outlawed by the Eighth and Fourteenth Amendments. In addition, they claimed that failure to give notice and hold a hearing prior to the punishment are violations of the due process clause of the Fourteenth Amendment.

If you were a school administrator, how would you reply to this line of reasoning? Do you think being punished without prior notice and a hearing is a denial of due process?

You could point out that forty-eight states sanction corporal punishment. Troublemakers set bad examples, and unless they are controlled, the school atmosphere can become chaotic. With discipline lax in many homes and in many schools, corporal punishment is an effective way of disciplining students and maintaining a learning environment in the school.

You could also argue that hearings are not so necessary here as they are in suspension or expulsion cases. Corporal punishment leaves temporary marks, while suspensions and expulsions leave permanent marks on a student's record.

Each state has the police power necessary to protect the lives, health, morals, welfare, and safety of its people. When a state delegates some of this power to its school officials, it is acting in the best interests of the children, the parents, and the people of the state.

How do we settle this conflict of values? It is agreed that the students were severely beaten. Does this create a constitutional issue? Perhaps they ought to sue the officials who injured them without trying to convert their situation into a constitutional case. What do you think? How would you vote on this issue?

Once again, we have a five-to-four decision. This time, Justice Powell, who had written the minority opinions in the *Goss* and *Wood* cases, spoke for the majority. The opinion, concurred in by Chief Justice Burger and Justices Blackmun, Rehnquist, and Stewart, began with a historical look at the use of corporal punishment.

The use of corporal punishment in this country as a means of disciplining school children dates back to the colonial period. It has survived the transformation of primary and secondary education from the colonials' reliance on optional private arrangements to our present system of compulsory education and dependence on public schools. Despite the general abandonment of corporal punishment as a means of punishing criminal offenders, the practice continues to play a role in the public education of school children in most parts of the country. Professional and public opinion is sharply divided on the practice, and has been for more than a century. Yet we can discern no trend toward its elimination.

At common law a single principle has governed the use of corporal punishment since before the American Revolution: teachers may impose reasonable but not excessive force to discipline a child . . . The basic doctrine has not changed. The prevalent rule in this country today privileges such force as a teacher or administrator "reasonably believes to be necessary for [the child's] proper control, training, or education." . . . *To the extent that the force is excessive or unreasonable, the educator in virtually all States is subject to possible civil and criminal liability.*

Although the early cases viewed the authority of the teacher as deriving from the parents, the concept of parental delegation has

Spare the rod and . . .

In the nineteenth century, students toed the line—or else.

Cynthia A. Kelly

"We observe with pain an increasing spirit of insubordination in some of our schools, cherished, as we believe, by many parents who advocate the doctrine that corporal punishment ought to be totally discarded."

Does this sound like something from an editorial you read recently? It might have been written last week, but it was actually part of an 1836 report by the Massachusetts Teachers Association. The debate about using corporal punishment in schools is clearly nothing new.

In colonial times and the early 1800's, corporal punishment was widely accepted. Flogging was a standard practice under the civil law of Egypt, Rome, and England, and was also countenanced by certain religious sects. In the United States, corporal punishment was common in military discipline.

In schools, corporal punishment was the cornerstone of discipline. Scenes such as the following were typical: A new teacher seized a long rod by both ends, and lifting it high over his head, said fiercely, as his first words to his class: "Do you see that rod? Would you like to *feel* it? If you would, just break any of the 49 rules I'm going to read to you!"

Flogging became such a routine way of handling discipline problems that in one Massachusetts school (with 250 students) there were 328 floggings in one week, or an average of more than 65 each day. . . .

The teacher who wouldn't administer corporal punishment was also likely to find himself unemployed. As one commentator warned in the 1850's, "no man can long satisfy the demand of the school, or satisfy the public around him, whatever else his qualifications may be, if he is not able to govern his school." . . .

By the mid-1800's, educational reformers who were appalled by the all too frequent instances of cruelty in the schools began to campaign against corporal punishment. Reformers like Horace Mann, Secretary of the Massachusetts Board of Education, proposed to limit the teacher's power to inflict such punishments.

As a result of pressure for reform, school committees in cities across the country passed regulations limiting the use of corporal punishment in schools. These regulations didn't outlaw corporal punishment, but rather set up guidelines designed to limit abuses. For example, a Brooklyn regulation in 1867 specified that "corporal punishment shall be resorted to only in cases of persistent misconduct, after failure of all other reasonable means of persuasion." . . .

Teachers' manuals also reflected the changes in attitude and law by recommending that corporal punishment never be administered in anger or in front of other pupils, that an adult witness should be present, that the parents' consent be attained beforehand if possible, and that a record be made listing the offense, type of punishment, and the time and manner of its infliction. . . .

Today, school discipline still ranks as a major concern of not only teachers and administrators, but increasingly of students who are victims of disruptive and

Source: Adapted from Update *(Fall 1977), pp. 16–17. Reprinted from* Update on Law-Related Education, *a magazine published by the American Bar Association.*

Corporal punishment was often used in public schools in the nineteenth century to enforce discipline.

violent acts in the school. The debates about the necessity of corporal punishment which raged in the middle of the last century thus continue to the present day, and we still seem very close to the position set forth in a treatise on school government written over 100 years ago: "This is corporal punishment. Now is this desirable, or admissible, or necessary? We answer that it is not desirable. But it is admissible and necessary in a system of school government."

been replaced by the view—more consonant with compulsory education laws—that the State itself may impose such corporal punishment as is reasonably necessary for the proper education of the child and for the maintenance of group discipline." . . . All of the circumstances are to be taken into account in determining whether the punishment is reasonable in a particular case. Among the most important considerations are the seriousness of the offense, the attitude and past behavior of the child, the nature and severity of the punishment, the age and strength of the child, and the availability of less severe but equally effective means of discipline. [emphasis added]

Justice Powell then examined the history of the Eighth Amendment's prohibition against cruel and unusual punishments. He concluded that it was the historical intent to protect those convicted of crimes and that it was not meant to and "does not apply to the paddling of children as a means of maintaining discipline in public schools."

Does this interpretation afford greater protection to a criminal than to a student in school? Justice Powell faced this question by differentiating the situation of a prisoner, who can be the victim of brutality, from that of the student.

The schoolchild has little need for the protection of the Eighth Amendment. Though attendance may not always be voluntary, the public school remains an open institution. Except perhaps when very young, the child is not physically restrained from leaving school during school hours; and at the end of the school day, the child is invariably free to return home. Even while at school, the child brings with him the support of family and friends and is rarely apart from teachers and other pupils who may witness and protest any instances of mistreatment.

The openness of the public school and its supervision by the community afford significant safeguards against the kinds of abuses from which the Eighth Amendment protects the prisoner. In virtually every community where corporal punishment is permitted in the schools, these safeguards are reinforced by the legal constraints of the common law. Public school teachers and administrators are privileged at common law to inflict only such corporal punishment as is reasonably necessary for the proper education and discipline of the child; *any punishment going beyond the privilege may result in both civil and criminal liability* . . . As long as the schools are open to public scrutiny, there is no reason to believe that the common law constraints will not effectively remedy and deter excesses such as those alleged in this case.

We conclude that when public school teachers or administrators impose disciplinary corporal punishment, the Eighth Amendment is inapplicable. The pertinent constitutional question is whether the imposition is consistent with the requirements of due process. [emphasis added]

Do you agree or disagree with this line of reasoning? What do you think of the emphasized portions?

Justice Powell turned to the second constitutional issue: Does the Fourteenth Amendment's due process clause apply to this case? Once again he looked to history for the answer. The amendment prohibits the state from depriving a person of life, liberty, or property without due process of law. What was it intended to mean?

The Due Process Clause of the Fifth Amendment, later incorporated into the Fourteenth, was intended to give Americans at least the protection against governmental power that they had enjoyed as Englishmen against the power of the Crown. The liberty preserved from deprivation without due process included the right "generally to enjoy those privileges long recognized at common law as essential to the orderly pursuit of happiness by free men." Among the historic liberties so protected was a right to be free from and to obtain judicial relief, for unjustified intrusions on personal security.

While the contours of this historic liberty interest in the context of our federal system of government have not been defined precisely, they have always been thought to encompass freedom from bodily restraint and punishment. It is fundamental that the state cannot hold and physically punish an individual except in accordance with due process of law.

This constitutionally protected liberty interest is at stake in this case. *There is, of course, a* de minimis *level of imposition with which the Constitution is not concerned.* But at least where school authorities, acting under color of state law, deliberately decide to punish a child for misconduct by restraining the child and inflicting appreciable physical pain, we hold that Fourteenth Amendment liberty interests are implicated. [emphasis added]

If a student about to be punished by school officials has a liberty interest, what protective procedures are available? The answer offered by the majority is quite complex and somewhat surprising.

Justice Powell's opinion repeated that moderate corporal punishment is permissible under the common law and that present-day state laws accentuate the need for moderation. Since teachers usually paddle students for offenses committed in their presence, there is little chance of their being mistaken about the offense and there is no serious violation of the rights of the students.

If the punishment is excessive, unjustified, or malicious, civil or criminal proceedings are available to the injured party. The common law remedy of damages, as well as criminal prosecutions, should discourage abuse of the common law right to punish students. The Florida penal code made malicious punishment of a child a felony.

Granted that this is so, would not the student's liberty interest be better protected if, in addition to these common law remedies, he or she had the safeguard of prior notice and a hearing? Justice Powell answered by asking us to weigh the benefits of such additional procedures with the administrative costs involved.

Such a universal constitutional requirement would significantly burden the use of corporal punishment as a disciplinary measure. Hearings—even informal hearings—require time, personnel, and a diversion of attention from normal school pursuits. School authorities may well choose to abandon corporal punishment rather than incur the burdens of complying with the procedural requirements. Teachers, properly concerned with maintaining authority in the classroom, may well prefer to rely on other disciplinary measures—which they may view as less effective—rather than confront the possible disruption that prior notice and a hearing may entail. . . . *We are reviewing here a legislative judgment, rooted in history and reaffirmed in the laws of many States, that corporal punishment serves important educational interests.* This judgment must be viewed in light of the disciplinary problems common-place in the schools. . . . Assessment of the need for, and the appropriate means of maintaining, school discipline is committed generally to the discretion of school authorities subject to state law. [emphasis added]

Corporal punishment "serves important educational interests," says Justice Powell. How would you answer this argument?

"At some point the benefit of an additional safeguard to the individual affected . . . and to society in terms of increased assurance that the action is just, may be outweighed by the cost." . . . We think that point has been reached in this case. In view of the low incidence of abuse, the openness of our schools, and the common law safeguards that already exist, the risk of error that may result in violation of a schoolchild's substantive rights can only be regarded as minimal. Imposing additional administrative safeguards as a constitutional requirement might reduce that risk marginally, but would also entail a significant intrusion into an area of primary educational responsibility. We conclude that the Due Process Clause does not require notice and a hearing prior to the imposition of corporal punishment in the public schools, as that practice is authorized and limited by the common law.

Why does Justice Powell oppose notice and a hearing prior to corporal punishment? Explain why you agree or disagree.

The majority opinion concluded:

Petitioners cannot prevail on either of the theories before us in this case. The Eighth Amendment's prohibition against cruel and unusual punishments is inapplicable to school paddlings, and the Fourteenth Amendment's requirement of procedural due process is satisfied by Florida's preservation of common law constraints and remedies. We therefore agree with the Court of Appeals that petitioners' evidence affords no basis for injunctive relief, and that petitioners cannot recover damages on the basis of any Eighth Amendment or procedural due process violation.

This time Justice White, who had spoken for the majority in the *Goss* and *Wood* cases, wrote the opinion for the minority. Justices Brennan, Marshall, and Stevens joined him. He began by pointing out that the Eighth Amendment places "a flat prohibition against the infliction" of cruel and unusual punishment. It does not limit its scope to criminal cases. It reflected "a societal judgment that there are some punishments that are so barbaric and inhumane that we will not permit them to be imposed on anyone, no matter how opprobrious the offense." He went on to say:

If there are some punishments that are so barbaric that they may not be imposed for the commission of crimes, designated by our social system as the most thoroughly reprehensible acts an individual can commit, then . . . similar punishments may not be imposed on persons for less culpable acts, such as breaches of school discipline. Thus, *if it is constitutionally impermissible to cut off someone's ear for the commission of murder, it must be unconstitutional to cut off a child's ear for being late to class. Although there were no ears cut off in this case, the record reveals beatings so severe that if they were inflicted on a hardened criminal for the commission of a serious crime, they might not pass constitutional muster.*

No one can deny that spanking of school children is "punishment" under any reasonable reading of the word, for the similarities between spanking in public schools and other forms of punishment are too obvious to ignore. *Like other forms of punishment, spanking of school children involves an institutionalized response to the violation of some official rule or regulation proscribing certain conduct and is imposed for the purpose of rehabilitating the offender, deterring the offender and others like him from committing the violation in the future, and inflicting some measure of social retribution for the harm that has been done.* [emphasis added]

Justice White expressed concern about the severity of the beatings. Why do you think he used the terms "rehabilitating," "deterring," and "social retribution"?

Justice White attacked the majority's position that schoolchildren do not need the protection of the Eighth Amendment. Assuming that schools are open institutions, as the majority suggested, and are subject to public study does not mean that school children are not entitled to the protection of the Constitution, he said. Granting the children civil and criminal remedies against abusive treatment does not preclude their right to constitutional protection. Either the Eighth Amendment applies or it does not. It cannot apply only to prisoners or only to persons who cannot bring a civil suit, while leaving everyone else unprotected. The issue is whether the "punishment is so barbaric and inhumane that it goes beyond the tolerence of civilized society." If it does, it is cruel and unusual and the Eighth Amendment applies, regardless of the openness of the schools or the availability of legal remedies.

The dissenters concluded this part of their opinion with this important observation:

The issue presented in this phase of the case is limited to whether corporal punishment in public schools can ever be prohibited by the Eighth Amendment. I am therefore not suggesting that spanking in the public schools is in every instance prohibited by the Eighth Amendment. My own view is that it is not. I only take issue with the extreme view of the majority that corporal punishment in public schools, no matter how barbaric, inhumane, or severe, is never limited by the Eighth Amendment. Where corporal punishment becomes so severe as to be unacceptable in a civilized society, I can see no reason that it should become any more acceptable just because it is inflicted on children in the public schools. [emphasis added]

They then turned to the due process argument. The majority conceded that students had a liberty interest to be free from "bodily restraint and punishment" involving "appreciable physical pain" arising out of corporal punishment. This liberty interest is protected by the Fourteenth Amendment's due process clause. The question is, What is the actual process due to the student? The majority answered that the fact that the student could sue for damages if the punishment was "excessive" amounted to due process under the common law.

Justice White attacked this position on two grounds. First, the right to sue for damages applies only to excessive punishment, not to punishment given in error. If school authorities, acting in good faith but on mistaken information, inflict "moderate" punishment on a student for an act he or she did not commit, there is no cause for action. In the second place, even if the student could sue, the lawsuit would follow the punishment. "The infliction of physical pain is final and irreparable it cannot be undone in a subsequent proceeding," he said.

This approach, Justice White said, would lead to strange results.

The majority's conclusion that a damage remedy for excessive corporal punishment affords adequate process rests on the novel theory that the State may punish an individual without giving him any opportunity to present his side of the story, as long as he can later recover damages from a state official if he is innocent. The logic of this theory would permit a State that punished speeding with a one-day jail sentence to make a driver serve his sentence first without a trial and then sue to recover damages for wrongful imprisonment. Similarily, the State could finally take away a prisoner's good time credits for alleged disciplinary infractions and require him to bring a damage suit after he was eventually released. There is no authority for this theory, nor does the majority purport to find any, in the procedural due process decisions of this Court. Those cases have "consistently held that *some kind of hearing is required at some time before a person is finally deprived* of his property interests . . . [and that] a person's liberty is equally protected. . . ." [emphasis added]

According to Justice White, it is a denial of due process to allow "the State to punish first and hear the sudent's version of events later." He cited the *Goss* case, in which, writing for the majority, he had said that due process required prior to suspension "an informal give-and-take between student and disciplinarian" which gives the student "an opportunity to explain his version of the facts" as a "meaningful hedge" against wrongful punishment. He insisted that this same requirement should apply prior to physical punishment.

Justice White disagreed with the majority's view that such "rudimentary precautions" as a hearing and notice of charges would impose such great burdens on the administrators and teachers that the disciplinary process would be significantly and adversely affected. Quoting from the dissent in *Goss*, he wrote

The disciplinarian need only take a few minutes to give the student "notice of the charges against him and, if he denies them, an explanation of the evidence the authorities have and an opportunity to present his side of the story." . . . In this context the Constitution requires, "if anything, less than a fair-minded principal would impose upon himself" in order to avoid injustice.

22 QUESTIONS ANSWERED AND QUESTIONS RAISED

The Supreme Court has a way of answering some questions in important cases and, at the same time, raising other questions which, in turn, call for new or different answers. For example, the rule of law declared in *Goss* v. *Lopez* requires minimal due process of law in suspensions of ten days or less: a hearing prior to the suspension, notice of the charges and of the nature of the testimony and evidence against the student, and an opportunity to refute the charges. In longer suspensions, there may be the necessity of more formal hearings, including cross-examination of witnesses and the presence of an attorney. In emergencies or severe disciplinary cases, the suspension may precede the hearing, but the hearing must be held as soon as is practicable after the suspension. In all suspensions, the principal may provide protections beyond these minimal due process of law requirements.

Certain questions remain unanswered. When does minimal due process apply? Would it apply to a suspension of half a day? Of one day? Where do we draw the line between a suspension which may be *de minimis* (a minimal deprivation of due process) and one which is a serious deprivation of liberty without due process of law? Isn't it possible that the required hearing may, in reality, be a kangaroo court? In other words, it seems possible that the authorities may have made up their minds about a case before the hearing but go through the proceeding as a mere formality. Obviously this is not what the Court intended, and most educators would not engage in such a practice. But it can happen, and what guarantees are available to prevent it?

The decision in *Wood* v. *Strickland* strengthened the *Goss* rule by holding members of school boards personally liable in money damages for any violation of the established constitutional rights of students. Good faith is no longer an excuse for any members who do not know the "settled indisputable law" requiring due process hearings prior to punishment. Again questions remain unanswered. For example, does liability for damages extend to teachers, principals, and superintendents? Is there any "settled, indisputable law" which school board members must know beyond the due process requirement for hearings prior to decision-making in disciplinary cases?

The *Goss* and *Wood* cases direct our attention to what the law refers to as the capricious, arbitrary, and unreasonable exercise of power by members of school boards and other education officials. If the schools *are* the training grounds of democracy, those who preach democracy, the Court said, should practice it. Accusations of misconduct should be verified so that the innocent will be protected and the wrongdoer will be properly identified and punished.

If supporters of the rights of students were happy with these two cases, the Court subsequently blunted their enthusiasm. Lawsuits are expensive, and to engage in an action and then win only nominal damages of one dollar turns out to be a Pyrrhic victory. According to *Carey* v. *Piphus,* the student must prove actual injuries to the reputation or to the emotional or mental state in order to recover damages. This is not a very easy task in the case of suspensions or expulsions.

Although damages can be shown in some corporal punishment cases, as in *Ingraham* v. *Wright,* the Court ruled that the remedy had to be sought in the state courts. A civil action in tort for damages or a criminal action for malicious punishment or battery may be available.

The significance of the *Ingraham* case is that it leaves the issue of corporal punishment to the states. The majority of five Justices, supporting the state's rights approach to educational affairs, concluded that the states should handle this subject in their own ways. They refused to accept the legal argument that such punishment violated the cruel and unusual punishment provision of the Eighth Amendment. They also denied that the due process procedures of notice and a hearing were applicable to such situations.

Three of the four cases discussed in this section were resolved by five-to-four decisions. Obviously the Justices, like educators and the general public, are not of one mind on these issues. It may very well be that is not the end of the matter. Attempts will be made to reach the Court on issues relating to the conduct of students, board members, and school officials. It will be interesting to see whether the precedents set by such close votes will be sustained. At any event, these rulings are now the law of the land.

CONCLUDING THOUGHTS

The history of American Freedom is, in no small measure, the history of procedure.

Frankfurter in Malinowski *v.* New York,
324 U.S. 401, 414 (1945)

Procedure is to law what scientific method is to science.

Foster, Social Work, the Law and Social Action
in Social Casework, July 1964, pp. 383, 386

Justice, it has been said, is a gut feeling. We seem to feel that an act is unjust. Our glands react, suggests Edmund Cahn in *The Sense of Injustice,* even before our minds can think about it. There are certain things that we do not find acceptable: Convicting an accused without a fair trial; sentencing juveniles before they can present an adequate defense; suspending or expelling students from school without an opportunity to defend themselves against the charges; and imposing the death sentence without considering mitigating circumstances. The consciences of those who seek justice have breathed life into the phrase, due process of law. The result has been the creation of principles of law which define fair procedures designed to lead to what is popularly referred to as a fair trial or hearing and a just verdict.

The idea of justice has been a major concern of thinking men and women from the dawn of history. The opening words of King Hammurabi's Code of Laws proclaimed:

Law and Justice I established in the land, I made happy the human race in those days.

This concern with law and justice is evidenced in the history of the Jews, the Greeks, the Romans, medieval thinkers, and modern and contemporary philosophers. Moses is associated with the Ten Commandments. Plato's great book, *The Republic,* focuses on the just individual and the just society. Aristotle, another great Greek thinker, warned:

Man, when perfected, is the best of animals, but when separated from law and justice, he is the worst of all.

During the Middle Ages, this warning was heeded. It was in the year 1215 that the barons of England confronted King John with the

209

Magna Carta—the Great Charter—which has been cherished as a milestone on the road to human rights. Among the sixty-three chapters of this document limiting the powers of the English kings were two that have exerted an enduring influence on those concerned with the idea of justice as due process of law:

Chapter Thirty-Nine

No Freemen shall be taken or (and) imprisoned or disseised or exiled or in any way destroyed, nor will we go upon him nor send upon him, except by the lawful judgment of his peers or (and) by the law of the land.

Chapter Forty

To no one will we sell, to no one will we refuse or delay, right or justice.*

The charters and constitutions of colonial America, as well our Constitution and the Bill of Rights, echo these ideals.

THE CRIME CONTROL MODEL AND THE DUE PROCESS MODEL

The Due Process Model of Justice, which has been examined in this book in considerable detail, has not gone unchallenged in recent years. The tidal wave of criminal activity among adults and juveniles has aroused public debate over our methods of detection, apprehension, and prosecution of lawbreakers. Has the Due Process Model led to the "handcuffing of the police" and the "coddling of criminals" as has been claimed? What is the alternative that the critics of the Due Process Model offer us?

Herbert Packer in his book, *The Limits of the Criminal Sanction*, constructs the Crime Control Model as an alternative. The goal of the Crime Control Model is to suppress crime by placing a premium on police efficiency and judicial speed and finality. The "assembly-line conveyor belt" becomes the metaphor, with emphasis on "quantitative output." If the police and the prosecutors have probable cause to believe that the accused is guilty, it is important to "get the show on the road" as soon as possible so that the guilty can be punished. The presumption is one of guilt and "legal technicalities" are not to be permitted to interfere with the "management" of the system.

According to Packer, the Due Process Model, on the other hand, is like an "obstacle course" in which the adversary system and the presumption of innocence force the prosecution to prove "legal guilt." Since "things are not always what they seem to be," formal

*Samuel E. Thorne et al. The Great Charter. *New York: Random House, 1965. p. 132.*

fact-finding is necessary to avoid the possibility of factual error. What are "legal technicalities" to some are the fundamental rights of the accused to others. The protection of the accused is the major objective here, while the protection of society against crime is the intent of the supporters of the Crime Control Model.

Since each of these models represents a different set of American values, is it possible to have both? Are they mutually exclusive, or is there any way of meshing them into a pattern where we can have the best of each of the models?

The sociologist Jerome Skolnick, in *Justice Without Trial*, has translated the Packer models into the *work ethic* and the *legal ethic*. From the standpoint of the police officer on duty, there is a never-ending dilemma. He or she is hired to apprehend criminals with all possible speed, but the work ethic says you should do the job for which you were trained. However, surrounding all of the officer's movements is the legal ethic. As soon as he or she begins a criminal investigation, the legal ethic with its due process of law principles, comes into play. It is as though society says to the police "Full speed ahead" and then warns them "Not so fast."

The Due Process Model and the Crime Control Model, as well as the legal ethic and the work ethic, represent American value systems. We ask of the state policies designed to protect our lives, health, morals, welfare, and safety. At the same time we expect the state to respect the principles of the Bill of Rights. When the state's police power and the individual's right to due process of law find themselves on a collision course, a choice has to be made. Which is to be given priority?

For many, due process of law has come to mean a series of technicalities which enable a criminal to escape punishment. For others, due process has come to mean concern for the dignity of the individual. Those who try to modify due process procedures must keep in mind that they were developed over centuries by men and women who protested the authoritarian and totalitarian policies of governments. Due process of law was the weapon used against arbitrary, capricious, and unreasonable acts by government officials. It represents an ideal in which, in reality, may permit some criminals to escape their just deserts, but which also protects the innocent. Principles which developed in response to serious needs and which took so many years to become part of our value system should not be changed lightly. It is easy to turn the clock back to the practices of the past, but it is easier to retain a precious heritage than to restore it.

The Anatomy of a Criminal Case: The Record of *Mapp* v. *Ohio*

The people are not made for courts, but courts for people; and yet a court sitting at the top of a great ladder, deciding only a few cases a year chosen on the basis of their general importance, must keep its eye on the whole picture as well as on the particular case.

John P. Frank. *The Marble Palace*, p. 148

Justice is truth in action.

Benjamin Disraeli

For me the background is respect for that privision of the Bill of Rights which is central to the enjoyment of the other guarantees of the Bill of Rights. How can there be freedom of thought or freedom of speech or freedom of religion, if the police can, without warrant, search your home and mine from garret to cellar merely because they are executing a warrant of arrest? How can men feel free if all their papers can be searched, as an incident to the arrest of someone in the house, on the chance that something may turn up, rather, be turned up?

Justice Felix Frankfurter,
dissenting in *Harris* v. *United States*,
331 U.S. at 163 (1947)

When the Supreme Court of the United States hands down an opinion, only the tip of the judicial process is visible. Long before a case reaches the highest court, there is much activity in the lower courts.

When the nine Justices sit down to decide a case, how do they know what the facts are? Where do they learn about the actual trial with its examination of witnesses and the judge's charge to the jury? How do they know what the lower courts decided and the reasons for their rulings.?

On June 19, 1961, the Supreme Court handed down its decision in the case of Mapp v. Ohio. When the Justices met in their conference room prior to announcing their decision, they had the transcript of the trial and other documents, which were the principal sources of information that the Justices used in deciding this important case.

All the documents that follow have been reproduced as originally written with minor editorial changes. Inconsistencies in the original documents, such as the spelling of Mrs. Mapp's first name, have been retained.

Document 1

The Arraignment

This document sets out the charge against Dollree Mapp; she was informed of the charge against her at the arraignment before a judge in examining court.

IN CLEVELAND MUNICIPAL COURT
Examining Court

THE STATE OF OHIO,
CUYAHOGA COUNTY, ss.:

———

THE STATE OF OHIO

CHARGE

Poss. of Obscene Pictures & Books

Defendant arrested on a warrant founded on an affidavit charging Dollree Mapp with Poss. of Obscene Pictures & Books as therein set forth; said affidavit being made before the Clerk of this Court, by Michael Haney on the 25 day of May A. D. 1957.

Warrant returned on the 27 day of May A. D. 1957, by FRANK T. KELLY, Bailiff of Cleveland Municipal Court, with the body of the defendant and after the examination before Andrew Kovachy Judge of the Court, it is ordered and required of the said defendant that he furnish bail for his personal appearance at the present term of the Court of Common Pleas of Cuyahoga County on the first day of the term thereof, in the sum of $5000.00 or $2500.00 R.E. dollars, or in default thereof to stand committed.

State of Ohio, City of Cleveland, ss.

I, JOHNNY KILBANE, Clerk of Cleveland Municipal Court, do hereby certify that the foregoing is a true transcript of the proceedings had before the said Court in said cause as fully as the same appears on record.

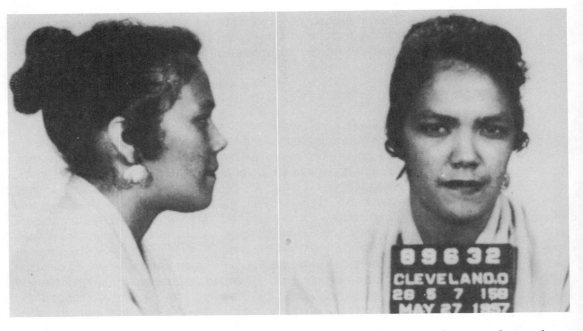

This is the Cleveland police department's mug shot of Mrs. Dollree Mapp that was taken at the time of her arrest on May 27, 1957. The Supreme Court ruled in 1965 that her arrest had resulted from an illegal search and thereby overturned her conviction.

Given under my hand and the seal of said Court this 25 day of June, 1957.

Helen J. Lyons, Clerk of Cleveland Municipal Court.

Document 2

Grand Jury Indictment

Because the crime charged was a felony, a grand jury indictment was necessary.

COURT OF COMMON PLEAS OF CUYAHOGA COUNTY
STATE OF OHIO

INDICTMENT FOR POSSESSION OBSCENE LITERATURE
R C 2905.34—Filed October 8, 1958

THE STATE OF OHIO,
CUYAHOGA COUNTY, ss.:

Of the term of September In the Year of our Lord one thousand nine hundred and fifty seven.

The Jurors of the Grand Jury of the State of Ohio, within and for the body of the County aforesaid, on their oaths, IN THE NAME AND BY THE AUTHORITY OF THE STATE OF OHIO,

Do Find and Present, That Dolly Mapp on or about the 23rd day of May 1957, at the County aforesaid, unlawfully and knowingly had in her possession and under her control, certain lewd and lascivious Books, Pictures and Photographs, said Books, Pictures and Photographs being so indecent and immoral in their nature that the same would be offensive to the Court and improper to be placed upon the records thereof contrary to the form of the statute in such case made and provided, and against the peace and dignity of the State of Ohio.

John T. Corrigan, Prosecuting Attorney.

Document 3

The Ohio Statute under Which the Defendant Was Charged

Pertinent Statutes of the State of Ohio. Section 2905.34 (13035) Selling, exhibiting and possessing obscene literature or drugs, for criminal purposes.

No person shall knowingly sell, lend, give away, exhibit, or offer to sell, lend, give away, or exhibit, or publish or offer to publish or *have in his possession or under his control an obscene, lewd, or lascivious book, magazine, pamphlet, paper, writing, advertisement, circular, print, picture, photograph, motion picture film, or book, pamphlet, paper, magazine not wholly obscene but containing lewd or lascivious articles, advertisements, photographs, or drawings, representation, figure, image, cast, instrument, or articles of an indecent or immoral nature,* . . . .

Whoever violates this section shall be fined not less than two hundred nor more than two thousand dollars or imprisoned not more than seven years, or both. [emphasis added]

Document 4

Motion to Suppress Evidence

A motion to suppress evidence which the defense believes has been illegally seized helps to determine, before the trial has begun, whether the prosecution has sufficient evidence to prove its case. If the motion is granted, this avoids a waste of time and the expense of a trial, since the prosecution may then not have sufficient evidence to proceed.

IN THE COURT OF COMMON PLEAS

Case No. 68326

[Title omitted]

MOTION TO SUPPRESS EVIDENCE—Filed

September 3, 1958

Now comes the defendant by her attorney, A. L. Kearns and moves this honorable court for an order suppressing the evidence procured by the police officers, to wit:

Certain claimed lewd and lascivious Books, Pictures and Photographs and intended to be used in evidence in the trial of the aforesaid cause.

For the reason that the aforesaid evidence was not procured by a proper search warrant as provided by Section 2905.35 of the Ohio Revised Code.

A. L. Kearns, Attorney for Defendant.

NOTICE

The State of Ohio will take notice that the defendant has filed the aforesaid motion and that the same will be set for hearing in Court Room No. 1 of the Court of Common Pleas Criminal Branch in accordance with the rules of said court.

A. L. Kearns, Attorney for Defendant.

[fol. D] Copy of aforesaid motion received this 3rd day of September, 1958.

John T. Corrigan, Prosecuting Attorney. [emphasis added]

Document 5

Transcript of the Pretrial Motion to Suppress

IN THE COURT OF COMMON PLEAS
CRIMINAL BRANCH
No. 68326

———

STATE OF OHIO, Plaintiff,
vs.
DOLLREE MAPP, Defendant.

———

Defendant's Bill of Exceptions

———

State of Ohio,
County of Cuyahoga, *ss.*:
IN THE COURT OF COMMON PLEAS
CRIMINAL BRANCH
No. 68326

STATE OF OHIO, Plaintiff,
vs.
DOLLREE MAPP, Defendant.

———

Be It Remembered That, heretofore, to-wit, on Wednesday, the 3rd day of September, 1958, being one of the regular days of the September, 1958, term of said court, this cause came on for trial before Hon. Donald F. Lybarger, one of the judges of said court, and a jury, in Courtroom No. 1, and the following proceedings were had:

Judge Lybarger, presiding in the Criminal Branch of the Court of Common Pleas, ruled on the defense's motion to suppress evidence prior to trial of the case. He ruled against the motion.

The Court: This is the matter of the State of Ohio versus Dollree Mapp. The defendant and counsel are in court, the prosecutor is in court. I have before me a motion to suppress evidence. Mr. Kearns, you bring that on behalf of the defendant?

Mr. Kearns: Yes. May it please your honor, this motion to suppress the evidence in this case is based upon Section 2905.35 of the Ohio Revised Code, which became effective October 6, 1955 . . . So we say to your honor that it is necessary under these statutes enacted by our legislature, that a search warrant . . . shall issue *warrants* to search such house or place upon written complaint, supported by oath or affirmation, that any person within the jurisdiction of such magistrate or court, has violated or is violating the several sections thereto . . . .

Now we say that the State of Ohio did not have a search warrant setting forth the items that are mentioned in this indictment, and which the State of Ohio intends to use as evidence in this cause against this defendant, and for that reason we are asking that that particular evidence be suppressed.

September 3, 1958: The Court: This cause came on this day for hearing on defendant's motion to suppress evidence, and the court upon hearing overrules the same. [emphasis added]

Document 6

Transcript of the Trial of Dollree Mapp

The prosecution, represented by Mrs. Mahon, begins the trial with direct examination of its first witness: Officer Michael Haney.

Direct examination.

By Mrs. Mahon:

Q. State your name, please.
A. Michael Haney.
Q. Your address?
A. 14026 Berwald Avenue, Cleveland.
Q. Are you a member of the Cleveland police department?
A. I am.
Q. And assigned to what department?
A. The bureau of special investigations.
Q. What is your title?
A. I am a patrolman assigned to the bureau of special investigations.
Q. How long have you been a police officer?
A. Twelve and a half years.
Q. Do you have a partner that you work with, officer?
A. Yes, I have two partners.
Q. What are their names?
A. Sergeant Carl Delau and patrolman Thomas Dever.
Q. Directing your attention to May 23 of last year, 1957, did you and your partners have occasion to go to the home of one Dolly Mapp?
A. Yes, we did.
Q. And where did she live at that time?
A. 14705 Milverton Road, upstairs.
Q. Can you describe that place, officer?
A. It is a two-family brick dwelling, suite down and suite up; there is a front entrance and a side entrance, full basement underneath the premises; there is a living room, kitchen, dinette, two bedrooms and bath on the second floor.

Q. Did she live on the second floor?
A. Yes, she did.
Q. Is that a brick or a frame home?
A. That is a brick home.
Q. Were you with Delau and Dever then?
A. Yes.
Q. About what time did you get out there?
A. About one or one-thirty in the afternoon.
Q. Do you see the Dolly Mapp that you refer to in the courtroom here?
A. Yes, I do.
Q. Will you point her out?
A. She is seated opposite yourself at the table behind Mr. Kearns.

Mrs. Mahon: Indicating the defendant.

Q. Do you know her by any other name?
A. Yes, by Dollree Mapp, or Dollree Bivins.
Q. What was the purpose of you officers in going to her home on that particular day?
A. On that particular day we had received information from a confidential source that there was a person hiding out in the home, who was wanted for questioning in connection with a recent bombing, and that there was a large amount of policy paraphernalia being hidden in the home, either in the basement or the suite on the second floor.
Q. Do you know who occupied the first floor suite?
A. No.
Q. Did you have occasion while you were out there to go into the first floor suite at all?
A. Only to the door of the first floor suite.
Q. After you arrived there what happened?
A. Upon our arrival at the address we rang the bell at the side of the house for the second floor; Mrs. Mapp came to the window and asked us what we wanted. We stated we would like to come in and talk to her, and she stated—first, she wouldn't let us in, and then she stated—after several minutes of conversation she said, "I'll call my attorney, Mr. Green, and see if he thinks I should let you in." She then re-

moved herself from the window and came back and she said "I have been advised by my attorney not to let you in without a search warrant." *A search warrant was brought out after an hour and a half or two hour delay, brought to the premises, and the officers were admitted by Mrs. Mapp from the sidewalk.* [emphasis added]

Q. Then what happened?

A. I remained outside until a considerable length of time, and see that nobody left the premises. After they had been admitted Sergeant Delau called me and said "Come on in." I went to the second floor, where he proceeded to search the second floor of the residence there, and went to the rear bedroom there, which, as we were about to enter, Mrs. Mapp said "This is my room." Mrs. Mapp sat on the bed when Delau proceeded to search the chest of drawers on the left wall as you leave the room. I began searching a dresser which would be located on the rear wall beside the bed in that room. In searching through the dresser I came upon four books. In removing them Mrs. Mapp saw them and said, "Better not look at those; they might excite you." I then looked at the books and found them to be obscene. I further made search of the dresser and found nothing else in that. I searched the suit cases and found a photo album pictures of herself. Among other stuff a pencil drawing on paper of a very obscene nature. Upon showing it to Mrs. Mapp she refused to say anything more about it, offer any more comment, what it was and why it was there.

Q. You say that was in the suit case?

A. That was in the suit case beside the bed in the rear bedroom.

Q. The same bedroom?

A. The same bedroom, yes.

Q. Do you know who that belonged to?

A. Mrs. Mapp stated it was her suitcase. Also in the suitcase we found personal papers with Mrs. Mapp's name on them.

Q. Then what did you do?

A. During this time we were up in the bedroom together, Sergeant Delau found four separate groups of vulgar pictures. We took all the evidence, put it together, conveyed Mrs. Mapp and the stuff to the Central Police Station, and consulted the police prosecutor, and warrant was issued for the arrest of Mrs. Mapp.

Q. Where were the pictures found?

A. In the chest of drawers, the same bedroom in which we had found the other stuff.

Q. Was any other person in that suite at the time you were conducting this search, officer?

A. There were other police officers there.

Q. I mean besides police officers?

A. Not to my knowledge.

Q. Did you have any conversation with Mrs. Mapp as to who occupied her suite?

A. We questioned who occupied her suite, and she said her and her daughter, Barbara, occupied the suite at that particular time, yes.

Q. You said there were two bedrooms?

A. Yes, there were two bedrooms, one coming off the hallway by the bath, bedroom off to the left, which we checked. It had child's clothing, child's paraphernalia, child's room. Directly to the rear of the residence is the room occupied by Mrs. Mapp. She stated at the time the stuff might belong to Morris Jones, who had lived in that room, yet there was no men's clothing, clothing men would have.

Q. There were ladies' clothing in that bedroom?

A. Yes, in that bedroom.

Q. Ladies paraphernalia?

A. Cosmetics, and so forth.

Q. How long were you out there altogether that day?

A. I would say we were out there two and a half or three hours.

Q. Did you have any occasion to go into the basement at that place while you were there?

A. I don't believe I was in the basement at all.

Q. Did any of the other officers go there?

A. Yes, patrolman Dever searched the basement; I don't know whether Sergeant Delau was down there or not.

Q. You say you took Mrs. Mapp into the station then?

A. Yes, we did.

Q. What did you do with those books and pictures, and so forth?

A. They were marked for identification and turned over to the property room at Central Police Station.

Q. This home of Mrs. Mapp's, is that in Cuyahoga County?

A. Yes, it is.

Q. Is that Cleveland?

A. That is in Cleveland.

Q. In Cleveland proper?

A. Yes.

Mrs. Mahon: Mark these.

(Thereupon booklets were marked by the reporter for identification State's Exhibits 1, 2, 3, 4, respectively.)

Q. You were present when Sergeant De-lau found the pictures here in the dresser?

A. Yes, I was.

Q. Officer, showing you what is identified as State's Exhibit 1, what can you tell us about that?

A. That is a book entitled "The Affairs of the Troubador." It has my initials, "M.H.", the date "5-23-57." It was one of the books found in the dresser drawer on this date.

Q. Showing you what has been identified as State's Exhibit 2, what can you tell us about that?

A. This book is entitled "Little Darlings," has my initials, and the date 5-23-57, inscribed on the second page, which was found at the residence of Mrs. Mapp May 23, 1957, in the dresser drawer.

Q. Showing you what has been identified as State's Exhibit 3, do you recognize it?

A. Yes, I do.

Q. And what is it?

A. That is a book entitled "London Stage Affairs," has my initials inscribed on the second page, date May 23, 1957. That is another of the books found in the dresser drawer at Mrs. Mapp's residence.

Q. Showing you what has been identified as State's Exhibit 4, do you recognize that?

A. Yes, I do.

Q. And that is what?

A. It is a book entitled "Memories of a Hotel Man," has my initials inscribed on the inner page, and date 5-23-57. That is the fourth of the four books found in the dresser drawer of Mrs. Mapp's residence, May 23, 1957.

Mrs. Mahon: Mark these. . . .

What conclusions can you draw from the testimony of Michael Haney?
If you were to cross-examine him, what questions would you ask?

The defense, represented by Mr. Kearns, now cross-examines Officer Haney.

Cross examination of Michael Haney.

By Mr. Kearns:

Q. Officer Haney, who was the person that you went out there to try to find?

A. We didn't know who the party would be at that address.

Q. You testified you received confidential information that somebody involved in a bombing would be found at that address?

A. Our information was somebody was wanted for bombing in the home, found in the home. We were not told ahead of time who the particular person was, other than it was a man for questioning wanted in the bombing.

Q. Who went out with you?

A. Sergeant Delau and patrolman Thomas Dever.

Q. After you arrived there the lady defendant here said through the window she would call her lawyer to see whether you should be admitted to search without a search warrant; is that right?

A. That's right.

Q. And to your knowledge, as far as you know, she did call me?

A. As far as I know; yes, sir.

Q. Well, didn't one of my assistants get out there, Mr. Walter Green?

A. Yes, Mr. Green arrived after the lieutenant had gotten there. *The search warrant arrived in approximately two hours after we originally got there.* [emphasis added]

Q. And you did procure a search warrant?

A. I did not, no.

Q. Well, some of the officers?

A. That's right.

Q. But when the search was made there were more officers than you and Sergeant Delau and patrolman Dever that were there?

A. That's right.

Q. How many all together?

A. There was Sergeant Delau, patrolman Dever, Lieutenant White come with a search warrant; Inspector Barrett of the fourth district was there; the captain was there; it could be the captain was there; I am not certain.

Q. Who else?

A. There was a patrolman from one of the zone cars there.

Q. That is seven?

A. Yes.

Q. Four beside the three of you that you counted, you and the sergeant and patrolman Dever?

A. That's right.

Q. Who was the inspector that came?

A. Carl Barrett, in charge of the fourth district.

Q. Any other police officers there at the time this place was entered and search was being made?

A. Not that I recall.

Q. Well, do you know what the other police officers were doing besides you and the sergeant that were upstairs in the bedroom?

A. I didn't see what they were doing.

Q. You know what they were doing?

A. Some was searching the basement, yes.

Q. Now, officer, you are speaking of a suitcase in which you found some of these items that have been shown to you; weren't there other things found in the suitcase?

A. There was a photo album, and other obscene pictures which were there, yes.

Q. Did you yourself make a search of the suitcase?

A. Yes, I did.

Q. But you didn't search the dresser drawers?

A. I did search the dresser drawers on the far wall, yes.

Q. Did the sergeant do some searching in the drawers in that room?

A. Yes, the chest of drawers.

Q. Didn't he find anything?

A. He found the four pictures which were presented in evidence here.

Q. And then he brought them out and handed them to you?

A. Yes, he did; he showed them to me and handed them to me.

Q. In other words, you didn't find them, you were present. Did you know as to where they came from, that is, what the sergeant gave to you?

A. I was in the room when the sergeant found them.

Q. You know you were in the room. Were you looking at them at the time he pulled them out of the drawer?

A. No, I was not.

Q. So that all you know as to where they actually came from, from your own personal knowledge, is what the sergeant told you when he handed them to you?

A. The sergeant searching the drawer turned around and said "Here."

Q. His back was to you when he was searching the drawer?

A. Yes.

Q. So you didn't see him take them out of the drawer, is that right?

A. That's right.

What is the defense attorney trying to suggest to the jury?

Q. Now in the suitcase wasn't there other things besides the photograph you spoke of, the album—wasn't there a man's shirt in that suitcase?

A. No, there was not.

Q. Wasn't there anything pertaining to men's clothing in the suitcase?

A. No, sir.

Q. Nothing?

A. Nothing.

Q. Did you talk to Mrs. Mapp about that particular suitcase, as to who it belonged to?

A. Yes, we did.

Q. And she told you it belonged to her?

A. Yes, she did.

Q. What else, if anything, did she tell you?

A. Nothing.

Q. Didn't she tell you she had loaned the suitcase to Morris Jones, to put some of his things in there?

A. No, she did not.

Q. Isn't it a fact you found a gun in that suitcase?

A. I did not.

Q. Wasn't there a gun in that suitcase?

A. No, there was not.

Q. I will hand you here a standard text book of Cosmetology, and ask you if that wasn't in the suitcase?

A. If it was in there I didn't see it.

Q. Isn't it a matter of fact you took that book out and said you weren't going to take it along, it wasn't necessary—isn't that a fact?

A. No, it is not.

Q. Isn't it a fact you said about the album, the pictures that you spoke of, that you said that wasn't necessary to take along?

A. The album of pictures was put back in the suitcase.

Q. But you saw the albums of pictures of Mrs. Mapp, didn't you?

A. Most of them were, yes.

Q. Yes, and you brought other things with her name on it. Why didn't you bring the album out to show that was all in the suitcase?

A. I felt her statement it was her suitcase and the pictures were there, I didn't need any more.

Q. You didn't even need the suitcase itself?

A. No.

Q. And you say there wasn't a gun in the suitcase?

A. No, there wasn't.

Q. Isn't it a fact you asked her whose gun that was?

A. No.

Q. Isn't it a fact she said it belonged to Morris Jones?

A. No, that is not a fact.

Q. Isn't it a fact you asked her who this standard text book of Cosmetology belonged to?

A. No, it is not.

Q. And isn't it a fact that you saw the name on the book itself, "Morris Jones," and that is the reason you refused to take it?

A. That is not a fact.

Q. Now you say that the State's Exhibit 6, which is a diet of Mrs. Mapp's, that was in the suitcase?

A. That was in the suitcase; yes, sir.

Q. Did you yourself find it in that suitcase?

A. Yes, I did.

Q. Did anybody search the desk in the living room?

A. I don't know whether they did or not.

Q. Didn't you?

A. No, I didn't.

Q. And isn't it a fact that that diet was not found in the suitcase but in the drawer of the desk in the living room?

A. No, it is not a fact; it was found in the suitcase.

Q. Now, officer, I want you to tell this jury, isn't it a fact that some obscene matters were found in a box in the basement where the lottery slips were found?

A. Not to my knowledge. Anything they found and presented here was found in the bedroom.

Q. Didn't you learn that some things were found in the box?

A. Nothing obscene; there was no box found other than the trunk, the policy paraphernalia.

Q. That was in the basement, wasn't it?

A. Yes.

Q. And in the box where that policy paraphernalia was found, was a small brown box with most of this evidence that you have introduced here and state you found; isn't that true, to your knowledge?

Mrs. Mahon: Objection.
The Court: He may answer.

A. That is not true.
Q. Now, you did find lottery paraphernalia in the basement, didn't you?
A. I didn't, but there was some found; yes, sir.
Q. Some of the seven police officers that made a search found it; is that right?
A. That's right.
Q. And you or no one in the police department ever charged Mrs. Mapp with any possession of any of this policy paraphernalia, did you?
A. Mrs. Mapp was charged with policy paraphernalia in police court.
Q. She was?
A. She was; she was tried.
Q. As a result of this search?
A. Yes, sir.
Q. You mean as a misdemeanor?
A. As a misdemeanor; yes, sir.
Q. To your knowledge, Mr. Green from my office, at the time the search was made, was not permitted inside of the house to watch the search, or what was being done; he was kept outside of the house?

Mrs. Mahon: I am objecting to the form of the question.
The Court: Yes, you made a statement.
Mr. Kearns: I said "To your knowledge."
The Court: Whether or not that is a fact. Can you answer?

A. Mr. Green remained outside with me. Whether he was kept out or remained out, I couldn't say, because I was outside when Mr. Green went to the house to gain admission.
Q. And you don't know one of the uniformed officers, whether it was the lieutenant or captain, told him he should not go in; do you know that as a fact?

A. I don't know who told him; I don't know whether somebody did; all I know I stayed outside and Mr. Green also remained outside.
Q. Isn't it a fact Mr. Green tried to get in the front door and was refused admission, and he tried to get in the side door and was refused admission by the same officer?
A. I don't know whether he was refused or not; I know he remained outside with me, but I don't know whether he was refused admission.

Why is the defense attorney stressing the fact the Mr. Green was not permitted to enter the house?

Q. Now you say Mrs. Mapp was charged with possession of these policy slips and policy paraphernalia?
A. Yes, sir.
Q. And was discharged in the court, wasn't she?
A. Yes, she was.

Mr. Kearns: That's all.

• • • • • • •

The State has the right to follow the cross-examination of its witness. The defense can then follow with recross-examination.

Recross examination of Michael Haney.

By Mr. Kearns:

Q. Officer, isn't it a fact all of the police officers at one time or another were inside of that house?
A. I don't know if they were all in or not.
Q. Most of them were?
A. Most of them, yes, were in the house.

• • • • • • •

Q. Officer, isn't it a fact that Mrs. Mapp was handcuffed to one of the uniformed police officers while the search was going on?

A. Mrs. Mapp was handcuffed, but there was a uniformed officer there; I couldn't testify whether she was handcuffed to him or merely handcuffed.

. . . . . .

By Mr. Kearns:

Q. Where is that search warrant?
A. I don't know.
Q. Do you have it here?
A. I don't have it.
Q. Would you tell the jury who has it?
A. I can't tell the jury who has it; no, sir.
Q. And you were one of the investigating officers in the investigation by the police department?
A. Yes.
Q. But you can't tell us where the search warrant is?
A. No, I cannot.
Q. Or what it recites?
A. No.

. . . . . .

Q. You yourself did not obtain the search warrant, did you, officer?
A. No, I did not.
Q. Do you know who did?
A. I was told Lieutenant White obtained it.

. . . . . .

Once again, the defense attorney asks about the search warrant. What point is he trying to make?

Now the prosecution presents its second witness, Officer Carl Delau.

Thereupon the State, further to maintain the issues on its part to be maintained, called as a witness, CARL DELAU, who, being first duly sworn, was examined and testified as follows:

Direct examination.

By Mrs. Mahon:

Q. Your name, please?
A. Carl Delau.
Q. What is your address?
A. 1063 Cove Avenue, Lakewood, Ohio.
Q. And you are a member of the Cleveland Police Department?
A. I am.
Q. And in what department are you employed, officer?
A. I am assigned to the Bureau of Special Investigation.
Q. You are a sergeant in the department, aren't you?
A. I am.
Q. How long have you been on the police force?
A. Twelve and a half years.
Q. During the course of your duties, officer, did you have occasion to go to the home of one Dollree Mapp on May 23rd last year?
A. Yes, I did.
Q. Were you alone at the time?
A. No, at that time I had patrolman Haney and patrolman Tom Dever with me.
Q. About what time did you get there?
A. Got there shortly after one o'clock p.m., in the afternoon.
Q. That is the Dolly Mapp who is sitting in the courtroom?
A. Seated at the table, yes.
Q. Did you know her by any other name?
A. Dollree Mapp, Dollree Bivens. And just suspected—I'll skip that; there was another name with that she had gone by.

Mr. Kearns: May I ask the court to instruct the jury to disregard that last statement, of his suspicion.
The Court: Sustained; the last statement will be disregarded, ladies and gentlemen of the jury.

Q. Will you tell us, officer, what happened when you arrived at her home?
A. We arrived there approximately a little

after one p.m.—well, first we went by the home shortly after one p.m. when we seen her car in the drive; we went down the street, parked down the street, made observation until approximately one-thirty; no one had left; at one-thirty that date we went to the brick home, two floors, two families, one on each floor; we attempted to gain entrance, rang the side door bell, when Mrs. Mapp put her head out the window and asked what we wanted: we said we wanted to search the house, that we had information there was evidence in there which we desired. At that time she said she wouldn't let us in, but would make a phone call; she left and came back and said she spoke to her attorney and her attorney told her not to let us in. At that time we left the scene and I called Mr. Cooney and told him we were unable to gain entrance. He said to remain on the scene and he will talk to her; he did speak to her on the phone and asked her to open the door.

Mr. Kearns: Object. [hearsay]
The Court: Sustained.
Mrs. Mahon: Don't relate the conversation.

A. (continuing) Close to four p.m. that afternoon Lieutenant White arrived on the scene with a search warrant. When we told her we had a search warrant she opened the door. Before that she said she wouldn't; at that time we did pry the screen door to gain entrance to the building itself. We went upstairs, myself and Lieutenant White; Inspector Barrett had arrived on the scene. She demanded to see the warrant; that is when she grabbed it out of his hand and concealed it on her person. We recovered the warrant, and she was quite belligerent at that particular time. So I told her we were going to search her apartment on the second floor. Patrolman Dever came upstairs briefly, and he went down to search the basement; he come from outside where he had remained and come upstairs with me. Patrolman Haney, a uniformed policeman who was on the scene, and myself, searched Mrs. Mapp's bedroom. There are two bedrooms in the rear, hers is on the right. At

that time she remained seated on the bed, remained in the bedroom while I was searching the bedroom.
    Q. She was present?
    A. She was in my presence during the complete search of the bedroom. It was at that time I was searching the chest of drawers and found four photographs, which have been entered in as evidence; and in the chest of drawers I found a 25 caliber Colt automatic gun.
    Q. Where did you find that?
    A. It was in the chest of drawers which I had searched. I found a lot of other stuff, tape recorders and such, confiscated that outfit that was in the chest of drawers there.
    Q. In her bedroom?
    A. In her bedroom. I was in that bedroom when patrolman Haney found the four books which have been introduced as evidence, in the dresser that he was searching. As soon as he had found them he showed me what he had found.

    Mr. Kearns: *I ask at this time the testimony patrolman Haney found these be stricken from the record because it is hearsay.* He said the police officer showed them to him and told him where he had found them. [emphasis added]
    The Court: Were you in the room at that time?
    The Witness: I was in the room at that time, yes.
    The Court: Did you observe what he was doing?
    The Witness: I wasn't watching him completely all the time, no. He had them in his hand and said, "Look what I found."
    The Court: The testimony may stand; his conclusion as to the finding will be stricken, but the observation may stand.
    Mr. Kearns: He just said patrolman Haney told him he had found it, "Look what I found."
    The Court: He may testify as to what took place at that time.

    Q. Was the defendant present while this conversation went on between you?
    A. Yes, she was.

Q. What size bedroom was this, officer?

A. It was a normal size bedroom; I'll say probably twelve by twelve, perhaps eleven by twelve; it wasn't too large; it contained a bed, chest of drawers and the dresser, and there is a closet for this particular bedroom.

The Court: We will have to stop here for lunch. So we will adjourn for lunch, ladies and gentlemen. *I charge you while you are absent from the courtroom not to have any conversation about this matter with anyone and above all draw no conclusions in your own minds until you have heard the whole case and received the evidence and the charge of the court. Have no contacts of any sort, and permit no one to talk to you, and you are not to contact them.* You will return from lunch and be ready to proceed at one-thirty. You may leave the courtroom. [emphasis added]

Thereupon the court adjourned until 1:30 p.m.

Trial resumed, pursuant to adjournment, at one-thirty p.m.

Thereupon the witness, CARL DELAU, resumed the witness stand for further direct examination, and was examined and testified as follows:

Direct examination.

By Mrs. Mahon:

Q. Officer, I believe you testified you found a gun in that bedroom?

A. Yes, I did.

Q. Where was that?

A. That was in the one dresser I was searching where I found four pictures.

Q. Did you have any conversation with this defendant concerning that gun?

A. I asked her who it belonged to; she just said it was in there, didn't say to who it belonged.

Q. You did observe that suitcase that was in the bedroom?

A. Yes, I had.

Q. And will you state whether or not it was a man's or woman's suitcase?

A. It appeared to me to be—

Mr. Kearns: I object.
The Court: Sustained.

Q. Officer, did you have any conversation with the defendant concerning that suitcase?

A. Yes, in company with patrolman Haney.

Q. And what did she say about it?

A. She said it was her suitcase at that time. This was on the premises in the bedroom.

Q. Did you make any further examination of the clothes closet in that suite?

A. In the both bedrooms I did.

Q. What did you find?

A. The bedroom where we found the confiscated evidence had nothing but feminine wearing apparel and other clothing, and women's personal things, adult woman, grownup clothing; and there was no men's clothing at all in that particular bedroom. The second bedroom contained children's clothing, and we questioned the defendant, and she said that was her daughter's bedroom, and we found nothing in there but clothing for a young girl.

Q. Did you search any other rooms in that suite?

A. I searched the entire second floor.

Q. You did?

A. Yes, I did.

Q. What did you find, if anything?

A. Other than in the one bedroom, I searched that bedroom, searched the daughter's bedroom, searched the kitchen, the living room, with small dinette in the rear of it. We found nothing else other than just some policy books, blank policy books.

Q. Where did you find them?

Mr. Kearns: May I object, if the court please?
The Court: Does that have any bearing on the issue?
Mrs. Mahon: Just to show—
The Court: I will sustain it.

Q. Officer, did you search the basement of that home?

Mr. Kearns: Object to leading the witness. Let him tell.

The Court: Well, he may tell. Have you told where you did search?

A. I searched the basement also.

The Court: That may stand.

Q. Did any other police officers besides patrolman Haney and your partner, Dever, help you in this search that you made?

A. The other policemen were on the premises, but they did not assist in the search at all.

Q. They didn't?

A. No.

Q. Did you find anything in the basement?

A. Yes, I did.

Q. What did you find?

A. I will qualify that. My partner found a foot locker, quite a large foot locker, and it contained policy paraphernalia in the foot locker.

Q. That was in the basement?

A. Yes.

Q. Anything else in the basement?

A. No, other than the usual things found in the basement, that was the only thing which we were interested in.

Q. Officer, did you have any conversation with this defendant concerning what you found in her bedroom?

A. I had a conversation with her, yes.

Q. What was the conversation?

A. In the bedroom itself, when we found those items she wouldn't say anything as to what they were doing there, what the confiscated evidence was doing in her bedroom, other than making the only explanation which I overheard her say to patrolman Haney he would be excited to see them, she wouldn't comment on those things. After we brought her down to Central Station we questioned her again, and it was there she said those books were left behind by Morris Jones, who had lived with her before that and who had roomed at her home on Milverton Road.

Q. Did you have any further conversation with her at any later time as to those books?

A. No, other than in the station and when she gave a statement the following day, we had no conversation with her, and she said those books were left behind by this roomer she had.

At this point in the trial, the defense attorney cross-examines Officer Delau.

Cross examination of Carl Delau.

By Mr. Kearns:

Q. Sergeant Delau, you went out to the residence of Mrs. Mapp with whom?

A. Patrolman Haney and patrolman Dever.

Q. You say that you have known Mrs. Mapp for some time, is that correct?

A. I probably have known her for four or five years.

Q. And you have known that her name is Dollree Mapp, isn't that right?

A. One of her names; also Dollree and Dolly.

Q. You had her charged in this case as Dolly?

A. She is also known as Dolly.

Q. But you did know that her right name was Dollree Mapp?

A. I did not know what her right name was.

Q. Well, you knew her name was Bivens at one time?

A. Yes, I did.

Q. And that is by reason of the fact that she was the wife of the prize fighter Bivens, is that correct?

A. That is correct.

Q. Now, after you went to this home which, by the way, is a private home in the city of Cleveland, isn't it?

A. Yes, it is.

Q. And after you called Mrs. Mapp's attention to the fact that you wanted to go in, she told you through the window she would call her lawyer and see if it is okay, is that correct?

A. That is correct.

Q. And after a little time passed she then came down to open the door for you, didn't she?

A. No, she did not.

Q. Well, as a matter of fact she told you then that she had talked to her lawyer, and asked you if you had a search warrant?

A. Yes, she did.

Q. And you said no, but we can get one?

A. That is correct.

Q. And then she told you that you better get a search warrant, then you could go into her house?

A. Correct.

Q. And it was then that you called Lieutenant White and told him you were having trouble getting in, and she insists on a search warrant?

A. I didn't call White; I called Lieutenant Cooney, my boss.

Q. Then sometime later when you and the other two police officers were on the scene, someone came out with a search warrant, didn't they?

A. That is correct.

Q. And who was it?

A. That was Lieutenant White.

Q. Lieutenant White came with a search warrant?

A. Yes.

Notice here that the defense attorney is continuing to emphasize the handling of the search warrant.

Q. By that time Mr. Walter Green, of my office, was also there, wasn't he?

A. He arrived a few minutes after that. . . .

Q. Did you give any one of your police officers instructions to keep Mr. Green out of the premises while you were searching?

A. I did not.

Q. Do you know anyone else who did give such orders, the inspector or the lieutenants?

A. I did not hear anyone pass out instructions.

Q. Whether you heard it or not, do you know whether any of them did?

A. I do not know.

Q. But in the basement of this residence you did find a large foot locker?

A. Patrolman Dever found it and called it to my attention; that is correct.

Q. Do you know how long before he found it that your attention was called to it?

The Court: What's that?

Q. How long before your attention was called to it had he found it?

A. To my knowledge it was a matter of a few minutes. He came up and said, "Sergeant, I want to show you what I found down in the basement." And I went down in the basement with him.

Q. And these things were confiscated by your department and taken to headquarters?

A. Yes, they were.

Q. And that was a large foot locker, is that right?

A. That is correct.

Q. Have any name on it, any identification on it?

A. No, there was no name on it.

Q. Well, was there any material in it that you could identify as belonging to Morris Jones?

A. There was not.

Mr. Kearns: I think that is all, your honor.
The Court: Anything else?

• • • • • • •

When the prosecution rested its case against Mrs. Mapp, the defense attorney made a motion for a directed verdict of discharge. A motion for a directed verdict asks the judge to rule that the prosecution has not succeeded in showing that the accused person committed the crimes for which he or she is being tried. In this case, the motion was made and was overruled by the judge.

At this point, the defense attorney called the defense's first witness, Walter Greene [whose name appears in the printed trial transcript with the spelling "Green"], for direct examination.

Defense

Whereupon the defendant, to maintain the issues on her part to be maintained, called as a witness, WALTER GREEN, who, being first duly sworn, was examined and testified as follows:

Direct examination.

By Mr. Kearns:

Q. Will you tell the court and jury your full name?

A. Walter Green.

Q. And your address?

A. 4394 Silsby Road, University Heights.

Q. What is your profession?

A. I am an attorney.

Q. Where is your law office?

A. 1101 Hippodrome Building.

Q. And who are you associated with?

A. With yourself and my father.

Q. On or about the 23rd day of May, 1957, do you recall a telephone call that you had with Mrs. Dollree Mapp?

A. Yes, I do.

Q. And how long have you known Mrs. Dollree Mapp?

A. I estimate it a couple of years.

Q. During that period of time have you spoken to her quite frequently?

A. Many times.

Q. Have you spoken to her on the telephone?

A. Many times.

Q. And are we now handling a civil lawsuit for her?

A. Yes, we are.

Q. And have we been handling that civil lawsuit for over two and a half years?

A. Well, as long as I have known her we have been handling this matter for her.

Q. And do you know that she was the person on the telephone that you talked to?

A. She so identified herself, and I recognized her voice.

Q. What did she say to you?

A. The exact words I can't repeat, but it was to the effect that the police had her house surrounded, and they wanted to gain admission, and should she let them in.

Q. What advice did you give her?

A. I said, "If they can produce a warrant,

and show you that warrant, let you read it to see it is in proper order, then let them in."

Q. Did you hear any more from her on that day?

A. Well, there were two, possibly three telephone calls on that particular date from Mrs. Mapp.

Q. To you?

A. To me. Well, originally she called you; I believe you were in court at the time when I took the call.

Q. Now what did you do after the telephone conversations, if anything, pertaining to her residence?

A. Well, eventually I went out to the residence at her request.

Q. And will you describe to his honor, Judge Lybarger and this jury what you saw there with reference to the action and activity?

A. Well, Mrs. Mapp lives on Milverton—the address I don't know—140th and Milverton; as I drove up I saw several police cars and what appeared to me policemen all over the place.

Q. At this time can you give this jury some idea of how many policemen you saw, as you say, all over the place?

A. My estimate at this time would be ten to fifteen officers.

Q. And were there men in uniform?

A. Yes, there were.

Q. Can you give this jury some idea, approximately, how many men in uniform were there, to your best recollection?

A. Well, I would say half to two-thirds of the men present were in uniform.

Q. What happened from then on?

A. Well, it was difficult finding a parking place right in front of the house, and I pulled up possibly a house or two beyond hers. As I walked back a couple of officers started to walk towards me, then they turned around and walked back, and I saw Sergeant Delau, I believe, attempting to kick in the door.

Q. Is this the gentleman sitting in the courtroom?

A. Yes, the second officer, and I think I—I believe I stopped and asked him what they were doing; he said they wanted to get in. I asked if they had a warrant, if they had a search warrant it wasn't necessary, just show it to Mrs. Mapp. He said he had a warrant; they refused to show it to anybody. I never did see a warrant.

Q. Go ahead and tell it to the court, what happened.

A. The sergeant tried, as I say, to kick in the door, and she wouldn't come down. Then he got a sharp instrument—I mean a metallic instrument; I don't know what it was—and broke the glass in the door and somebody reached in and opened the door and let them in. Inspector Behr was there at the time, and had plainclothes men; I don't know how many men walked in ahead or behind. I started to walk in somewhere behind Inspector Behr, and he instructed the uniformed captain to keep me from entering the premises. As I recall now the captain opened his tunic, and I got a glimpse of a revolver that he had on his belt. I didn't go any further; I asked him to let me in several times, and several times Inspector Behr came to the door and notified me I would not be allowed to walk in the premises. I walked to the front door and the side door, and I didn't gain access to the premises.

Q. You spoke of inspector Behr. Could that have been Barrett?

A. I think it was Behr, an inspector.

Q. He was an inspector of police, to your knowledge?

A. To my knowledge.

Q. And you did not gain entrance to the place at all?

A. No, sir.

Q. Give this jury some idea of approximately how long these people were in these premises—I mean the police officers—and before they left.

A. My best recollection at this time would be about an hour from the time I got there.

Q. Then what did you do?

A. As I say, I walked from door to door, yelled in, asked the inspector to let me in to observe what was going on. Either I got no answer, or if I got an answer I wasn't going to be admitted. There were policemen walking up and down, up and down. I heard some loud talking.

Q. When you speak of walking up and down, will you tell this jury walking up and down where?

A. Well, there is a front stairway—there is a stairway directly to the left of the front door as you walk in. I stood there and policemen were walking up and down to and from Mrs. Mapp's apartment, which is on the second floor; there was another lower apartment on the first floor. They would walk up and down; I assume they went into the basement; I don't know. As I say, there was a great deal of commotion and loud talk, and I heard Mrs. Mapp call out several times.

Q. Did you hear what she said?

A. One time she said "Take your hand out of my dress."

Q. What else do you recall? Did you get any chance to see her, see whether or not she was handcuffed?

A. No, I didn't see her until they took her out. At the time I heard this particular statement I was standing at the front door, which was somewhere on those steps; from the direction of the voice, the volume of the voice, I deduced she was somewhere on the steps.

Q. Then when they took her out will you describe whether or not she was wearing handcuffs or not?

A. I can't say, Mr. Kearns; I don't recall. I know they took her to the police car; Sergeant Delau got in the back with her.

Q. What did the other police officers do?

A. Eventually they all vacated the house; I don't know who went downtown in cars; I know they eventually went down; I believe they took a trunk out of the house; where they got it I don't know. I followed them in my car.

Q. Where did you follow them?

A. Central police station.

Q. Did you stop at Central Police station?

A. Yes. I believe I saw Mrs. Mapp there.

Q. Did you talk to her?

A. Yes, I believe I did.

Q. And what did they do with her?

A. Well, she was detained in jail; I don't know what they did to her.

Q. What did you do?

A. I believe I arranged bail for her.

Mr. Kearns: You may inquire.

How does Mr. Greene's testimony differ from that of the police officers?

Following the defense attorney's direct examination of Mr. Greene, Mrs. Mahon, the prosecutor, cross-examines him.

Cross examination of Walter Green.

By Mrs. Mahon:

Q. Mr. Green, you are an associate of Al Kearns? You are partners in the law business?

A. Yes.

Q. You have an office with him?

A. Yes ma'am.

Q. So that you are very close friends, aren't you?

A. Yes.

Q. When you went out to that house you weren't trying to prevent the police from making a lawful search, were you?

A. I wasn't trying to prevent them from doing anything; I simply wanted to observe what they were doing to Mrs. Mapp. She was terrified and asked that I come out.

Q. Just answer my questions. You are a lawyer, aren't you?

A. Yes.

Q. When you got out there you took a lot of pictures, didn't you?

A. No.

Q. You didn't take any pictures?

Q. You took three of the house there?

A. The sergeant's foot against the door.

Q. Do you have that picture?

A. They didn't come out.

Q. You didn't get his foot?

A. No; it was a little camera I frequently carry; I guess in the excitement I didn't pull the film through; they didn't come out.

Q. Where were you standing when you took that picture?

A. I was standing, I would say, about two yards away from that side door, next to Mr. Haney's—

Q. What other pictures did you take?

A. I tried to take pictures of the people as they were being taken away, but I was kind of shooting from the hip, not looking through the camera; got a bunch of trees and scenes like that.

Q. You didn't get any pictures?

A. Just trees and scenes, and the double exposure of the sergeant.

Q. You are not good with a camera at all.

A. Not at that time.

Q. You were with patrolman Haney outside of the house?

A. Yes, ma'am.

Q. That is this officer here?

A. Yes, ma'am.

Q. And patrolman Haney never told you that you couldn't go into that house, did he?

A. I don't know whether—I wouldn't say he didn't; I don't know; I don't recall.

Q. And he was the only officer you were talking to?

A. Oh, no.

Q. That is when you arrived at the home?

A. When I arrived at the home several of the officers started to move towards me, because I didn't know any of them at that time. As a matter of fact, it was only later that I learned their names; and, as I say, I stood there and watched the sergeant attempt to break in the door. They saw I had a camera; officer Haney said, "He's got a camera, he's got a camera." Then he threatened me.

Q. Who do you mean by "he"?

A. Officer Haney. He told me I was invading his privacy, he was going to do something about it. I explained my legal rights.

Q. Just answer my question. You say you don't recall Haney never told you to go into the house?

A. I wouldn't say.

Q. Don't you remember Haney telling you that you would have to answer to the police if you go in?

A. That I couldn't say.

Q. What officer did you ask?

A. I spoke directly to inspector Behr. As I say, the first man who stopped me was a captain, uniformed captain.

• • •

Q. You testified here one time while you were out there you heard her say, "Take your hand out of my dress"; is that right?

A. Something to that effect.

Q. Did you know, Mr. Green, that she had taken the search warrant away and shoved it down her bosom at that time?

A. I didn't know there was a search warrant, because I haven't seen it to this day; I asked them for it.

Q. You don't know why she said that, do you?

A. No, I haven't the slightest idea.

Q. Did you know she tussled with Lieutenant White when he tried to serve her with a search warrant?

A. I don't know Lieutenant White.

Q. You didn't know he was out there?

A. Well, I don't know; if you show him to me I will identify him.

Q. You had every opportunity to talk to this defendant when she was in the police station, didn't you?

A. If I am not mistaken, the—

Q. Please answer my question.

A. I don't think I had every opportunity. If I am not mistaken, officer Haney and another officer were in close proximity, and they permitted me to talk to her privately for a few minutes at a distance, not in a private room they have down the corridor.

Q. Did you ask them for a private room?

Mr. Kearns: Object.

The Court: Overruled.

A. I don't know whether I did or didn't.

Q. You weren't prevented in any way from talking to her at the police station?

A. That wasn't your original question.

Mr. Kearns: Object to that.

The Witness: Frankly, I don't see what bearing this has.

The Court: What was the question?

(Question read by the reporter.)

The Court: Overrule the objection.

A. No.

Q. You did have a conversation with her at the police station, didn't you?

Mr. Kearns: Object.

The Court: Overruled.

A. Yes.

Mrs. Mahon: That's all.

Mr. Kearns: That's all.

(Thereupon, after duly cautioning and instructing the jury, a short recess was had.)

After the prosecutor had cross-examined Mr. Greene, the defense called its second witness, Dolores Clark, for direct examination.

Thereupon the defendant, further to maintain the issues on her part to be maintained, called as a witness DOLORES CLARK, who, being first duly sworn, was examined and testified as follows:

Direct examination.

By Mr. Kearns:

Q. Now, Mrs. Clark, will you please speak to the last lady on this jury, loud enough so that they will all hear you. Tell us what your full name is.

A. Dolores Clark.

Q. And where do you live?

A. 5608 Utica.

Q. Do you know Mrs. Dollree Mapp?

A. Yes.

Q. How long have you know her?

A. A long time.

Q. Can you give this jury some idea, how many years approximately?

A. I first met her when she was married to Mr. Bivens.

Q. And that was approximately how long ago?

A. Thirteen, fourteen; thirteen years, probably; a long time.

Q. You and she have remained friends since?

A. Well, off and on, yes.

Q. Did you ever see me before today?

A. No.

Q. Did you ever see or speak to anyone in my office, or connected with me in the law business before today?

A. No.

Q. Do you recall on or about the latter part of April or first part of May of 1957, whether or not you were at Dollree Mapp's home when certain things were done with reference to packing?

Mrs. Mahon: Objection. Leading question.

Mr. Kearns: I am trying to get her down to the point that we want instead of taking a lot of time.

The Court: Sustained.

Q. Do you recall being at the home where Dollree Mapp lives?

A. Yes.

Q. Where?

A. On Milverton Road.

Q. In 1957 did you visit her quite often?

A. Yes, I visited her.

Q. And do you recall at any time on or about the latter part of April or first part of May, 1957, helping her to any packing?

A. Yes.

Q. Will you tell this jury in your own language what took place at that time when you helped her pack?

A. Well, I couldn't tell you all the details because it has been so long ago.

Q. Tell us what you remember of it.

The Court: Let's get set when this was. When did this happen?

A. I can't say the exact date; it has been a long time ago.

Mrs. Mahon: I am objecting to the answer.

Q. Can you tell us approximately what month?

A. Say May.

Q. Will you tell us what took place?

A. I don't know the exact date, but she called me and asked what was I doing; I said nothing; she said, "How about coming out and straightening my room." Okay. When I got out there she said she needed someone to change the room, rearrange the furniture. When I got there she proceeded to pack some things—clothing, saying she was going to clean the room out, pack the stuff before she rearranged the furniture. She said she had had a room rented out to a man. So when I got there she started to pack the stuff, pack the stuff in the box to take to the basement.

Q. What kind of clothes were they, ladies or men's clothes?

A. Men's clothes. A lot of junk, letters, shoes, just general stuff, put them in (sic) . . .

Q. You will have to speak a little louder.

A. When we got the stuff up off the floor and put it in the box, started to clean out the dresser drawers, and things like that. She was looking in the drawer, and all of a sudden she had this bag, a brown paper bag; she opened it up, she said, "Look what's in here." Then when she took the stuff out of the bag it was a bunch of dirty books and some pictures." She said, "Look at what filthy stuff men read." So we laughed it off, put it in the bag and put it with the man's stuff.

Q. You put it in the bag with the man's stuff?

A. Yes.

Q. And where, if you remember, did you take this bag eventually?

A. We took the whole box of junk down in the basement.

Q. Would you be able to identify the things that she showed you, if I show them to you?

A. I wouldn't say too clearly; it was just some dirty books; it wasn't important; I didn't want to see the stuff, so I didn't pay too much attention.

Q. Handing you what has been marked for identification State's Exhibits 1, 2, 3, and 4. I will ask if you identify any of these as the things she took out of that drawer and put it in this box and carried it in the basement?

A. It was something like—it was more than this, more bags and cards and things; I didn't pay too much attention to it.

Q. Would you say this was some of it?

A. I would say it was some of it, yes.

Q. Handing you what has been marked for identification as State's Exhibit 10, 11, 12, 13. Look at these and tell us if you have ever seen them before? (handing to witness) Did you?

A. Yes.

Q. And where did you see these?

A. In the paper bag that came out of the dresser.

Q. That is the paper bag that was put in this big box and taken down to the basement?

A. Yes.

Mr. Kearns: You may inquire.

Now the prosecutor cross-examines Dolores Clark, the defense's witness.

Cross examination of Dolores Clark.

By Mrs. Mahon:

Q. Did you ever help Mrs. Mapp pack or move her things around before?

A. Yes.

Q. How often have you done that?

A. Go to the house and be doing something.

Q. I am asking how often you helped Mrs. Mapp pack before, or move her furniture around?

A. This is the first time I ever helped pack stuff. The men moved and she wanted me to help her. Whenever I am at her house we make coffee, wash dishes; we usually do whatever is to be done.

Q. Do you know which bedroom she was sleeping in?

A. She was sleeping in the room, we were cleaning up this room so she could get back into her room.

Q. You didn't take this bag yourself and put it in the box?

A. I handed them back to her, put all the stuff in the big box.

Q. Those cards you just identified, you say they were in the paper bag with the books?

A. Put this stuff together.

Q. Please answer the question. You say those cards were in the paper bag with the books?

A. Yes.

Q. Where did she find those?

A. In the dresser drawer.

Q. In the dresser drawer?

A. Yes.

Q. And you say both you and she took the books and the cards and put them in a box?

A. Put them back in the bag, then put them in the box.

Q. And then took them down to the basement with a whole lot of more stuff?

A. It was all men's stuff.

Q. Did you know, Mrs. Clark, the police found those books in her dresser drawer on May 23rd of last year?

Mr. Kearns: Object.
The Court: Objection sustained as to the form of the question.

Q. Can you tell me what was in that room when you were in there packing?

A. Yes.

Q. What was in there? I mean by way of furniture?

A. It was a large bed, a great, huge dresser, a chest.

Q. Was there a suitcase in the room?

A. I didn't see a suitcase.

Q. And you can't tell us what date you were over there, can you?

A. No, I can't remember that long ago.

Q. You can remember the bags but you can't remember the date; is that right?

A. I remember the bag because she asked me to help her clean up and take up the stuff; I don't know what day of the week it was; all I know I was there.

Q. You say you can't remember the date because it was long ago, is that right?

A. Yes.

Q. You don't know, as a matter of fact, whether it was in April or May, or what month in '57, is that right?

A. It was near the end of April or first of May; still kind of cold out.

Why is the prosecution asking the witness to identify the date?

Q. You remember that, don't you?

A. Yes.

Q. And you remember seeing those bags, don't you?

A. Yes.

Q. And you saw those pictures too, didn't you?

A. Yes.

Q. Don't shake your head; answer.

A. Yes.

Q. What else did you take down to the basement?

A. A lot of stuff—boots, hats, papers, shavings and stuff; everything out of the drawers, off the floor, got in the box; everything in this box, then taken to the basement. Then we straightened it up.

Q. You say there were some men's clothes too?

A. It was all men's clothes, everything we put in the box.

Q. Were there some men's clothes?

A. I suppose you would call hats and shoes men's clothes.

Q. In other words, the man who lived in that room didn't take his clothes with him?

A. I don't know what he took with him, but he left quite a bit there.

Q. He left some clothes, is that right?

A. Yes.

Q. Well, let's get specific on this; just what besides those bags and cards did you take down to that basement?

A. Some boots—shoes.

Q. Men's shoes?

A. Yes; and a hat, some shaving stuff; just a whole lot of things, men's things. I remember the books, she showed it to me, and I didn't like it at all. We laughed about it; I said, "Don't show it; put it in the bag." And when we finished we took it all to the basement.

Q. Were there any women's clothes in that room?

A. No, there was nothing in it but these things a man left. We were cleaning the room out so she might move back into the room.

Mrs. Mahon: That's all.
Mr. Kearns: That's all.

At this point in the trial, Dollree Mapp, the defendant, took the stand and testified as a witness on her own behalf. She was not required to do this and could have refused to testify by reason of the Fifth Amendment privilege against self-incrimination. The defense attorney begins with direct examination of Mrs. Mapp.

Thereupon the defendant. DOLLREE MAPP, further to maintain the issues on her part to be maintained, offered herself as a witness in her own behalf, and, being first duly sworn, was examined and testified as follows:

Direct examination.

By Mr. Kearns:

Q. Please speak direct to the jury in answering all questions. Give us your full name, please.

A. Dollree Mapp.

The Court: Spell the first name.
The Witness: D-o-l-l-r-e-e.
The Court: I think I will therefore change the form to the actual fact of her name.
Mrs. Mahon: We will amend the indictment.

The Court: Yes. All right.

Mr. Kearns: No objection.

Q. Have you at any time used the name Dolly, or to your knowledge have you been called Dolly by anyone?

A. Well, I am called Dolly.

Q. By friends?

A. My friends, yes.

Q. But your real name is Dollree now?

A. Yes.

Q. You are now single?

A. That is correct.

Q. And you are the mother of a daughter?

A. That's correct.

Q. And what is her name?

A. Barbara Bivens.

Q. And how old is she?

A. Fifteen.

Q. Where does she live?

A. With me.

Q. And why is her name Barbara Bivens?

A. I was at one time married to Jimmy Bivens. I am now divorced.

Q. Is he the father of Barbara?

A. That is correct.

Q. Did you at any time go by any other name than Bivens or Mapp?

A. Never.

Q. Where do you live?

A. 14705 Milverton Road.

Q. Will you describe the living quarters, as to the type of house?

A. It is a two-family brick, with front and side entrance and full basement.

Q. It had a full basement?

A. It has a full basement, yes.

Q. Now, on or about the 23rd day of May, 1957, were you at home?

A. Yes.

Q. Did anything unusual happen?

A. Yes.

Q. Will you tell this jury, please, what happened?

A. At one-thirty someone rang the door bell, and I looked out upstairs, and it was Sergeant Delau, Haney and Dever, and I asked them what they wanted; they said they wanted to come in; I asked for what;

they said they wanted to question me about something. I still insisted what he wanted to question me for. He said, "I'll tell you when we come upstairs." And I told them I wouldn't let them in, and they insisted that I should open the door. I told them I would call my attorney, if he tells me to let them in, I would. At that time I called for you, and you were in court, and Mr. Green advised me not to let them in without a search warrant. I went back to the window and told Sergeant Delau what Mr. Green had told me.

Q. Was there anything else said about this search warrant?

A. Sergeant Delau said something like this, "Well, we'll get in."

Q. I mean Mr. Green; did he say anything else to you?

A. No. He told me to make sure that it was a search warrant, and they should let me see it and read it, and then I should let them in.

Q. Then you advised Sergeant Delau of that fact, what your attorney said?

A. Yes. I told him my attorney said get a warrant, and he said he would have his boss to call me, which he did—Lieutenant Cooney.

Q. Who was his boss?

A. Lieutenant Cooney.

Q. And you talked to the Lieutenant?

A. Yes.

Q. And what did you say to him?

A. I told him the same thing I told Sergeant Delau—I wouldn't let them in without a warrant.

Q. Then what?

A. Well, I hung up on him, and I called Mr. Green back; I was still trying to locate you; Mr. Green told me not to let them in unless they produced a search warrant, and they had to give the warrant to me to let me read it, and I refused to open the door.

Q. You told them that?

A. Yes. They went across the street, and I could see Sergeant Delau standing in the neighbor's yard. It went on for hours; when I say hours, they were there shortly after one. About four-thirty they started—police started arriving in cars. I think Mr. Green got there around the same time; and he called to me and asked me if I was going to open the door. I said "Yes, I'll come down. I want to see the search warrant."

Q. Who was it that called to you?

A. I don't know: one of them. At that time I talked to Mr. Green out of the window, and he—he was outside at the back door. They were all at the side door, and they were still coming. At that time I went downstairs to the front door; without opening I called through the door if I could see the search warrant. I was standing on the landing when Sergeant Delau came in; he was the first one in there.

Q. This gentleman? (indicating)

A. Yes. The back door was broken.

Q. Tell us about the breaking.

A. When they came in I said, "Inspector, I want to see the search warrant." And I was standing on the top landing of the stairs, and I didn't know who the inspector was when he was in plain clothes. He said, "Here is the search warrant." He held it back from me, and I remember Mr. Greene told me I should see it and read it, and I told him I wanted to see it. He said, "You can't see it." At that I reached over, took the search warrant from his hand and put it down in my bosom.

Q. Was that after the door was broken in?

A. That is correct, and they were inside.

Q. Give this jury some idea how many police officers, plain clothes and uniformed were there.

A. There were at least a dozen, some plain clothes, some uniform, also the paddy wagon.

Q. Then what?

A. When I grabbed the search warrant off him and put it down in my bosom, one of them said "What are we going to do now?" The one that grabbed me said "I'm going down after it." I said, "No, you are not." He went down anyway.

Q. What did you do that for?

A. Because Mr. Green told me I should

read it, and I wanted to read it to make sure it was a search warrant.

Q. Then what happened?

A. He grabbed me, twisted my hand, some lieutenant behind me, and it was hurting. I yelled, I pleaded with him to turn me loose. At this time they were all going upstairs and some downstairs. He asked for handcuffs, I believe, from one of the men in uniform, and he put the handcuffs on me, then later he changed it to a man with a uniform.

Q. You mean he handcuffed you to himself at first?

A. I was handcuffed to him at first; that was the one I grabbed the warrant from.

Q. Then he took the handcuff off himself and handcuffed you to a uniformed man?

A. Yes.

Q. Then what happened?

A. One said to the other. "They are all in the house." He said, "Take her upstairs." I was led upstairs handcuffed to this policeman.

Q. You were led upstairs in the apartment that you occupied is that right?

A. Yes.

Q. And who came in there with you?

A. When I got upstairs Sergeant Delau was in my bedroom, and there was someone else searching my living room; they were all over the place.

Q. Well, was Haney searching?

A. I didn't see Haney at that time; I did not see him; I saw him later.

Q. You say they were all over the place searching. Who do you mean?

A. There were others; they were not the only ones there; there were eight or ten others besides Dever, Haney and Delau.

Q. And they were searching the entire premises?

A. Yes, that is correct.

Why does her attorney ask Mrs. Mapp to describe the search? To help you answer this question, read the Ohio constitutional provision on page 215.

Q. Men in uniform and without uniform?
A. That is correct.
Q. Now, tell what happened then?
A. Well, naturally, being handcuffed, he pulled me into the bedroom and I sat on the bed. This policeman that I was handcuffed to stood over to me; Sergeant Delau was going in the drawers. About that time Haney walked in and asked me—he had this brown bag, and asked me—
Q. Walked in from where?
A. I don't know where he came from, but he walked into my bedroom door, and he said, "Does this belong to you?" I asked him not to look at it, it might embarrass him. He asked me again if it belonged to me. I said "no." He said, "Oh, yes, that's the kind of trash you read."
Q. Had you seen these things before?
A. Yes, they were in my bedroom, that I had rented out to this fellow.
Q. What was his name?
A. Morris Jones.
Q. What did you do with them?
A. Well, when he left he didn't move, he went to New York on vacation, and he didn't come back; when I found out why he didn't come back—he had paid up for the month—I was going to clean the room out, take the room for myself, because I was sharing the room with my daughter.
Q. Did you have anyone at all to help you clean the room out?
A. Well, I called Dolores and if she wasn't busy I would pick her up and have her come over to help me. I was going to take my daughter's room and change the furniture.
Q. Is Dolores the girl that just testified before you did?
A. Yes.
Q. Handing you what have been marked for identification State's Exhibits 1, 2, 3 and 4, I want to ask you if you identify these books?
A. Yes.
Q. Where did you first see them?
A. I first saw them when I was in his room during his absence.

Q. When you speak of "him" tell the jury to whom you are referring?
A. Yes, I had rented my room out to this fellow.
Q. Do you know his name?
A. Morris Jones. He was leaving there, he was going to open a cosmetology school on Cedar. He was there about a month before he moved. Now I meant during his absence when in the school I went to his room, and that was my first knowledge of the books. When he went to New York and didn't come back is when I packed his things, I packed all of the things in this box.
Q. Are these Exhibits 1, 2, 3 and 4 the books that you took out of the room that he occupied and packed with his stuff?
A. Yes.
Q. What did you do with them?
A. I put them all in this box and I took them downstairs, with the help of Dolores, and put them in the corner of the basement.
Q. Now, handing you what have been marked for identification as State's Exhibits 10, 11, 12 and 13, please look at them and tell us where you saw those?
A. With the books in his room.
Q. Do these State's Exhibits 1, 2, 3 and 4, and Exhibits 10, 11, 12 and 13, belong to you?
A. No.
Q. Did you ever own them?
A. No.
Q. Did you ever have possession of them?
A. No.

Why is the defense attorney asking Mrs. Mapp whether she owned or had possession of them? To help you answer this question, check the wording of the statute under which she was being tried found on page 215.

Q. They were things taken out of the drawer of Morris Jones', is that correct?
A. That is correct.
Q. Now I will hand you what have been

marked for identification State's Exhibits 8 and 9. Exhibit 8 is what?

A. That is me, and Mr. Keeley, a real estate man, and Mrs. Lena Derry.

Q. These pictures were taken where?

A. Chatterbox Musical bar and grill.

Q. And State's Exhibit 9? (handing to witness)

A. The same.

Q. Where did you keep these State's Exhibits 8 and 9?

A. Those were in my desk in the living room.

Q. And at the time the police officers made the search of your premises, where were State's Exhibits 8 and 9?

A. They were on the desk in the living room, because they had just been made a couple of years before.

Q. Handing you what has been marked for identification State's Exhibit 6, will you tell us what that is?

A. It is a diet; that is my diet.

Q. And where did you get that?

A. From the doctor.

Q. And where was that at the time these police officers made this search?

A. That is always kept in my kitchen.

Mrs. Mahon: Objection.

Q. Where was it that night or that day? Where was it that day that the search was made?

A. I was using this diet; it had to be in the kitchen.

Q. Handing you what is marked for identification State's Exhibit 7, will you tell this jury what that is?

A. This is a chattel mortgage on carpeting that I purchased quite some time ago; this was kept in papers, important papers I had in my daughter's bedroom, top drawer, with other papers.

Q. At the time the search was made where was it?

A. It was with the other papers in my daughter's bedroom I was sharing with her.

Q. Were any of these exhibits, 8 and 9, 6 and 7, in a suitcase in your room?

A. No; not at any time.

Q. Were they in any of the drawers in your room?

A. No.

Q. Handing you what has been marked for identification State's Exhibit 5, please look at it and tell us if you ever saw that before?

A. Yes, I have.

Q. And where did you see it?

A. It was in the drawer of the room that Morris occupied.

Q. And what, if anything, did you do with it when you cleaned out Morris Jones' room?

A. I used my suitcase and packed some of his things away and put them under the bed, and this is one of the things that was in the suitcase that belonged to me.

Q. You say Morris Jones had paid a month's rent?

A. That is correct.

Q. And had his rental run out at the time the police officers came in and made the search?

A. No, it would have been out June 1st.

Q. And you expected him to come back for his things?

A. I knew he wasn't coming back, that's why I was packing them.

Q. Was there anything else belonging to Morris Jones that you had packed in this suitcase?

A. Yes, there was a gun, and there was a shirt, silk shirt, there were ties; they were small items; there were socks.

Q. This State's Exhibit 5, did this ever belong to you?

A. Not at any time.

Q. Was it filed in your personal possessions as yours?

A. Absolutely not.

Q. Now there was some evidence here of a 25 caliber gun. At the time the police officers made the search of your premises, where was that gun kept?

A. Well, I had packed the gun along with that sketch you just gave me, and other things, in my suitcase and put it under the bed.

Q. With the other things belonging to Morris Jones?

A. That is correct.

Q. Did you know at that time whether Morris Jones would come back, or not?

A. I knew he wouldn't come back; I had talked to his mother long distance.

Q. And was there anything else with this gun, that you haven't yet described, in this suitcase?

A. Well, just his effects; there were letters, there was a cosmetology book; there were school papers.

Q. There was what?

A. School papers.

Q. Was he studying cosmetology?

A. That is correct.

Mrs. Mahon: I haven't seen that at all.

Mr. Kearns: I am going to show it to you. (handing to prosecutor.) Mark these.

(Thereupon book was marked Defendant's Exhibit A, and papers marked Defendant's Exhibits B and C, respectively, for identification.)

Q. Handing you what has been marked for identification as Defendant's Exhibit A, I want to ask you whether you ever saw this before?

A. Yes, I did.

Q. And where did you see it?

A. It was in the drawer and I put it in the suitcase along with Morris' other things.

Q. When you were in this room and officer Haney or Sergeant Delau searched this room, do you know, or did you see where they found that book?

A. Yes, they found it in the suitcase because I was sitting on the bed, and he put the suitcase on the bed with me, and when I told him it belonged to Morris Jones, he said he didn't need it.

Q. He said what?

A. He didn't need it.

Q. Who said that?

A. Haney said it.

Q. Handing you what has been marked for identification as Defendant's Exhibits B and C, have you ever seen them before?

A. Yes.

Q. And where?

A. This is some of his school work, Morris Jones' school work.

Q. And where were they in connection with this book of Cosmetology?

A. They were in the suitcase also.

Q. They were in the suitcase?

A. Yes.

Q. But where were they taken from, if you know?

A. From the suitcase.

Q. By whom?

A. By Haney.

Q. Now we spoke of State's Exhibits 1, 2, 3 and 4, which are these books. Where were these books on the day of this search by the police officers?

A. They were in the basement in a box, along with other things that belonged to Morris Jones.

Q. And who had put them there?

A. I had put them there myself.

Q. And where were State's Exhibits 10, 11, 12 and 13 on the day of this search?

A. They were also there in the basement, in the same bag, as a matter of fact.

Q. And is that the bag that officer Haney walked into the bedroom with that you spoke of?

A. Yes.

Q. And these things were in that bag?

A. Yes.

Q. And prior to that date, to your knowledge, they were in the basement, is that right?

A. They were in the basement.

Q. And when you were taken down to Central Police Station and questioned by Sergeant Delau, you told him that these things belonged to Morris Jones?

A. That is correct.

Q. Were you ever given an opportunity to read that search warrant?

Once again the search warrant is mentioned. Why?

A. I never had—I never read one word on there.

Q. Now, there was some testimony here about crayons, child's crayons. Where were they and where did the police officers find them?

A. Well, Sergeant Delau went in my daughter's room; I did not go with him; but the crayons, they were on my daughter's— she has a little desk with crayons and drawing board on the desk, and they were there.

Q. Did they show you these crayons at any time and ask you about them?

A. Yes.

Q. Who did that?

A. Sergeant Delau showed them to me in the police station.

Q. And what did he say about that?

A. He asked me if they belonged to my daughter.

Q. And what did you say?

A. Yes, they were hers.

Q. That they were hers?

A. That is correct.

Q. Did he tell you then at the police station where he found them?

A. No, he did not.

Q. I am going to ask you, finally, whether State's Exhibit 5, which is this drawing, was ever in your possession except as you have described?

A. Not at any time.

Q. Did it ever belong to you?

A. No.

Q. I am going to ask you whether State's Exhibits 1, 2, 3 and 4, or any of them, were ever your property?

A. Not at any time.

Q. Or did you ever have possession of them except as you have described to this jury?

A. No.

Q. I am going to ask you whether State's Exhibits 10, 11, 12 and 13 were ever your property?

A. No.

Q. Did you ever have possession of them except as you have described to this jury?

A. No.

Mr. Kearns: That is all, your honor.

If you have been following the transcript to this point, you have probably noticed that Mrs. Mapp's attorney is asking her questions about ownership and possession as well as about the search warrant. What is her attorney trying to convey to the jury?

In your opinion, is Mrs. Mapp's testimony believable? If you could cross-examine her, what questions would you ask?

Now the prosecutor cross-examines Mrs. Mapp.

Cross examination of Dollree Mapp.

By Mrs. Mahon:

Q. How long did Morris Jones live at your place?

A. Off and on for about a year—off and on.

Q. Off and on. What do you mean by off and on?

A. He was traveling back and forth to New York.

Q. Well, did he rent the rooms at intervals, monthly, or what?

A. No, it was a permanent thing.

Q. It was a permanent thing?

A. Yes.

Q. Well, his rent hadn't run out in May, had it, when you were moving his things out?

A. I knew he wouldn't be back; his mother called me long distance. He got in trouble and she called me.

Q. Didn't you testify here his rent hadn't run out?

A. It had.

Q. At the time?

A. At the time I was packing his things, no, it hadn't run out.

Q. All of these things you related—rather none of it that you related here did you tell the police at the time of your arrest, did you?

A. Yes, I did tell the police.

Q. Did you tell them that these various books, pictures and everything, that you had taken them down to the basement?

A. I told them just like I am telling you now, that they didn't belong to me, and told them before they took me to the jail who they belonged to, all of them.

Q. Did you tell them you had taken them down to the basement?

A. They didn't ask me.

Q. They didn't ask you?

A. No.

Q. Did you tell them about the pictures, that you put them into a box and took them down to the basement?

A. That was the only thing they asked me; I told them no.

Q. As a matter of fact, they found these things in your bedroom, didn't they—the books and pictures?

A. No, they did not.

Q. You say you took the pictures and the books and put them down in the basement?

A. No, the other things that belonged to Morris Jones.

Q. How come you put things in the suitcase?

A. Because I took all the things that belonged to him; he had powder, pencils, fingernail polish, everything that you use for cosmetology.

Q. Well, you were packing his things in a box?

A. His mother asked me to pack his things.

Q. I didn't ask you that. You say you were taking his things down to the basement, and you put them back in your suitcase, is that right?

A. That is correct.

Q. The suitcase belonged to you?

A. That is correct.

Q. And it was a woman's suit case?

A. That is correct.

Q. And in this suitcase you had this souvenir, State's Exhibit 8, didn't you?

A. No, not in my suitcase.

Q. Where did you have it?

A. In the living room on the desk.

Q. You say that is where the police got them, not out of the suitcase?

A. I know where they got them, yes, both of those.

Q. Both of these were in the living room?

A. Yes, both of those; they were on the desk.

Q. So that these officers are lying here, is that right, when they say they got them out of your suitcase?

Mr. Kearns: Object. Just a minute, please.

Q. Well, you heard both police officers testify, rather patrolman Haney testified concerning this diet sheet of yours, State's Exhibit 6, this chattel mortgage, State's Exhibit 7, this souvenir photo taken at the Chatterbox, State's Exhibits 8 and 9—you heard patrolman Haney testify that he got these out of your suitcase in your bedroom. Is that right?

A. No.

Q. Didn't you hear him so testify?

A. Yes, I heard him say that.

Q. And you say they were found on the desk?

A. I am telling you where they were found; they were on my desk in the living room. I live there, I put them there.

Q. You were present when Haney was searching your bedroom?

A. I was present.

Q. He was present there when they were searching?

A. Yes, I was sitting on the bed.

Q. You were present when he was searching your suitcase?

A. Yes. He did not take them out of my suitcase.

Q. He didn't?

A. No, he did not.

Q. And in searching your suitcase patrolman Haney found State's Exhibit 5; you heard him so testify?

A. He is correct; he did find that there.

Q. In your suitcase?

A. In my suitcase, with the things that belonged to Morris Jones; I put them there.

Q. You put them in the suitcase and the book?

A. Along with the cosmetology book.

Q. What else was in that suitcase that belonged to Morris Jones?

A. Everything in there belonged to Morris Jones.

Q. The suitcase was yours, however, wasn't it?

A. Yes.

Q. But you do say that patrolman Haney did get this out of your suitcase, State's Exhibit 5?

A. Yes; I put it there.

Q. Now you heard officer Delau testify that he found these four groups of pictures in a dresser drawer in your bedroom?

A. Yes.

Q. You heard him testify to that?

A. Yes.

Q. Is he telling the truth?

Mr. Kearns: Object, if the court please.
The Court: She may answer that.

A. So far as I am concerned he is not.

Q. Sergeant Delau is not telling the truth when he said he found them in your presence—you were present, were you?

A. Yes, I was present with two other officers.

Q. Was Sergeant Delau searching your bedroom when you were there?

A. Yes.

Q. He was?

A. Yes.

Q. Where do you say they were?

A. I packed them along with the bags, put them in the cardboard box and took them with other things belonging to Jones; I put the books and the pictures together.

Q. So Sergeant Delau is mistaken when he said he found these in a dresser drawer in your bedroom?

Mr. Kearns: Object.
The Court: Objection overruled.

A. Yes.

Q. Now you heard patrolman Haney tes-

tify that he found these four books, State's Exhibits 1, 2, 3 and 4 in your bedroom in a dresser also?

A. Yes.

Q. You heard him so testify?

A. Yes, I heard that.

Q. And you say these were not in the bedroom, that they were down in the basement?

A. They were in the basement.

Q. They were in the basement?

A. Yes; he walked in the door with the bag in his hand and asked me if they belonged to me; I was sitting on the bed.

Q. You were sitting on the bed?

A. That is correct.

Q. You are telling us now that patrolman Haney found these in the basement instead of, as he testified here, in a dresser in your bedroom?

A. He did not find them in my bedroom.

Q. He didn't?

A. He did not.

Q. When did Morris Jones start this beauty course that he was taking?

A. He started in the latter part of '56.

Q. The latter part of '56?

A. Yes.

Q. Where did he attend the cosmetology class?

A. Beatrice School on Cedar.

Q. How long did he attend it?

A. I would say about three or four months.

Q. You didn't turn this book over to the police at any time, did you, as belonging to Morris Jones and being in the suitcase?

A. Yes, I offered it to patrolman Haney; he said he didn't need it.

Q. This book has been in your possession all this time up until this trial?

A. No.

Q. Who did you turn it over to?

A. My attorney.

Q. Mr. Green?

A. Yes.

Q. When did you turn this book over to him?

A. I don't remember, but it was after—it was after I was arrested.

Q. Do you know where Morris Jones is now?

A. No, I do not.

Q. Was this Jones employed?

A. I think he started at Republic Steel, because they sent a telegram there for him; I do believe he worked there a very short time.

Q. What did he do there, do you know?

A. No, I don't know.

Q. Did he at any time work at any beauty school?

A. He is a student.

Q. At this place, you own that home, don't you?

A. No, I do not own it.

Q. You are not just renting there, are you?

A. I am renting.

Q. Well, you yourself collected rent from the downstairs suite, didn't you?

A. I collected rent from the downstairs suite? Yes.

Q. For the owner?

A. For the owner.

Q. What is her name?

A. Mrs. Miller.

Q. Did you pay rent to her?

A. Absolutely.

Q. How much rent?

A. Ninety dollars.

Q. Ninety dollars a month?

A. Yes.

Q. Mrs. Mapp, you heard patrolman Haney testify here that when he found those books you said to him, "Don't read them, they might excite you"; do you remember he testified that?

A. I heard him say that, yes.

Q. You said that to him, didn't you?

A. I told him not to look at them, they might embarrass him.

Q. You did say that?

A. Yes, I did say that.

Q. You were questioned about that gun that was found in the room?

A. No, I was not.

Q. You weren't.

A. No.

Q. You never told the police anything about it?

A. They might have asked; I don't say they didn't.

Q. To whom did that gun belong?

A. To Morris Jones.

Q. That was some property of his that you didn't take to the basement?

A. No, it wasn't in the basement.

Q. That was where?

A. That was upstairs.

Q. Where?

A. In the suitcase.

Q. In the suitcase the gun was?

A. Yes, along with a box of cartridges; I put them there.

Q. On one of these souvenir photos, perhaps both of them, you said a man was Mr. Keeley?

A. Yes.

Q. That is State's Exhibit 9. That is Mr. Keeley with you?

A. Yes.

Q. Who is the lady?

A. Mrs. Derry.

Q. Is Keeley a boy friend of yours?

Mr. Kearns: Objection.
The Court: Objection sustained.

Q. Have you been going around with Mr. Keeley?

Mr. Kearns: Object.
The Court: Sustained.
Mrs. Mahon: On what ground?
The Court: It doesn't bear on the issue of the case.

Q. To this day has Morris Jones ever come to your home to get any of his property?

A. His mother came.

Q. His mother came?

A. Yes.

Q. When?

A. Oh, it was later; I think it was October, somewhere along there; it was chilly.

Q. She came to get his property?

A. Yes.

Q. What did you turn over to her?

A. Everything that I had I gave to her.

Q. You had this book?
A. My lawyer had it.
Q. You didn't turn this over?
A. My attorney had the book.
Q. But that belonged, you say, to Morris Jones?
A. Yes, it does.
Q. Did you explain to the mother about the books and the photographs?

Mr. Kearns: Object.

A. No.

The Court: Overruled.

Q. Where did the mother come from?
A. Tennessee.
Q. Tennessee?
A. Yes.
Q. How did you know you had anything belonging to Morris Jones?

Mr. Kearns: Object.
The Court: Objection sustained.

Q. What is his mother's name?
A. Mrs. Jones is all I know.
Q. Mrs. Jones?
A. Yes.
Q. Had you ever met her before?
A. Only when she came there to my house to get his things.

Mrs. Mahon: That's all.

Mr. Kearns: Just one question. This box you speak of that you had packed Morris Jones' stuff in and put in the basement, that was not the large foot locker that has been mentioned in this case?
The Witness: No, the foot locker, that is an entirely different thing.
Mr. Kearns: That's all.
Mrs. Mahon: That's all.
Mr. Kearns: Now, may it please your honor, on behalf of the defense we would like to introduce Defendant's Exhibits A, B and C, as they were identified.
Mrs. Mahon: Objection.
The Court: What is your ground of objection, Mrs. Mahon?
Mrs. Mahon: She has testified here that

that book belonged to him; we don't have any testimony of any Morris Jones here that is his property.
The Court: Well, they may be received.
Mr. Kearns: She also testified it was taken out of the suitcase.
The Court: They may be received, all three of them, A, B and C, may be received.
Mr. Kearns: And with that the defense rests.
The Court: Is there anything by way of rebuttal?
Mrs. Mahon: No rebuttal.
Thereupon the State rested.
Thereupon the defense rested.
Testimony closed.

After the prosecutor and the defense attorney deliver their closing arguments, Judge Lybarger instructs the jury on what law to apply to this case, how to apply it, and the burden of proof needed for conviction.

CHARGE OF THE COURT

LYBARGER, J.:

Ladies and gentlemen of the jury, it now becomes the duty of the court to instruct you in the law that governs this case. *It likewise becomes your duty to accept the law as this court gives it to you*, to adopt it as a guide for your determination of what the facts actually are in this matter, and by that means to arrive at a verdict which will be just and fair. *You, ladies and gentlemen of the jury, must determine what the facts are, what is the truth in this matter*. You should approach this task with an open mind, and in all fairness, having in mind your oath as jurors that you would not be influenced by sympathy or prejudice against either the State or the accused.

At the outset the court should define for you what is meant by evidence, and how you are to weigh the testimony in this case. Throughout the course of the trial on occasion the court has ruled for or against the admission of evidence when objections were raised, either by the State or the defense. You will draw no inference of any kind from any of the rulings of the court as on questions of law; neither will you because of any such rulings, or any other expression of the court, infer that the court has any opinion as to the guilt or innocence of the accused in this case. *You are the exclusive judges of all the facts in this case,* and the court must not and does not invade the province of the jury by reflecting upon the facts at issue in any manner whatsoever.

At the opening of the case, and presently at the close of the case, very able counsel on both sides of the trial table addressed you, first the opening statements and then closing arguments in summation. They were entitled to do so under the law, and you will keep in mind, however, that anything that was said was not to be received as evidence, but may or may not be of assistance in helping you to arrive at a conclusion in the case, depending on how you view the argument.

The indictment in this case, which the court will soon read to you, is not to be considered as evidence; it serves to inform the defendant of the charge made against her by the State; the mere fact that the defendant was indicted by the grand jury does not constitute evidence, or raise any presumption of the guilt or innocence of the accused. The evidence upon which you must decide this case is what was presented to you from the witness stand, together with any exhibits which were received into evidence. *You, ladies and gentlemen of the jury, are the sole and exclusive judges in this case in determining where the truth lies;* it is your duty to weigh the testimony of all the witnesses and decide what faith, credit and confidence you will give to the testimony.

In passing upon the credibility of the witnesses you may consider, among other things, their manner of testifying on the witness stand, their apparent intelligence, candor and truthfulness, or the lack of these qualities; their interest, bias or prejudice; their means of knowing and remembering the facts about which they testified, and the reasonableness or unreasonableness of

what they had to say; did a witness appear to be telling a full, honest story, or to be withholding or exaggerating or understating certain facts.

Applying this test to the witnesses, which ones appear to you to be "telling a full, honest story"? Which ones appear to be "withholding or exaggerating . . . certain facts"?

It is your privilege to believe all that a witness said, or to believe none; or you may believe a part and disbelieve another part of a witness's testimony. Take all these things into consideration and give to the testimony of each witness such weight and credit as in your honest judgment it deserves.

The defendant, Dollree Mapp, comes into this court for trial by reason of an indictment returned by the grand jury in essentially these words: "The grand jury do find and present that within and for, on or about the 23rd day of May, 1957, at the county aforesaid, (being Cuyahoga County, Ohio) unlawfully and knowingly had in her possession and under her control certain lewd and lascivious books, pictures and photographs, said books, pictures and photographs being so indecent and immoral in their nature that the same would be offensive to the court and improper to be placed upon the records thereof."

To this indictment the defendant has returned a plea of not guilty; by this plea the defendant puts at issue every material element of the indictment and of the offenses charged therein. The defendant denies the existence of each element which constitutes the crime charged in the indictment. *The plea of not guilty entered by the defendant clothes her with the legal presumption of innocence. This presumption is not a mere matter of form, but is rather a shield which the law throws about the defendant.* The presumption of innocence is accorded to the defendant from the moment that protection was first cast upon her, and remains with her throughout the trial.

The presumption of innocence is only overcome when you, the jury, find the evidence is such as to exclude every reasonable doubt of the guilt of the defendant. This plea of not guilty tendered by the defendant places upon the State of Ohio the burden of proving beyond a reasonable doubt each and every element that constitutes the allegations in the indictment, and of proving beyond a reasonable doubt each and every element of the offense that is charged therein. The law of Ohio has this to say concerning the presumption of innocence: A defendant in a criminal case is presumed to be innocent until he is proved guilty of the crime charged, and in case of a reasonable doubt whether his guilt is satisfactorily shown he shall be acquitted.

This presumption of innocence places upon the State the burden of proving the guilt beyond a reasonable doubt. *The law also requires that I read to you from the statute this definition; reasonable doubt is defined as follows: "It is not a mere possible doubt because everything relating to human affairs or depending upon moral evidence is open to some possible or imaginary doubt. It is that state of the case which, after an entire comparison and consideration of all the evidence, leaves the minds of the jurors in that condition that they cannot say they feel an abiding conviction to a moral certainty of the truth of the charge."*

To doubt is to be honestly uncertain of the truth or of a fact; *a reasonable doubt is a substantial doubt;* it is not an unreasonable doubt; it is not a capricious doubt based merely upon conjecture, but it is a doubt based upon reason; it must be a doubt honestly uncertain and not a doubt originating in your mind from a desire to avoid the performance of a disagreeable duty; it is not a doubt created by any feeling of sympathy, passion or information not based upon the evidence in the case.

The rule of law which clothes every person accused of crime with the presumption of innocence, and casts upon the State the burden of proving him guilty beyond a rea-

sonable doubt, is a humane provision of the law, intended to guard against the danger of an innocent person being unjustly punished; but the rule is not intended to aid a person who is in fact guilty to escape.

When after a full and impartial consideration of all the evidence, *the judgment of the jury is convinced to a moral certainty that the defendant is guilty as charged* in the indictment, and there is no reasonable explanation of the fact proven except upon the hypothesis that the defendant, in fact, committed the crime charged, then every reasonable doubt is removed and a verdict of guilty should follow.

What is meant by the phrase "presumption of innocence"? How does the judge explain the meaning of a "reasonable doubt"? The judge says that the jury must be "convinced to a moral certainty" that the defendant is guilty. Explain the meaning of a moral certainty.

You should examine all the evidence with an honest purpose to ascertain the truth and render your verdict accordingly, irrespective of what consequences may follow your verdict.

I come now to define for you the law that bears particularly upon this case. The Revised Code of Ohio contains this section, which I shall read for you only in part as it may apply to the charges here made, omitting those parts which have no reference, since the statute is all-inclusive and covers many subjects.

"No person shall knowingly have in his possession or under his control an obscene, lewd or lascivious book, magazine, pamphlet, paper, writing, advertisement, circular, print, picture, photograph, or pictures and stories of immoral deeds, lust or crime."

In order to find the defendant, Dollree Mapp, guilty as charged in the indictment, the State must prove beyond a reasonable doubt each and all of the following elements, which I shall enumerate:

(1) That the crime was committed in this state and county on or about the date alleged in the indictment.

(2) That the act was done unlawfully, that is, in violation of a statute of Ohio; and that it was done knowingly, that is, voluntarily, of one's own choice, not accidentally. This signifies an act of the will, an intention to possess and have under one's control the things alleged in the indictment, which knowledge and intention must have been present at the time when the act complained of was done. The law presumes that a sane person intends the ordinary consequences of his own voluntary acts.

(3) *That the defendant had in her possession and under her control the books, pictures and photographs mentioned in the indictment.* "Possession" means the act or state of detaining a thing; it is the act of holding or keeping it. Now, such detention does not mean that it is necessary always to have in one's sight the thing possessed. For example, one who deposits articles in a place of concealment may still be deemed to have them in his possession. To have something under one's control is to have the present right and power to do with it as one will.

Neither possession or control necessarily means ownership. If a person possesses something it does not necessarily mean that he owns it. The test is whether or not the defendant had some degree of possession and control over the material as alleged in the indictment.

(4) That the books, pictures and photographs set forth in the indictment are obscene, lewd or lascivious. To be obscene the material must be calculated to appeal to a reader's or viewer's prurient interest, that is to say, it must have as its dominant purpose and effect erotic allurement, a calculated and effective excitement to sexual desire.

The term "lewd" as used in the law means lustful, sensual, pornographic. "Las-civious" means wanton, tending to produce voluptuous emotions. "Prurient" means inclined to or characterized by lascivious thought. The standard for judging obscenity is whether to the average person applying contemporary community standards, the dominant theme of the material, taken as a whole, appeals to prurient interest.

Ladies and gentlemen of the jury, if beyond a reasonable doubt you are convinced that the State has proved that on or about the 23rd day of May, 1957, in this county, Dollree Mapp unlawfully and knowingly had in her possession and under her control, certain lewd and lascivious books, pictures and photographs, and that the State has proved beyond a reasonable doubt all of the essential elements of the crime as I have defined them for you, then it will be your duty to return a verdict of guilty; on the other hand, if the State has not proved to you beyond a reasonable doubt any one of the elements which I have just defined for you, then it will be your duty to return a verdict of not guilty. It is for you to decide. I have charged you to pay strict attention to the evidence and the law, the evidence as given in court and the law as given to you by the judge.

You will now retire to your jury room; *there you will elect one of your number as foreman, which may be either man or woman.* The foreman will have no greater authority than anyone else, except he will preside and see that your deliberations are regular and orderly. You will have with you in the jury room the indictment, which the court admonishes you again is not to be considered as evidence; you will have with you in the jury room the exhibits, which are to be considered as evidence. During your deliberations and until you have reached a verdict, you will be kept together, unless you are otherwise discharged by the court, or permitted to separate for a good purpose. Should you desire to address any communication to the court during your deliberations concerning this case, you will do so in writing, signed by your foreman, and deliver to Mr. O'Grady, the court bailiff, in whose charge you will be while deliberating.

In order to arrive at a verdict in this case it is necessary that all twelve of you be of one mind in agreement. So far as conviction goes, there can be no conviction until all twelve are of one mind, and if twelve of you do not so agree then there is no conviction.

You will be handed two forms of verdict; you will use the one which meets with your unanimous approval. One says, "We the jury in this case, being duly impaneled and sworn, do find the defendant, Dollree Mapp, not guilty." The other says, "We the jury in this case, being duly impaneled and sworn, do find the defendant Dollree Mapp guilty of possession of obscene literature as charged in the indictment."

The fact that the court submits these to you and reads them to you should raise no presumption in your minds as to which one you should use; that is entirely up to you. The court charges you that in determining the question of guilt or innocence of the accused, you are not to consider for a minute anything concerning punishment. Punishment is entirely a province of the court and not the jury.

One final word, ladies and gentlemen. This case is of great importance to the State, and it is of great importance to the defendant, Dollree Mapp. You as citizens and jurors are now called on to decide the important question of the guilt or innocence of the accused. It is essential for the welfare of society that those who are guilty of crime should be found guilty, but it is also essential that anyone that is innocent should be found innocent. So I charge you to deliberate carefully, in accordance with your oath, and to return a verdict which will respond to the facts in the case as you find them to be, and the law as this court has given it to you. [emphasis added]

The Court: Is there anything further?
Mrs. Mahon: No, your honor.
Mr. Kearns: Nothing on behalf of the defense, your honor.

The emphasized portions of the judge's charge to the jury are so important that they call for thought and discussion.
1. Why is there a division of authority: the law explained by the judge and the facts determined by the jury?
2. Why is there a "presumption of innocence"?
3. What is meant by "burden of proof"?
4. When is a doubt "reasonable"?
5. Explain the statement, "The judgment of the jury is convinced to a moral certainty that the defendant is guilty."
6. How does the judge distinguish possession from ownership?
7. Why do you think there is no mention of the warrant and of the nature of search and seizure?

Following the judge's charge, the jury retired for deliberation. In due course, the jury delivered its verdict.

And the said jury having heard all the testimony adduced by the parties, the arguments of counsel, and the charge of the court, retired to their room, in charge of the bailiff, for deliberation. And now come the jury, conducted into court by the bailiff, and return the following verdict in writing, to-wit: "We, the jury in this case, being duly impaneled and sworn, do find defendant Dollree Mapp guilty of possession of obscene literature as charged in the indictment."

The sentence for this crime was one to seven years in prison.

Document 7

The Supreme Court's Majority Opinion in the Case of *Mapp* v. *Ohio*

Following her conviction in the criminal court in Cleveland, Mrs. Mapp's attorneys ap-

pealed her case to the Ohio appellate court and then to the Ohio Supreme Court. In that court, they were not able to get her conviction overturned, so they appealed the case to the U.S. Supreme Court. Based on the facts in the trial record, and after considering the law which the attorneys for each side argued in support of their clients, the Justices handed down their opinion on June 19, 1961. Justice Tom Clark, speaking for the majority, posed the issues in the Mapp *case as follows:*

At the trial no search warrant was produced by the prosecution, nor was the failure to produce one explained or accounted for. At best, "There is, in the record, considerable doubt as to whether there ever was any warrant for the search of defendant's home." . . . The Ohio Supreme Court believed a "reasonable argument" could be made that the conviction should be reversed "because the 'methods' employed to obtain the [evidence] . . . were such as to 'offend "a sense of justice," ' " but the court found determinative the fact that the evidence had not been taken "from defendant's person by the use of brutal or offensive physical force against defendant." . . .

The State says that even if the search were made without authority, or otherwise unreasonably, it is not prevented from using the unconstitutionally seized evidence at trial, citing *Wolf* v. *Colorado,* 338 U.S. 25 (1949), in which this Court did indeed hold "that in a prosecution in a State court for a State crime the Fourteenth Amendment does not forbid the admission of evidence obtained by an unreasonable search and seizure." . . . On this appeal, of which we have noted probable jurisdiction, . . . it is urged once again that we review that holding.

*In other words, the majority is going to take another look at a precedent (*Wolf *v. Colorado) upon which the state of Ohio based its arguments and the Ohio Supreme Court based its decisions.*

I.

Seventy-five years ago, in *Boyd* v. *United States,* . . . considering the Fourth and Fifth Amendments as running "almost into each other" on the facts before it, this Court held that the doctrines of those Amendments

"apply to all invasions on the part of the government and its employés of the sanctity of a man's home and the privacies of life. It is not the breaking of his doors, and the rummaging of his drawers, that constitutes the essence of the offence; but it is the invasion of his indefeasible right of personal security, personal liberty and private property . . . . Breaking into a house and opening boxes and drawers are circumstances of aggravation; but any forcible and compulsory extortion of a man's own testimony or of his private papers to be used as evidence to convict him of crime or to forfeit his goods, is within the condemnation . . . [of those Amendments]."

The Court noted that "constitutional provisions for the security of person and property should be liberally construed. . . . It is the duty of courts to be watchful for the constitutional rights of the citizen, *and against any stealthy encroachments thereon.*"

In this jealous regard for maintaining the integrity of individual rights, the Court gave life to Madison's prediction that "independent tribunals of justice . . . will be naturally led to resist every encroachment upon rights expressly stipulated for in the Constitution by the declaration of rights." . . . Concluding, the Court specifically referred to the use of the evidence there seized as "unconstitutional."

Less than 30 years after *Boyd,* this Court, in *Weeks* v. *United States,* stated that

"the Fourth Amendment . . . put the courts of the United States and Federal officials, in the exercise of their power and authority, under limitations and restraints [and] . . . forever secure[d] the people, their persons, houses, papers and effects against all unreasonable searches and seizures under the guise of law . . . and the duty of giving to it force and effect is obligatory upon all entrusted under our Federal system with the enforcement of the laws."

Specifically dealing with the use of the evidence unconstitutionally seized, the Court concluded:

"If letters and private documents can thus be seized and held and used in evidence against a citizen accused of an offense, the protection of the Fourth Amendment declaring his right to be secure against such searches and seizures is of no value, and, so far as those thus placed are concerned, might as well be stricken from the Constitution. The efforts of the courts and their officials to bring the guilty to punishment, praiseworthy as they are, are not to be aided by the sacrifice of those great principles established by years of endeavor and suffering which have resulted in their embodiment in the fundamental law of the land."

Finally, the Court in that case clearly stated that use of the seized evidence involved "a denial of the constitutional rights of the accused." . . . Thus, in the *year 1914, in the* Weeks *case, this Court "for the first time" held that "in a federal prosecution the Fourth Amendment barred the use of evidence secured through an illegal search and seizure"* . . . . [emphasis added]

Part I of the Court's opinion applies the Fourth Amendment to federal officials. In Part II which follows, Justice Clark applies it to state officials.

II.

In 1949, 35 years after *Weeks* was announced, this Court, in *Wolf* v. *Colorado, supra,* again for the first time, discussed the effect of the Fourth Amendment upon the States through the operation of the Due Process Clause of the Fourteenth Amendment. It said:

"[W]e have no hesitation in saying that were a State affirmatively to sanction such police incursion into privacy it would run counter to the guarantee of the Fourteenth Amendment."

Nevertheless, after declaring that the "security of one's privacy against arbitrary intrusion by the police" is "implicit in 'the concept of ordered liberty' and as such enforceable against the States through the Due Process Clause," . . . and announcing that it "stoutly adhere[d]" to the *Weeks* decision, the Court decided that the *Weeks* exclusionary rule would not then be imposed upon the States as "an essential ingredient of the right." . . . The Court's reasons for not considering essential to the right to privacy, as a curb imposed upon the States by the Due Process Clause, that which decades before had been posited as part and parcel of the Fourth Amendment's limitation upon federal encroachment of individual privacy, were bottomed on factual considerations. . . .

At this point the opinion discusses the experiences of the states with illegal searches and seizures. Justice Clark pointed out that twenty-three states have experimented with laws imposing criminal liability on those who maliciously procure search warrants, on magistrates who issue search warrants without supporting affidavits, on officers who willfully exceed the authority of the search warrant, and on officers who search with no warrant or with an invalid warrant. Finding these remedies "worthless and futile," more than half of those states have turned to the exclusionary rule as the only effective remedy against unreasonable searches and seizures. Under this rule, evidence illegally seized is excluded from the trial.

III.

Today we once again examine *Wolf's* constitutional documentation of the right to privacy free from unreasonable state intrusion, and, after its dozen years on our books, are led by it to close the only courtroom door remaining open to evidence secured by official lawlessness in flagrant abuse of that basic right, reserved to all persons as a specific guarantee against that very same unlawful conduct. *We hold that all evidence obtained by searches and seizures in violation of the Constitution is, by that same authority, inadmissible in a state court.* [emphasis added]

IV.

Since the Fourth Amendment's right of privacy has been declared enforceable against the States through the Due Process Clause of the Fourteenth, it is enforceable against them by the same sanction of exclusion as is used against the Federal Government. Were it otherwise, then just as without the *Weeks* rule the assurance against unreasonable federal searches and seizures would be "a form of words," valueless and undeserving of mention in a perpetual charter of inestimable human liberties, so too, without that rule the freedom from state invasions of privacy would be so ephemeral and so neatly severed from its conceptual nexus with the freedom from all brutish means of coercing evidence as not to merit this Court's high regard as a freedom "implicit in the concept of ordered liberty." . . . This Court has not hesitated to enforce as strictly against the States as it does against the Federal Government the rights of free speech and of a free press, the rights to notice and to a fair, public trial, including, as it does, the right not to be convicted by use of a coerced confession, however logically relevant it be, and without regard to its reliability. . . . Why should not the same rule apply to what is tantamount to coerced testimony by way of unconstitutional seizure of goods, papers, effects, documents, etc.? We find that, as to the Federal Government, the Fourth and Fifth Amendments and, as to the States, the freedom from unconscionable invasions of privacy and the freedom from convictions based upon coerced confessions do enjoy an "intimate relation" in their perpetuation of "principles of humanity and civil liberty [secured] . . . only after years of struggle. . . ." They express "supplementing phases of the same con-

stitutional purpose—to maintain inviolate large areas of personal privacy. . . ." The philosophy of each Amendment and of each freedom is complementary to, although not dependent upon, that of the other in its sphere of influence—the very least that together they assure in either sphere is that no man is to be convicted on unconstitutional evidence. . . .

In this portion of the opinion, the Court joins the Fourth and Fifth Amendments of the Bill of Rights in its explanation of the right to privacy. What connection do you see between the Fourth Amendment's prohibition against unreasonable searches and seizures and the Fifth Amendment's privilege against self-incrimination?

V.

Moreover, our holding that the exclusionary rule is an essential part of both the Fourth and Fourteenth Amendments is not only the logical dictate of prior cases, but it also makes very good sense. There is no war between the Constitution and common sense. Presently, a federal prosecutor may make no use of evidence illegally seized, but a State's attorney across the street may, although he supposedly is operating under the enforceable prohibitions of the same Amendment. Thus the State, by admitting evidence unlawfully seized, serves to encourage disobedience to the Federal Constitution which it is bound to uphold. Moreover, as was said in *Elkins*, "[t]he very essence of a healthy federalism depends upon the avoidance of needless conflict between state and federal courts." . . . Such a conflict, hereafter needless, arose this very Term, in *Wilson* v. *Schnettler*, . . . in which, . . . we gave full recognition to our practice in this regard by refusing to restrain a federal officer from testifying in a state court as to evidence unconstitutionally seized by him in the performance of his duties. Yet the double standard recognized until today hardly put such a thesis into practice. In nonexclusionary States, federal officers, being human, were by it invited to and did, as our cases indicate, step across the street to the State's attorney with their unconstitutionally seized evidence. Prosecution on the basis of that evidence was then had in a state court in utter disregard of the enforceable Fourth Amendment. If the fruits of an unconstitutional search had been inadmissible in both state and federal courts, this inducement to evasion would have been sooner eliminated. . . .

Justice Clark is discussing a practice that has been labeled "the silver platter doctrine." Can you explain the use of this term?

Federal-state cooperation in the solution of crime under constitutional standards will be promoted, if only by recognition of their now mutual obligation to respect the same fundamental criteria in their approaches. "However much in a particular case insistence upon such rules may appear as a technicality that inures to the benefit of a guilty person, the history of the criminal law proves that tolerance of shortcut methods in law enforcement impairs its enduring effectiveness." . . . *Denying shortcuts to only one of two cooperating law enforcement agencies tends naturally to breed legitimate suspicion of "working arrangements" whose results are equally tainted.* . . . [emphasis added]

What is meant by "short cuts" and "working arrangements"?

There are those who say, as did Justice (then Judge) Cardozo, that under our constitutional exclusionary doctrine "[t]he criminal is to go free because the constable has blun-

dered." . . . In some cases this will undoubtedly be the result. But, as was said in *Elkins*, "there is another consideration—the imperative of judicial integrity" . . . *The criminal goes free, if he must, but it is the law that sets him free. Nothing can destroy a government more quickly than its failure to observe its own laws, or worse, its disregard of the charter of its own existence. As Mr. Justice Brandeis, dissenting, said in* Olmstead v. United States, *"Our Government is the potent, the omnipresent teacher. For good or for ill, it teaches the whole people by its example. . . . If the Government becomes a lawbreaker, it breeds contempt for law; it invites every man to become a law unto himself; it invites anarchy."* [emphasis added]

Do you think it is fair to set the criminal free because "the constable has blundered"? Would it be better to punish the criminal and the constable? Would this be possible on a practical level?

The ignoble shortcut to conviction left open to the State tends to destroy the entire system of constitutional restraints on which the liberties of the people rest. Having once recognized that the right to privacy embodied in the Fourth Amendment is enforceable against the States, and that the right to be secure against rude invasions of privacy by state officers is, therefore, constitutional in origin, we can no longer permit that right to remain an empty promise. Because it is enforceable in the same manner and to like effect as other basic rights secured by the Due Process Clause, we can no longer permit it to be revocable at the whim of any police officer who, in the name of law enforcement itself, chooses to suspend its enjoyment. Our decision, founded on reason and truth, gives to the individual no more than that which the Constitution guarantees him, to the police officer no less than that to which honest law enforcement is entitled, and, to the courts, that judicial integrity so necessary in the true administration of justice.

The Supreme Court ruled that the evidence against Dollree Mapp should have been excluded because the Cleveland police had violated the First and Fourteenth Amendment. Did you notice, however, that the court's opinion makes no reference to the issue of obscenity? All the briefs by the attorneys had emphasized this issue. Why do you think the majority simply passed over that issue?

Document 8

The Concurring Opinions

In his concurring opinion on the Mapp *case Justice Hugo Black wrote:*

Reflection on the problem, *however*, in the light of cases coming before the Court since *Wolf*, has led me to conclude that when the Fourth Amendment's ban against unreasonable searches and seizures is considered together with the Fifth Amendment's ban against compelled self-incrimination, a constitutional basis emerges which not only justifies but actually requires the exclusionary rule.

Justice William Douglas, who also concurred with the majority opinion, wrote:

As stated in the *Weeks* case, if evidence seized in violation of the Fourth Amendment can be used against an accused, "his right to be secure against such searches and seizures is of no value, and . . . might as well be stricken from the Constitution" . . .

When we allowed States to give constitutional sanction to the "shabby business"

of unlawful entry into a home . . . we did indeed rob the Fourth Amendment of much meaningful force. There are, of course, other theoretical remedies. One is disciplinary action within the hierarchy of the police system, including prosecution of the police officer for a crime. Yet as Mr. Justice Murphy said in *Wolf* v. *Colorado*, . . . "Self-scrutiny is a lofty ideal, but its exaltation reaches new heights if we expect a District Attorney to prosecute himself or his associates for well-meaning violations of the search and seizure clause during a raid the District Attorney or his associates have ordered."

The only remaining remedy, if exclusion of the evidence is not required, is an action of trespass by the homeowner against the offending officer. Mr. Justice Murphy showed how onerous and difficult it would be for the citizen to maintain that action and how meagre the relief even if the citizen prevails. . . . The truth is that trespass actions against officers who make unlawful searches and seizures are mainly illusory remedies.

Do you agree that trespass actions against police or disciplinary actions against them for illegal searches and seizures are "illusory remedies"? Explain your reasons for agreeing or disagreeing.

Moreover, continuance of *Wolf* v. *Colorado* in its full vigor breeds the unseemly shopping around. . . . Once evidence, inadmissible in a federal court, is admissible in a state court a "double standard" exists which, as the Court points out, leads to "working arrangements" that undercut federal policy and reduce some aspects of law enforcement to shabby business. The rule that supports that practice does not have the force of reason behind it.

"Double standard" and "shabby business" are harsh descriptions. What do you think of them?

Justice Potter Stewart also wrote as follows:

Memorandum of MR. JUSTICE STEWART.

Agreeing fully with Part I of MR. JUSTICE HARLAN'S dissenting opinion, I express no view as to the merits of the constitutional issue which the Court today decides. I would, however, reverse the judgment in this case, because I am persuaded that the provision of § 2905.34 of the Ohio Revised Code, upon which the petitioner's conviction was based, is, in the words of MR. JUSTICE HARLAN, not "consistent with the rights of free thought and expression assured against state action by the Fourteenth Amendment."

Here is a noteworthy point. Justice Stewart found the Ohio obscenity law unconstitutional because it violated freedom of thought and expression, an issue which the majority did not consider. He also agreed with part of the reasoning of the dissenting opinion.

Document 9

The Dissenting Opinion

Justice John Marshall Harlan wrote the dissenting opinion in the Mapp *case, which was joined by Justices Felix Frankfurter and Charles E. Whittaker.*

MR. JUSTICE HARLAN, whom MR. JUSTICE FRANKFURTER and MR. JUSTICE WHITTAKER join, dissenting.

In overruling the Wolf *case the Court, in my opinion, has forgotten the sense of judicial restraint which, with due regard for* stare decisis, *is one element that should enter into deciding*

whether a past decision of this Court should be overruled. Apart from that I also believe that the Wolf *rule represents sounder Constitutional doctrine than the new rule which now replaces it.* [emphasis added]

There are two differing philosophies concerning the court's role in deciding issues. One is judicial restraint, which is mentioned above in the emphasized sentence. The other is judicial activism, which the passage above criticizes without mentioning it by name. Can you identify the difference between these two approaches to judicial decision making?

I.

From the Court's statement of the case one would gather that the central, if not controlling, issue on this appeal is whether illegally state-seized evidence is Constitutionally admissible in a state prosecution, an issue which would of course face us with the need for re-examining *Wolf*. However, such is not the situation. For, although that question was indeed raised here and below among appellant's subordinate points, the new and pivotal issue brought to the Court by this appeal is whether §2905.34 of the Ohio Revised Code making criminal the *mere* knowing possession or control of obscene material, and under which appellant has been convicted, is consistent with the rights of free thought and expression assured against state action by the Fourteenth Amendment. That was the principal issue which was decided by the Ohio Supreme Court, which was tendered by appellant's Jurisdictional Statement, and which was briefed and argued in this Court.

In this posture of things, I think it fair to say that five members of this Court have simply "reached out" to overrule *Wolf*. With all respect for the views of the majority, and recognizing that *stare decisis* carries different weight in Constitutional adjudication than it does in nonconstitutional decision, I can perceive no justification for regarding this case as an appropriate occasion for re-examining *Wolf.*

The action of the Court finds no support in the rule that decision of Constitutional issues should be avoided wherever possible. For in overruling *Wolf* the Court, instead of passing upon the validity of Ohio's §2905.34, has simply chosen between two Constitutional questions. Moreover, I submit that it has chosen the more difficult and less appropriate of the two questions. The Ohio statute which, as construed by the State Supreme Court, punishes knowing possession or control of obscene material, irrespective of the purposes of such possession or control (with exceptions not here applicable) and irrespective of whether the accused had any reasonable opportunity to rid himself of the material after discovering that it was obscene, surely presents a Constitutional question which is both simpler and less far-reaching than the question which the Court decides today. It seems to me that justice might well have been done in this case without overturning a decision on which the administration of criminal law in many of the States has long justifiably relied.

Since the demands of the case before us do not require us to reach the question of the validity of *Wolf,* I think this case furnishes a singularly inappropriate occasion for reconsideration of that decision, if reconsideration is indeed warranted. Even the most cursory examination will reveal that the doctrine of the *Wolf* case has been of continuing importance in the administration of state criminal law. . . .

Justice Harlan went on to say that in the lower courts the issue of overruling the Wolf *case had not been adequately briefed or argued. Therefore, either the case should be reargued on that point or the court should wait for another properly argued case to reach its docket.*

I am bound to say that what has been done is not likely to promote respect either for the Court's adjudicatory process or for the stability of its decisions. Having been unable, however, to persuade any of the majority to a different procedural course, I now turn to the merits of the present decision.

Justice Harlan argued that the federal system permits the states to manage their problems of criminal law enforcement without the Supreme Court's stamp of approval or disapproval.

The preservation of a proper balance between state and federal responsibility in the administration of criminal justice demands patience on the part of those who might like to see things move faster among the States in this respect. Problems of criminal law enforcement vary widely from State to State. One State, in considering the totality of its legal picture, may conclude that the need for embracing the *Weeks* [exclusionary] rule is pressing because other remedies are unavailable or inadequate to secure compliance with the substantive Constitutional principle involved. Another, though equally solicitous of Constitutional rights, may choose to pursue one purpose at a time, allowing all evidence relevant to guilt to be brought into a criminal trial, and dealing with Constitutional infractions by other means. Still another may consider the exclusionary rule too rough-and-ready a remedy, in that it reaches only unconstitutional intrusions which eventuate in criminal prosecution of the victims. Further, a State after experimenting with the *Weeks* rule for a time may, because of unsatisfactory experience with it, decide to revert to a non-exclusionary rule. And so on. . . . For us the question remains, as it has always been, one of state power, not one of passing judgment on the wisdom of one state course or another. In my view this Court should continue to forbear from fettering the States with an adamant rule which may embarrass them in coping with their own peculiar problems in criminal law enforcement.

Further, we are told that imposition of the *Weeks* rule on the States makes "very good sense," in that it will promote recognition by state and federal officials of their "mutual obligation to respect the same fundamental criteria" in their approach to law enforcement, and will avoid " 'needless conflict between state and federal courts.' " . . .

A state conviction comes to us as the complete product of a sovereign judicial system. Typically a case will have been tried in a trial court, tested in some final appellate court, and will go no further. In the comparatively rare instance when a conviction is reviewed by us on due process grounds we deal then with a finished product in the creation of which we are allowed no hand, and our task, far from being one of over-all supervision, is, speaking generally, restricted to a determination of whether the prosecution was Constitutionally fair. The specifics of trial procedure, which in every mature legal system will vary greatly in detail, are within the sole competence of the States. *I do not see how it can be said that a trial becomes unfair simply because a State determines that evidence may be considered by the trier of fact, regardless of how it was obtained, if it is relevant to the one issue with which the trial is concerned, the guilt or innocence of the accused.* Of course, a court may use its procedures as an incidental means of pursuing other ends than the correct resolution of the controversies before it. Such indeed is the *Weeks* rule, but if a State does not choose to use its courts in this way, I do not believe that this Court is empowered to impose this much-debated procedure on local courts, however efficacious we may consider the *Weeks* rule to be as a means of securing Constitutional rights. . . .

I regret that I find so unwise in principle and so inexpedient in policy a decision motivated by the high purpose of increasing respect for Constitutional rights. *But in the last analysis I think this Court can increase re-* *spect for the Constitution only if it rigidly respects the limitations which the Constitution places upon it, and respects as well the principles inherent in its own processes. In the present case I think we exceed both, and that our voice becomes only a voice of power, not of reason.* [emphasis added]

What is your reaction to Justice Harlan's concluding charge that, in this case, the voice of the Court is one of power, not of reason?

Summary

The anatomy of Mapp v. Ohio *discloses the workings of the judicial process from the arrest to the Supreme Court's ruling. What we have seen is a set of procedures designed to determine both the facts in a case and the principles of law applicable to the issues. In this case, the process from beginning to the end took four years. Obviously, due process of law can be a slow, deliberate, and costly procedure.*

One might well ask, How could Mrs. Mapp afford the lawyers and the appeal? She had to have some assistance in her quest for justice. It was the American Civil Liberties Union and its affiliate, the Ohio Civil Liberties Union, which helped to finance the case through the courts.

Why did these organizations intervene in what seems to be a rather ordinary criminal case? The answer to this question can be found in the issues raised in the proceedings. The first dealt with obscenity; the second focused on the exclusionary rule. It was in this second issue that the American Civil Liberties Union saw the making of a landmark ruling. If they could persuade the Supreme Court to extend the exclusionary rule to state police, then illegally seized evidence would have to be excluded from state courts as well as from the federal courts. The same rule of law would apply to all police officials. They took the chance and won. Mapp v.

Ohio *became a landmark ruling in the same sense that* Gideon *v.* Wainwright *and* In re Gault *were. Each of these cases announced a new principle of law guaranteeing a con-* stitutional right to the accused. Each of these cases added a new dimension to the concept of justice as due process of law in criminal and juvenile proceedings.

APPENDIX B

Constitutional Amendments Cited in the Text

Amendment IV (1791) [Searches and seizures] The right of the people to be secure in their persons, houses, papers, and effects, against unreasonable searches and seizures shall not be violated, and no Warrants shall issue, but upon probable cause, supported by Oath or affirmation, and particularly describing the place to be searched, and the persons or things to be seized.

Amendment V (1791) [Grand jury indictment; double jeopardy; self-incrimination; due process of law; compensation for property] No person shall be held to answer for a capital, or otherwise infamous crime, unless on a presentment or indictment of a Grand Jury, except in cases arising in the land or naval forces, or in the Militia, when in actual service in time of War or public danger; nor shall any person be subject, for the same offence, to be twice put in jeopardy of life or limb; nor shall be compelled in any criminal case to be a witness against himself, nor be deprived of life, liberty, or property, without due process of law; nor shall private property be taken for public use, without just compensation.

Amendment VI (1791) [Jury trial in criminal prosecutions; procedural rights] In all criminal prosecutions, the accused shall enjoy the right to a speedy and public trial, by an impartial jury of the State and district wherein the crime shall have been committed, which district shall have been previously ascertained by law, and to be informed of the nature and cause of the accusation; to be confronted with the witnesses against him; to have compulsory process for obtaining witnesses in his favor, and to have the Assistance of Counsel for his defense.

Amendment VIII (1791) [Excessive bail, fines, punishment] Excessive bail shall not be required, nor excessive fines imposed, nor cruel and unusual punishments inflicted.

Amendment XIII (1865) [Slavery abolished] Section 1. Neither slavery nor involuntary servitude, except as a punishment for crime whereof the party shall have been duly convicted, shall exist within the United States, or any place subject to their jurisdiction.

Section 2. Congress shall have power to enforce this article by appropriate legislation.

Amendment XIV
(1868)
[(Section 1) United
States citizenship; states
prohibited from
abridging rights of a
citizen or depriving any
person of due process
of law or equal
protection of the laws]

Section 1. All persons born or naturalized in the United States, and subject to the jurisdiction thereof, are citizens of the United States and of the State wherein they reside. No State shall make or enforce any law which shall abridge the privileges or immunities or citizens of the United States; nor shall any State deprive any person of life, liberty, or property, without due process of law; nor deny to any person within its jurisdiction the equal protection of the laws.

Section 5. The Congress shall have power to enforce, by appropriate legislation, the provisions of this article.

Amendment XV
(1870)
[Right to vote not
abridged on account of
race, color, or
previous servitude]

Section 1. The right of citizens of the United States to vote shall not be denied or abridged by the United States or by any State on account of race, color, or previous condition of servitude.

Section 2. The Congress shall have power to enforce this article by appropriate legislation.

APPENDIX C

Glossary

Adjudication A decision, judgment, or decree resolving a controversy handed down by a court.

Appellate Relating to appeals. An appellate court hears appeals from rulings of lower courts.

Appellant The person or party who appeals a case to a higher court.

Appellee The person or party against whom the appeal is taken.

Aggravated Made more serious or weighty. The term is used in law to designate something malicious or especially serious. Usually it describes conduct which creates risk of serious bodily injury; for example, assault may be aggravated if a weapon is used.

Aggravating circumstances Conditions which make a criminal act more serious; for example, to knowingly create a risk of death or serious injury to other persons in addition to the victim.

Arraignment The procedure in a criminal case in which an accused is brought before a judge to hear the charges and to enter a plea of guilty or not guilty.

Beyond a reasonable doubt The level of proof required to convict a defendant in a criminal case. A jury must be convinced to the utmost certainty by the evidence that the person is guilty.

Bail bond Written statement of money or property put up by an arrested person and others who back it up, promising that the person will show up in court or forfeit the amount of the bond.

Bifurcated trial Divided into two parts; one part to determine guilt, the other part to determine sentence.

Capital offense A crime for which the death penalty can be imposed.

Capital punishment The death penalty.

Challenge for cause To object or except to a juror for some reason or cause as, for example, bias or prejudice.

Class action A lawsuit brought on behalf of oneself and all other persons who are in the same situation. The persons share a common right or have suffered a common injury by the same defendant.

Complainant In civil actions, the one who starts a lawsuit (plaintiff). In a criminal case, it is the one who presses charges against the accused; the plaintiff in a criminal case, however, is the government entity—i.e., state or federal.

Contraband Articles which the law prohibits a person from possessing, importing, or exporting.

Common law The term generally refers to the "judge-made law" (case law or decision law). Originating in England, the common law meant the rulings of judges based on tradition and custom. These rulings became the law common to the land. Common law is distinguished from statutes (laws enacted by legislatures).

Corporal punishment Punishment inflicted on the body of a person; physical punishment.

Deterrence A correctional theory that fear of punishment, i.e. imprisonment or the death penalty, will discourage or prevent persons from committing criminal acts.

Docket An official list of cases to be tried in a court.

Double jeopardy A second prosecution for the same offense. It is prohibited by the Fifth Amendment.

Extenuating circumstances Conditions surrounding a crime which help to explain why it happened. They do not excuse the act, but may reduce the moral blame, and so the severity of the penalty.

Federalism or federal system As applied to the United States, a division of powers between the federal or U.S. government and the governments of the fifty states. The states have powers of their own, such as power to create a public school system. The federal government has powers such as the control over coinage and to regulate foreign trade. Both have concurrent powers in such areas as taxation and public health and welfare.

Felony A serious crime, generally punishable by more than one year in prison.

Hearsay A statement made by someone other than the witness testifying, which is offered as evidence in the trial; it is what the witness says he heard another person say (or see).

Indigent A poor person; one without financial resources. Poverty is defined by state statutes as it relates to such matters as the right to court-appointed counsel.

Impeach To raise doubt about the truthfulness of a witness. This is generally done by directly disproving the witness's testimony by cross-examination or by introducing evidence which conflicts with what the witness testified to on direct examination. It may be done by showing the witness to be unreliable.

Indictment An accusation by a grand jury that a person has committed a crime. This does not mean that the accused is guilty. It simply means that the grand jurors believe there is evidence that the person has been involved in a criminal act and that the evidence is sufficient to justify a trial.

Jeopardy The risk of conviction and punishment which the defendant faces in a criminal trial. See double jeopardy.

Jurisdiction The authority of a court to exercise its power over certain persons or matters or within a certain geographical area.

Misdemeanor A crime less serious than a felony and generally punishable by a fine or less than one year's imprisonment.

Mitigating circumstances Factors such as age, mental capacity, or duress, which lessen the degree of guilt in a criminal offense, and so the nature of the punishment.

Moot A disputed matter or legal issue which, if judicially determined would have no practical significance or effect because the facts and rights existing at the time the issue arose have changed.

Opinion A written statement of a judge setting forth the reasons for a decision and explaining his or her interpretation of the law applicable to the case. A *majority* opinion represents the views of more than half of the judges who participated in the case. A *plurality* opinion represents the views of the greatest number of judges, but less than half of those who heard the case. For example, suppose nine judges hear a case and decide it by a five to four vote. If all five agree in their reasons for the decision and join in an opinion stating those reasons, it would be a majority opinion. However, if three of the five agree on the reasoning and the other two agree with the decision but not with the reasoning, the opinion of the three would be a plurality opinion. A *dissenting* opinion is one which disagrees with the decision of the majority. A *concurring* opinion agrees with the decision of the majority, but differs with the reasoning of the majority opinion.

Per curiam opinion (By the court) An opinion stating the decision of all the judges, and not signed by any particular judge.

Peremptory challenge A kind of challenge (objection) to a juror which defense or prosecution may use to eliminate a certain number of jurors from serving. No reason need be given for this kind of challenge.

Plaintiff The person who starts a lawsuit.

Plea bargaining Negotiations in a criminal case between a prosecutor and an attorney for the defendant about the charges to which the defendant will plead guilty and the sentence the prosecutor will recommend to the judge.

Precedent A decision in an earlier case which is used as a model, authority, or example for deciding a case before the court in which the facts and issues are similar.

Preliminary hearing A hearing or examination before a judge or magistrate to determine whether an accused should be detained, freed, or released on bail.

Presentence investigation A study of a convicted person's background (education, family situation, employment, prior record, physical and mental condition, and reputation in the community) and potential for rehabilitation. A court-appointed social worker or probation officer makes the investigation and prepares a report to assist the judge in deciding what sentence to impose.

Probable cause A reasonable ground for believing that a crime has been committed or that a person has committed a crime. Probable cause is required to support the issuance of a search warrant or arrest warrant. Under certain circumstances, a police officer who has probable cause to believe a person has committed or is about to commit a crime may make an arrest without a warrant.

Punitive damages A money award to a person who has been injured, which is over and above the actual damages suffered. The compensation is designed to "punish" the one who caused the injury in order to discourage similar conduct in the future.

Reconstruction The period following the Civil War (1865 to 1876) during which the national government enacted legislation designed to "restructure" the seceded states and bring them back into the Union. The Civil War Amendments (XIII, abolishing slavery; XIV, extending citizenship rights to former slaves; XV, extending the right to vote to former slaves) were ratified during this period. The Civil Rights Acts of the period were intended to implement these amendments and to prevent violations of the rights of the freed slaves.

Remand To send back to a lower court. A higher court can remand a case to a lower court with instructions to carry out certain orders.

Retribution A correctional theory that views sentencing of convicted defendants as a means for society to retaliate and punish the offender for the harm done.

Rule of law A legal principle, recognized by authorities, and used a guide in deciding cases. Also, a system of government in which the law of the land is the highest authority and no individual or group can disregard or disobey the law without penalty; laws can be changed only through procedures provided by the law.

Sequester To isolate a jury from the news media and other outside influences which might affect its verdict.

Stare decisis To stand on the decisions of the past. A principle which holds that courts and judges should follow prior decisions and judicial rulings in the interest of predictability, fairness, and certainty.

Statute A law or act passed by a legislature.

Verbatim Word for word; in a trial, the court reporter takes down testimony in the exact words spoken.

Verdict The decision of a jury. In a criminal case, it is "guilty" or "not guilty".

Waive To give up or relinquish something to which one is entitled. The term is used in several ways. In a juvenile proceeding, the judge may waive jurisdiction and, thereby give up the right to hear the case, which is then transferred to the criminal court. A person who is entitled to a jury trial may waive that right. A defendant may waive immunity; that is give up the right not to testify in his or her own trial.

Waiver The act of giving up a right or claim. A legally enforceable statement that one gives up such a right.

Bibliography

**Section I
The Courtroom as
Theater: The Curtain
Rises**

General Buncher, Judith F. *Crime and Punishment in America.* New York: Facts on File, 1978.

Clark, Ramsey. *Crime in America: Observations on Its Nature, Causes, Prevention and Control.* New York: Touchstone Paperback Series, Simon & Schuster, 1971.

Goodykoontz, William, ed. *Law: You, the Police, and Justice.* New York: Scholastic Book Service, 1968.

President's Commission on Law Enforcement and the Administration of Justice. *The Challenge of Crime in a Free Society.* Washington D.C.: U.S. Government Printing Office, 1968.

Silberman, Charles E. *Criminal Violence, Criminal Justice.* New York: Random House, 1978.

Starr, Isidore. *The Supreme Court and Contemporary Issues.* Chicago: Encyclopedia Britannica Educational Corporation, 1969.

Due Process of Law Gora, Joel M. *Due Process of Law.* Skokie, Ill.: National Textbook Company, 1977.

Pennock, J. Roland, and Chapman, John W. *Due Process of Law.* New York: New York University Press, 1977.

Right to Counsel Lewis, Anthony. *Gideon's Trumpet.* New York: Vintage Books, Random House, 1964.

Starr, Isidore. *The Gideon Case.* Chicago: Encyclopedia Britannica Educational Corporation, 1968.

Judges Goulden, Joseph C. *The Bench Warmers: The Private World of the Powerful Federal Judges.* New York: Ballantine Books, 1974.

Jackson, Donald Dale. *Judges.* New York: Athenaeum, 1974.

The Jury Bloomstein, Morris J. *Verdict: The Jury System.* New York: Dodd, Mead and Co., 1972.

Gleisser, Marcus. *Juries and Justice.* New Jersey: Barnes & Co., 1968.

Saks, Michael. "Social Scientists Can't Rig Juries." *Psychology Today,* January 1976, pp. 48–57.

Schulman, Jay, et al. "Recipe for a Jury." *Psychology Today,* May 1973, pp. 37–44.

Villaseñor, Victor, *Jury: The People* vs. *Juan Corona.* Boston: Little Brown & Co., 1977.

Zerman, Melvyn B. *Call The Witness: The People* vs. *Darrell R. Mathes,* New York: Harper & Row, 1977.

The Grand Jury Frankel, Marvin E. and Naftalis, Gary P. *The Grand Jury: An Institution on Trial.* New York: Hill and Wang, 1977.

The Press Friendly, Alfred, and Goldfarb, Ronald L. *Crime and Publicity: The Impact of News on the Administration of Justice.* New York: Vintage Books, Random House, 1968.

Lofton, John. *Justice and the Press.* Boston: Beacon Press, 1966.

Political Trials Becker, Theodore L., ed. *Political Trials.* Indianapolis: Bobbs-Merrill Co., 1971.

Epstein, Jason. *The Great Conspiracy Trial: An Essary on Law, Liberty and the Constitution.* New York: Vintage Books, Random House, 1971.

Kirchheimer, Otto. *Political Justice: The Use of Legal Procedure for Political Ends.* Princeton, N.J.: Princeton University Press, 1961.

Plea Bargaining Downie, Leonard, Jr. "Crime in the Courts: Assembly Line Justice." *Washington Monthly,* May 1970, pp. 26–39.

Comparative Legal Abraham, Henry, J. *Judicial Process: An Introductory Analysis of the*
Systems   *Courts of the United States, England and France,* 2d ed. New York: Oxford University Press, 1968.

Karlen, Delmar. *Anglo-American Criminal Justice.* New York: Oxford University Press, 1967.

Orian, Lee, and Robertson, T. A. *"Moral Order" and the Criminal Law: Reform Efforts in the United States and West Germany*. The Hague, The Netherlands: Nijhoff Press, 1973.

The Supreme Court and Criminal Justice

Galloway, John. *Criminal Justice and the Burger Court*. New York: Facts on File, 1978.

Graham, Fred P. *The Due Process Revolution: The Warren Court's Impact on Criminal Law*. New York: Hayden Book Co., 1971.

Supreme Court Justices

Barnes, Catherine A. *Men of the Supreme Court: Profiles of the Justices*. New York: Facts on File, 1978.

Section II
The Courtroom as Theater: The Curtain Falls

Cruel and Unusual Punishment

Berns, Walter. *For Capital Punishment: Crime and the Morality of the Death Penalty*. New York: Basic Books, Inc. 1979.

Black, Charles L., Jr. *Capital Punishment: The Inevitability of Caprice and Mistake*. New York: W. W. Norton and Co., 1974.

Bowers, William. *Executions in America*. Lexington, Mass.: D. C. Heath and Co., 1979.

Meltsner, Michael. *Cruel and Unusual: The Supreme Court and Capital Punishment*. New York: William Morrow and Company, 1974.

Section III
Justice in the Juvenile Court

Fox, Sanford J. *Juvenile Courts*. St. Paul: West Publishing Company, 1977.

Johnson, Thomas A. *Introduction to the Juvenile Justice System*. St. Paul: West Publishing Company, 1975.

Katkin, Daniel; Hyman, Drew; and Kramer, John. *Juvenile Delinquency and the Juvenile Justice System*. North Scituate, Mass.: Duxbury Press, 1976.

Platt, Anthony M. *The Child Savers: The Invention of Delinquency*. Chicago: University of Chicago Press, 1969.

Senna, Joseph L., and Siegel, Larry J. *Juvenile Law: Cases and Comment*. St. Paul: West Publishing Company, 1978.

Teitelbaum, Lee E., and Gough, Aidan R. *Beyond Control: Status Offenders in the Juvenile Court.* Cambridge, Mass.: Ballinger Publishing Company, 1977.

Section IV
Justice in the Schools Levine, Alen H.; Cary, Eve; and Divoky, Diane. *The Rights of Students.* New York: Avon Books, 1974.

Schimel, David, and Fischer, Louis. *The Civil Rights of Students.* New York: Harper and Row, 1975.

La Morte, Michael W.; Gentry, Harold W.; and Young, D. Parker. *Student's Legal Rights and Responsibilities.* Cincinnati: W. H. Anderson Company, 1971.

Table of Cases

Apodaca v. *Oregon*
406 U.S. 404, 92 S.CT. 1628, 32 L.Ed.2d 184 (1972)

Argersinger v. *Hamlin*
407 U.S. 25, 92 S.Ct. 2006, 32 L.Ed. 2d 530 (1972)

Ballew v. *Georgia*
435 U.S. 223, 98 S.Ct. 1029, 55 L.Ed. 2d 234 (1978)

Bell v. *Ohio*
438 U.S. 637, 98 S.Ct. 2977, 57 L.Ed. 2d 1010 (1978)

Branch v. *Texas*
408 U.S. 238, 92 S.Ct. 2726, 33 L.Ed. 2d 346 (1972)

Breed v. *Jones*
421 U.S. 519, 95 S.Ct. 1779, 44 L.Ed. 2d 346 (1975)

Burch v. *Louisiana*
441 U.S. 130, 99 S.Ct. 1623, 60 L.Ed. 2d 96 (1979)

Carey v. *Piphus*
435 U.S. 247, 98 S.Ct. 1042, 55 L.Ed. 2d 252 (1978)

Cooper v. *Oregon*
406 U.S. 404, 92 S.Ct. 1628, 32 L.Ed. 2d 184 (1972)

Dennis v. *United States*
341 U.S. 494, 71 S.Ct. 857, 95 L.Ed. 1137 (1951)

Duncan v. *Louisiana*
392 U.S. 947, 88 S.Ct. 2270, 20 L.Ed. 2d 1412 (1968)

Durst v. *United States*
434 U.S. 542, 98 S.Ct. 849, 55 L.Ed. 2d 14 (1978)

Faretta v. *California*
422 U.S. 806, 95 S.Ct. 2525, 45 L.Ed. 2d 562 (1975)

Fuller v. *Oregon*
417 U.S. 40, 94 S.Ct. 2116, 40 L.Ed. 2d 642 (1974)

Furman v. *Georgia*
408 U.S. 238, 92 S.Ct. 2726, 33 L.Ed. 2d 346 (1972)

Gannett Co., Inc. v. *DePasquale*
443 U.S. 368, 99 S.Ct. 2898, 61 L.Ed. 2d 608 (1979)

Gideon v. *Wainwright*
372 U.S. 335; 83 S.Ct. 792, 9 L.Ed. 2d 799 (1963)

Goss v. *Lopez*
419 U.S. 565, 95 S.Ct. 729, 42 L.Ed. 2d 725 (1975)

Gregg v. *Georgia*
428 U.S. 153, 96 S.Ct. 2909, 49 L.Ed. 2d 859 (1976)

Harris v. *New York*
401 U.S. 222, 91 S.Ct. 643, 28 L.Ed. 2d 1 (1971)

Illinois v. *Allen*
397 U.S. 337, 90 S.Ct. 1057, 25 L.Ed. 2d 353 (1970)

Ingraham v. *Wright*
430 U.S. 651, 97 S.Ct. 1401, 51 L.Ed. 2d 711 (1978)

In re Burrus
403 U.S. 528, 91 S.Ct. 1976, 29 L.Ed. 2d 647 (1971)

In re Gault
387 U.S. 1, 87 S.Ct. 1428, 18 L.Ed. 2d 527 (1967)

In re Winship
397 U.S. 358, 90 S.Ct. 1068, 25 L.Ed. 2d 368 (1970)

Ivan V. v. *City of New York*
407 U.S. 203, 92 S.Ct. 1951, 32 L.Ed. 2d 659 (1972)

Jackson v. *Georgia*
408 U.S. 238, 92 S.Ct. 2726, 33 L.Ed. 2d 346 (1972)

Johnson v. *Louisiana*
406 U.S. 356, 92 S.Ct. 1620, 32 L.Ed. 2d 152 (1972)

Jurek v. *Texas*
428 U.S. 262, 96 S.Ct. 2950, 49 L.Ed. 2d 929 (1976)

Kent v. *United States*
383 U.S. 541, 86 S.Ct. 1045, 16 L.Ed. 2d 84 (1966)

Lockett v. *Ohio*
438 U.S. 586, 98 S.Ct. 2954, 57 L.Ed. 2d 973 (1978)

Louisiana ex rel, Francis v. *Resweber*
329 U.S. 459, 67 S.Ct. 374, 91 L.Ed. 2d 422 (1947)

McKeiver v. *Pennsylvania*
403 U.S. 528, 91 S.Ct. 1976, 29 L.Ed. 2d 647 (1971)

Madden v. *Oregon*
406 U.S. 404, 92 S.Ct. 1628, 32 L.Ed. 2d 184 (1972)

Mapp v. *Ohio*
367 U.S. 643, 81 S.Ct. 1684, 6 L.Ed. 2d 1081 (1961)

Miranda v. *Arizona*
384 U.S. 436, 86 S.Ct. 1602, 16 L.Ed. 2d 694 (1966)

Nebraska Press Assoc. v. *Stuart*
427 U.S. 539, 96 S.Ct. 2791, 49 L.Ed. 2d 683 (1976)

Proffitt v. *Florida*
428 U.S. 242, 96 S.Ct. 2960, 49 L.Ed. 2d 913 (1976)

Richmond Newspapers, Inc. v. *Virginia*
_____U.S. _____, 100 S.Ct. 2814, _____L.Ed. 2d _____(1980)

Roberts v. *Louisiana*
428 U.S. 325, 96 S.Ct. 3001, 49 L.Ed. 2d 974 (1976)

Robinson v. *California*
370 U.S. 660, 82 S.Ct. 1417, 8 L.Ed. 2d 758 (1962)

Santobello v. *New York*
402 U.S. 994, 91 S.Ct. 2172, 29 L.Ed. 2d 160 (1971)

Scott v. *Illinois*
440 U.S. 367, 99 S.Ct. 1158, 59 L.Ed. 2d 383 (1979)

Sheppard v. *Maxwell* (1960)
384 U.S. 333, 86 S.Ct. 1507, 16 L.Ed. 2d 600 (1966)

Terry v. *Pennsylvania*
403 U.S. 528, 91 S.Ct. 1976, 29 L.Ed. 2d 647 (1971)

Tinker v. *Des Moines Ind. School District*
393 U.S. 503, 89 S.Ct. 733, 21 L.Ed. 2d 731 (1969)

Trop v. *Dulles*
356 U.S. 86, 78 S.Ct. 590, 2 L.Ed. 2d 630 (1958)

United States v. *Dellinger, et al.*
472 F.2d 340 (1972)

United States v. *Mandujano*
425 U.S. 564, 96 S.Ct. 1768, 48 L.Ed. 2d 212 (1976)

United States v. *Seale*
461 F.2d 345 (1972)

Weems v. *United States*
217 U.S. 349, 30 S.Ct. 544, 54 L.Ed. 793 (1910)

Williams v. *Florida*
399 U.S. 78, 90 S.Ct. 1893, 26 L.Ed. 2d 446 (1970)

Wood v. *Strickland*
420 U.S. 308, 95 S.Ct. 992, 43 L.Ed. 2d 214 (1975)

Woodson v. *North Carolina*
428 U.S. 280, 96 S.Ct. 2978, 49 L.Ed.2d 944 (1976)

Index

A

Apodaca v. *Oregon*, 64–68
Appeals, 7
Appellate, 7
Argersinger v. *Hamlin*, 18
Aristotle, 210

B

Bailiff, 27
Ballew v. *Georgia*, 61
Bell v. *Ohio*, 120–121
Betts v. *Brady*, 15
Bill of Rights, 5
Black, Hugo L., 17, 49–51, 144, 151, 253
Blackmun, Harry A., 19–20, 21, 35–37,
    61–63, 100–101, 119, 156–157, photo
    p. 62
Borstal System, 170
Branch v. *State of Texas*. See *Furman* v.
    Georgia
Breed v. *Jones*, 163–165
Brennan, William J., 19, 51, 93–95,
    111–112, 148–150, 158, 167–168,
    photo p. 148
Burger, Warren E., 21, 34, 76–77, 99–100,
    118–119, 120, 150, 164–165, photo
    pp. 76, 99
Burch v. *Louisiana*, 68–69
Burrus, In Re. See *McKeiver* v. *Pennsylvania*
Burton, Harold H., 88

C

Cahn, Edmund (*The Sense of Injustice*), 210
Cardozo, Benjamin N., 46

Carey v. *Piphus*, 192–194
Cases
    civil, 7–8
    criminal, 7–8
Challenges
    for cause, 57
    peremptory, 57
*Challenge of Crime in a Free Society: Report
    of the President's Commission on Law
    Enforcement and the Administration of
    Justice*, 25, 169–170
Chessman, Caryl, 28–29
Chicago Conspiracy Trial. See *United
    States* v. *Dellinger et al.*
Civil Rights Act of 1871, pp. 189–191
Clark, Tom C., 249–253
Class action, 179
Clerk, 27–28
Code of Judicial Conduct, 12
Compurgation, 3–4
Cooper v. *Oregon*, 64–68
Counsel
    defense, 21–22
    prosecutor, 13–14
Corporal punishment. See *Ingraham* v.
    Wright
Court reporter, 26–27
Courtroom, 7
Courts
    appellate, 7
    federal, 7
    state, 7
    trial, 7
Crime Control Model, 211–212
Cross-examination, 39–40

D

Damages, 8–9
  compensatory, 193
  punitive, 193
Declaratory judgment, 8
Defendant, 8, 14
Defense. *See* Counsel
Dennis v. *United States*, 52
Direct examination, 39
Disraeli, Benjamin, 213
Double jeopardy, 163–165
Douglas, William O., 18, 51, 67, 77, 85,
  92–93, 158–159, 253–254
Due Process Model, 211–212
Duncan v. *Louisiana*, 59
Durham, Michael, 15–16
Durst v. *United States*, 167–168

E

English Bill of Rights (1689), 80
Exclusionary Rule, 45. *See* also *Mapp* v.
  Ohio, 250–254

F

Faretta v. *California*, 20–21
Federal Youth Corrections Act, 170
Fifth Amendment, 5
Fortas, Abe, 16, 139–144, 162
Fourteenth Amendment, 5–6
Frank, John P., 213
Frankfurter, Felix, 88, 213
Fuller v. *Oregon*, 20
Furman v. *Georgia*, 89–104

G

Gannett Co., Inc. v. *DePasquale*, 32
Gault, In Re, 137–145
Gideon v. *Wainwright*, 14–17
Goss v. *Lopez*, 179–188
Grand jury. *See* Jury
Great Charter. *See* Magna Carta
Gregg v. *Georgia*, 105–108

H

Habeas corpus, 137–138
Habeas Corpus Act, 137–138
Hammurabi's Code of Laws, 201
Harlan, John M., 144, 254–256
Harris v. *New York*, 42
Hearsay, 23, 41

I

Indigent, 14–16
Illinois v. *Allen*, 47–51, 54
Ingraham v. *Wright*, 195–205
In loco parentis, 176
Institute of Judicial Administration (Recommendations), 171–172
Ivan V. v. *City of New York*, 151

J

Jackson v. *Georgia*. See *Furman* v. *Georgia*
Johnson v. *Louisiana*, 64–68
Judge, 11–13
Jurek v. *Texas*, 108–110, 111–112
Jury,
  French, 70
  German, 70–71
  grand, 58–59
  history, 56
  of one's peers, 55
  petit, 59–71
  voir dire, 57
Juvenile Court, 9, 131–172
  appeal, 143–144
  confrontation of witnesses, 143
  counsel, 141
  cross-examination, 143
  double jeopardy, 163–165
  French, 155–156
  hearing, 141
  history, 133–136
  privilege against self-incrimination,
    142–143
  transcript, 143–144
  waiver of jurisdiction, 161–165

K

Kelly, Cynthia A., 198–199
Kent v. *United States,* 163–165

L

Legal aid, 22
Legal ethic, 212
Lettres de Cachet, 31
Lindsey, Judge Benjamin B., 135–136
Lockett v. *Ohio,* 117–120
Louisiana ex rel. Francis v. *Resweber,* 83, 87–88

M

Mack, Julian, 134
Magna Carta, 4–5, 210–211
Massachusetts Body of Liberties, 80
McKeiver v. *Pennsylvania,* 153–159
Madden v. *Oregon,* 64–68
Mapp v. *Ohio,* 46, Appendix A (213–257),
    arraignment, 214–215
    indictment, 215–216
    judge's instructions, 244–248
    jury's verdict, 248
    Supreme Court opinions, 248–256
    trial transcript, 217–244
Marshall, Thurgood, 27, 67, 96–98, 111–112, photo p. 97
Millett, Larry, 28–29
Miranda v. *Arizona,* 42
Miranda Rule, 41–44
Miranda Warning Card, 42

N

Nebraska Press Association v. *Stuart,* 37
Northwest Ordinance, 80

O

Oath, 23
Objections, 41
Ordeals, 3–4
Original jurisdiction, 7
Otis, James, 45

P

Packer, Herbert (*The Limits of the Criminal Sanction*), 211–212
Parens patria, 134
Perry, Ernest, 28–29
Perjury, 23
Plaintiff, 8
Powell, Lewis F., Jr., 34, 65, 101–103, 111, 184–188, 191–192, 194, 197–202, photo p. 186
Plea bargaining, 73–77
Presentence report, 40
Pretrial hearing, 32
Proffitt v. *Florida,* 110–112
Prosecutor. *See* Counsel
Public defenders, 22

R

Reed, Stanley, 87
Rehnquist, William H., 19, 21, 68–69, 103, 119–120, photo p. 69
Richmond Newspapers, Inc. v. *Virginia,* 37
Roberts v. *Louisiana,* 114–117
Robinson v. *California,* 83, 85–87

S

Santobello v. *New York,* 75–77
Schools
    corporal punishment. See *Ingraham* v. *Wright*
    due process, 179–192
    expulsions, 188–192
    suspensions, 179–188
School board members
    liability, 188–194
Scott v. *Illinois,* 18
Seale, Bobby, 52–53
Search warrants, 45–46
Sheppard v. *Maxwell,* 37
Skolnick, Jerome (*Justice Without Trial*), 212
Spanish Inquisition, 31
Star Chamber, 31

Status offenders, 9
Stevens, John Paul, 109–115, photo p. 116
Stewart, Potter, 20, 33–34, 67–68, 85, 95, 107–108, 113–114, 144–145, 162–163, 254, photo p. 86
Strasburg, Paul A., 115–116
Supreme Court, photo p. 8

T

Terry v. *Pennsylvania*, 153–159
Themis, ix
Tinker v. *Des Moines Independent School District*, 176
Trial, 39–41
    chart, 40
Trop v. *Dulles*, 82, 84–85

U

Unanimous verdict rule, 63–69
United States v. *Dellinger, et al.*, 52–53
United States v. *Mandujano*, 44–45
United States v. *Seale*, 52–53

V

Victim, 24–26
    compensation, 25–26
    compensation chart, 26–27
Voir dire. See Jury

W

Wager of law. *See* Compurgation
Warren, Earl, 84–85
Weems v. *United States*, 81, 84
White, Byron R., 63, 65–67, 86, 95–96, 110–111, 117, 157–158, 180–184, 190–191, 202–205, photo p. 182
Williams v. *Florida*, 60
Winship, In Re, 147–151
Witness, 23–24
    expert, 24
Wood v. *Strickland*, 188–192
Woodson v. *North Carolina*, 112–115
Work ethic, 212
Writs of Assistance, 45